Creating Sustainable Communities

Creating Sustainable Communities

Lessons from the Hudson River Region

Rik Scarce

excelsior editions

State University of New York Press
Albany, New York

Published by State University of New York Press, Albany

Printed in the United States of America

Excelsior Editions is an imprint of State University of New York Press

For information, contact State University of New York Press, Albany, NY
www.sunypress.edu

Production, Jenn Bennett
Marketing, Anne M. Valentine

Library of Congress Cataloging-in-Publication Data

Scarce, Rik, 1958–
    Creating sustainable communities : lessons from the Hudson River Region /
Rik Scarce.
        pages cm
    Includes bibliographical references and index.
    ISBN 978-1-4384-5643-0 (hardcover : alk. paper)
    ISBN 978-1-4384-5642-3 (pbk : alk. paper)
    ISBN 978-1-4384-5644-7 (e-book)
    1. Hudson River Valley (N.Y. and N.J.)—Environmental conditions.
2. Environmental policy—Hudson River Valley (N.Y. and N.J.)   3. Community
development—Hudson River Valley (N.Y. and N.J.)   4. Sustainable development—
Hudson River Valley (N.Y. and N.J.)   I. Title.

    GE155.H83S27 2015
    338.9747'307—dc23   2014027105

10 9 8 7 6 5 4 3 2 1

For Wendy, with whom
I joyfully walk, paddle, and travel
the Hudson region

Contents

Illustrations

Acknowledgments

I am deeply indebted to many for making this book possible. Foremost are the sixty-two folks who sat with me for interviews, fifty-nine of which were filmed for a documentary. Whatever this book is, it was made possible through their generosity of time, wisdom, and experience.

I had the good fortune to work with several wonderful students. In the early years of this project, Megan McAdams and I traveled to New York City and throughout the region looking at old maps and filming scenes; she also was a tremendous help in my grasp of the area's early history. Mary Rynasko and Katarra Peterson spent a summer working on the environmental justice data reported in chapter 5, and Jessica Aleman picked up that work and completed it with me. As I finished the research, Leah Docktor was an exceptional assistant. To all of them, my heartfelt gratitude.

Skidmore College supported this work in multiple ways. The Faculty Development Committee awarded me grants that made the extensive travel possible, and the Dean of the Faculty's office was similarly helpful. The Environmental Studies Program funded four summer collaborative projects with students, above and beyond my highest expectations, and supplied me with the video equipment used for filming the interviews.

I've always felt fortunate to be on the Skidmore faculty, never more so than as I look back on the ways large and small that my colleagues across campus, particularly in the Department of Sociology, aided this work. Outside of my department, Cathy Gibson thoughtfully reviewed an early draft of chapter 2, and A. J. Schneller shared comments on a late draft of the entire book.

Finally, my wife, Wendy Scarce, showed me far more forbearance and understanding than I deserved. This project has been with us throughout our marriage, and I know she is as happy as I am to see it fledge.

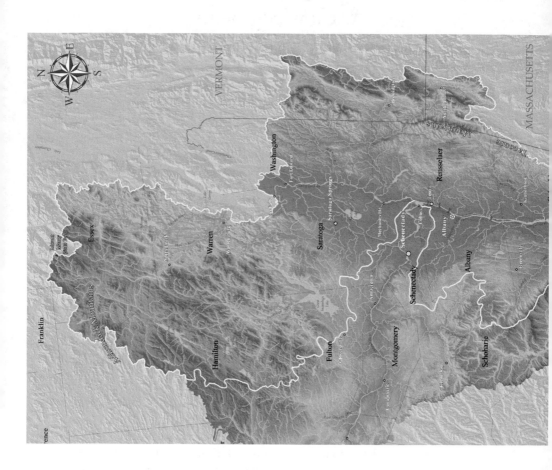

Figure 1.1. Hudson River Watershed

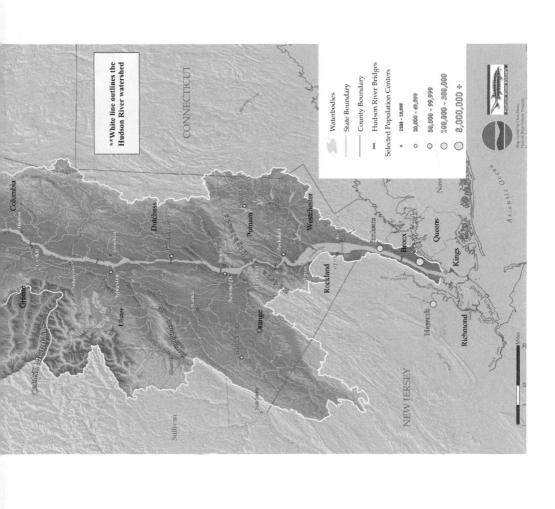

Introduction

Remaking a Region—Intentionally

> [R]emake, so far as humans
> can remake, all that humans
> have unmade. To you, whoever
> you may be, I say: Come,
> meaning to stay. Come,
> willing to learn what this place,
> like no other, will ask of you
> and your children, if you mean
> to stay.
>
> —Wendell Berry "XI"

Few settings in American society are home to richer landscapes than the Hudson River region of the Northeast and New England. Here we find formative places in the nation's history and in its consciousness: West Point, Sleepy Hollow, Hyde Park, and the World Trade Centers—which were built on land created by filling the Hudson River. This region is the home of the Mohicans and IBM, the craggy Adirondack Mountains and New York City's concrete canyons, General Electric and General Benedict Arnold's treason.

Increasingly, it is also the land of sustainability, a watershed like no other in the extent and intensity of efforts residents undertake to create a lasting bioregion.

One of the most studied, storied, painted, pampered, and abused landscapes in North America, the Hudson region has undergone relentless change over the last four centuries. It was a source of immense riches

1

to the Dutch, the region's first European colonists, who exploited it but never truly settled it. To the British who followed, it was a vital northern foothold on the continent, an opportunity to extend their domain and to push back those of their enemies.

And since our nation's founding, the Hudson region has been wracked with contradiction and conflict. The same setting that inspired some of our earliest literature and first great works of art, a place that was home and playground to working people and presidents, was savaged beyond recognition for lumber and leather tanning. The river that witnessed the turning point of the American Revolution and the voyage of the world's first viable steamship became an open sewer. A great city grew to a sprawling megalopolis, overrunning the farmland that made it viable in its early years and outstripping the capacity of the region's remaining farms to feed those who live there. And the aggressive industrialization of the region prompted a national backlash, a reinvigoration of environmentalism that has yet to wane—and that today embraces sustainability as its watchword.

Not surprisingly, until the environmentalists came along, few stopped to ask whether it was possible to simultaneously create livable cities, functioning environments, and permanent, workable economies in the Hudson region. Yet today that question is being asked, and answered in the affirmative, not only by avowed "greens" but many others as well.

This book tells the story of those working to create a region that grows much of its own food, that takes ecology to heart when making land use decisions, and where reinvigorated communities embrace environmental justice. It is a place where transportation systems depend less and less on automobiles, in part because jobs are closer to home and, as a result, our homes become central to living happier, more fulfilling lives. In this emerging Hudson River region, ski resorts produce their own energy, insulation is made from fungi, and children eat the vegetables they grow on the roofs of their schools.

Admittedly, there's a paradox at play here. There is no place,·no other river's drainage, like the narrow strip of land on either side of the Hudson for exemplars of sustainability. Yet the region as a whole remains a long way from sustainable. What makes it special is that so many who call it home are doing so much in such diverse ways to fulfill their vision of lasting, stable communities, economies, and ecosystems. For all the changes they've brought, they're only getting started. In the words of sustainability entrepreneur Melissa Everett, "What we do here will send a signal and will resonate, I believe, as other places see [what's happening in the Hudson region]." (The Hudson bioregion primarily lies in New York State and includes much of Manhattan and the Bronx in New York City; all or portions of seventeen New York counties; substantial areas of northwestern Massachusetts, northern New Jersey, and southwestern Vermont; and slivers of Connecticut.)

In *Getting Green Done*, Auden Schendler writes, "The environmental movement needs something like a world's fair today. We need a series of demonstration projects that will give us experience and inform policy."[1] Something like that is happening in the Hudson region. These are the tales of regular citizens who have curbed rampant development through creative land use laws that promise to reinvigorate rural villages. Others have opened the first legal distillery since Prohibition using corn grown practically within sight of the old barn where the mashing takes place; have countered our autocentric culture by making New York City streets safer for cyclists and pedestrians to ride and walk to work and to the park; have created an urban sustainability center on the site of an abandoned gas station; and have preserved old buildings that passively heat and cool in ways that are the envy of contemporary architects.

All the more remarkable, their efforts are largely disconnected from each other. There is no annual conference of Hudson region sustainability practitioners, no Facebook page, and the one organization dedicated to the purpose is energetically led but poorly funded and limited in its geographic scope. Yet, despite the lack of coordination, these farmers, elected officials, community organizers, business owners, scientists, planners, and social justice advocates persist and succeed. Most argue, as urban sustainability guru Scott Kellogg does, that "we don't have the luxury of time at this point. The transition needs to be urgent and rapid." He and others are not just bent on spreading that message; they show us the way to a lasting tomorrow today.

These stories only scratch the surface of what's happening in the Hudson region. For each of them there are dozens of others. Untold restaurants support local farms; in the same vein, one often sees knitting shops that stock locally produced yarn. Solar and small-scale wind power businesses proliferate in the Hudson region, as do sustainability-oriented magazines, health and wellness retreats, organic bakeries, and more. Nonprofits green former food deserts by promoting community gardening, and colleges vie with one another for the honor of being the most sustainable campus not only in the region but in the nation.

So what I present here is not intended to be representative, only illustrative of the intensely creative, exciting things going on between

Mount Marcy and Manhattan. It's also not a how-to guide in the genre of *Twenty Things YOU Can Do to Sustain the Planet.* Those primers have their place, but when you look closely at the individuals in this book, *all* of them are associated with organizations, even if the companies or non-profits were created by them. Like most of the important, lasting things in life, sustainability advocates work with others to accomplish what they do. Martin Luther King relied on churches and the Southern Christian Leadership Conference. Henry Ford created a massive corporation. Charles Lindbergh flew the first plane across the Atlantic, but he didn't build the thing—he didn't even make his own sandwiches for the trip! While sustainability organizations don't have to be large or complex, individuals alone find social change difficult to accomplish.

Inspiration and Insight

The idea behind this book is twofold. First, I hope to inspire those in this region and beyond to take their own chances—to become sustainability entrepreneurs, whether in the business sense or otherwise. The sixty-two people I interviewed have worked hard to fulfill their vision, yet few of them possess exceptional resources. Most do not work for powerful organizations, nor are they able to draw from depthless wells of capital or charisma. What they can call on, however, is a drive to make a difference in a place about which they deeply care. They are realistic optimists: fully aware of the roadblocks confronting them—they're the ones who have overcome the challenges, after all—they plow ahead in the belief that our collective future can and must be a sustainable one.

In addition to inspiring potential sustainability practitioners and advocates, I hope to provide insight about how the sustainability phenomenon can be conceptually understood. As I explain below, I weave the trope of "Landscape" throughout this book, defined here as *the intersection of place and people* and capitalized throughout to remind us of that connection.

These Landscapes are meaning-filled locales, and that meaning making occurs not only when we speak or write of a place such as the Hudson region but also when we pollute or nurture it, pave it over or plow it, mine it or set it aside as precious wilderness. Along multiple dimensions, the determined people and groups about which I write embrace, advocate for, and enact a new Hudson region Landscape, inevitably in the face of resistance.

What ties together these two purposes is that so much sustainability activity is occurring in this one area. Case studies of, and theories about, sustainability abound, but the Hudson region allows one to do both. Without a broad understanding of what so many individuals, organizations, and corporations in one region are attempting to accomplish, their efforts make little sense. And without examining those efforts in depth, theorizing becomes a hollow act.

Landscapes: Re-Meaning Place and People

By Landscape, I have in mind something conceptually richer than a painting, photograph, or view of an outdoor setting, though my choice of that word certainly isn't accidental. The academic notion underlying Landscape goes by the far from self-explanatory label "social construction of nature." It holds that our understandings of nature are packed with *meaning*. These meanings are not denotations, dictionary definitions, but rather are connotations; meaning that emerges from real life—from what people, organizations, corporations, and agencies say and do. Sociologists explore social constructions of nature through interviews, observations, and by gleaning insight from policies and behaviors.

Informed by this social construction approach, Landscape, as it develops on these pages out of the stories that sustainability practitioners shared with me, stands at the intersection of geographic place and society. In *Landscape and Memory* Simon Schama writes, "Before it can ever be a repose for the senses, landscape is a work of the mind. Its scenery is built up as much from strata of memory as from layers of rock."[2] Schama's memories are expressed as meanings passed from generation to generation. There is culture, history, and connection to people, wildlife, and geography in them.

Those same factors influence Landscape as I convey the concept here. But the takeaway message from this book is that the view does not have to be over the shoulder. Landscapes are not merely received and ready-made; future Landscapes don't have to be preformed or happened onto by accident. They may be created anew: new memories of place consciously crafted.

My efforts to identify the new Hudson region Landscape that is in-becoming today, then, have two purposes: to expose those novel meanings and by doing so to encourage discussion and debate over them and over the region's future. Tomorrow is too important to stumble into blindly.

Framing Landscape as the result of people interacting with one another and with place enables it to address a host of questions: How do we see and understand the places that mean the most to us? What is our relationship to the world around us? How does our treatment of air, water, soil, plants, and animals reflect our place in the world, and what insights can we take from those actions? How do our interactions with a geographical place influence our interactions with one another? How are nature and society connected—and how did they ever come to be disconnected? Perhaps most important for sustainability, what do we want our future Landscapes to look and live like?

Creating Sustainable Communities explores these questions, the Landscape concept providing us with a particularly insightful tool for grasping the commonalities and differences that bridge and distinguish the place-people-nature nexus that sustainability advocates seek to develop.

Beyond Meaning

All this talk of "meaning" can sound overly abstract, so it's worth pointing out that sociologists are not much interested in the old "if a tree falls in a forest and no one is there to hear it, does it make a sound?" philosophical conundrum, with its implication that reality itself comes down to human *perception*. To the contrary, reality comes down to its *construction*: it is a meaning-filled phenomenon created not in the individual's mind but through many people's shared connotations of the worlds they inhabit. From this socially constructed point of view, real, physical landscapes exist. Trees, mountains, fish, and you and I are there. But what they mean—what we make of them in word and deed—is not self-evident.

Social constructions of place, Landscapes for us, are uncovered by considering how people "speak" (talk, paint, photograph, film, and write) of their location. Landscape narratives are also revealed through how we physically make place: the shape of our towns and cities, whether we dam rivers or leave them free-flowing, the protections we erect for conservation, and how the powerful treat those less fortunate.

We infuse the places we settle with meaning, almost always unconsciously inscribing our interpretations of the land and one another through those ways of speaking and living. Whether and how we talk of place with neighbors and friends, what we build, how we treat the land—the ways we make place part of our lives or not—expose the connotative meanings of place commonly hidden in people's everyday lives.

As Schama would expect, everywhere we look in the Hudson River region we find intimations of past Landscapes. For example, on a sunny July day I drove through Catskill State Park past the tiny villages of Phoenecia and Fleischmanns, gradually gaining altitude, then leaving the Hudson River watershed and gliding down to Arkville to speak with Alan White, executive director of the Catskill Center. Formally the Catskill Center for Conservation and Development, the Center is oddly positioned somewhere between environmental advocacy and economic development, and it confronts challenges on both fronts.

Like another great range that partially lies within the watershed, the Adirondack Mountains, the Catskill Mountains now designated by New York's Constitution as "forever wild" were once all but completely tamed. White explained, "The Catskills are the poster child of a boom-bust economy, and we've seen it over and over again. It began with leather tanning in the mid-1800s, which took the hemlocks but opened the land for farming."

Logged almost to the last tree for firewood and to supply bark for leather tanning, the Catskills were transformed into thin-soiled farmland, much of which proved unfit for cropping and barely able to support dairy cattle. Then for a time the Catskills became a summer playground that attracted visitors eager for relief from a sweltering New York City; "Borscht Belt" comedians from Woody Allen and Billy Crystal to Phyllis Diller and Henny Youngman played now-defunct clubs. Today, White told me, the dwindling number of residents face challenging economic conditions with few employment opportunities in Catskill State Park (like Adirondack Park, about half of the land in "the Catskills," as the park is known, is privately owned). Yet before any development took place, the Catskills were so inaccessible, remote, and mysterious that Washington Irving situated his somnolent "Rip Van Winkle" there.

So what, exactly, *are* the Catskills? With the aid of even such a thumbnail version of history we can identify a host of meanings—several Landscapes—created for that place over the last two centuries: first, there was Irving's *forbidding wilderness*, then the tannery owners' *resource-filled land* available for economic gain, followed by the *hard-won livelihoods* experienced by generations of farmers, then city dwellers' *escape*, and, finally, today's residents' *imperiled home*.

Far from a comprehensive analysis of the socioecological history of the Catskills, that list of shifting Landscapes demonstrates a simple, frequently overlooked side of life: places matter to us. Integral facets of our lives, when we hold places dear we create meanings for them; the same is true when we despise them. Our home towns, favorite recreational spots, grandparents' farms, inner city blocks and parks, and even, I suppose, the denuded hillside one has handsomely profited from: the locales that touch (or scar) us reside in special corners of our hearts, psyches, even bank accounts. Whether we return to them nightly after work, a few times each year to visit family, or never again, our most important places never escape us.

∾

Some final thoughts on Landscapes, meaning, and reality to prepare us for what lies ahead: First, meaning does not exist in a social sense until it is shared. For example, it is only when we tell others what we think our local land use laws ought to look like that what rumbles around our brains shifts from mere musing to meaning. Once those ideas become public, there's one additional step necessary for meaning making: they must become adopted by others. The sharing of new meanings is about more and more of us accepting novel characterizations of some thing.

There are other ways to construct meanings than person-to-person interaction, of course. Governments, corporations, religions, and non-profit groups propagate meanings, too. What they have going for them is that they are established. With ready-made soapboxes and constituencies, they enjoy something that individual agents and small groups lack: power. In the scholarly literature on the social construction of nature, one frequently reads of the power dynamic between dominant and insurgent meanings that have been created for some phenomenon. Examples include the National Park Service versus wild horse advocates in Ozark National Park,[3] developers versus cattle egret sympathizers in Arkansas,[4] and the Massachusetts Department of Environmental Protection versus animal rights advocates.[5] My own research includes examinations of competing constructions of wolves between the U.S. Fish and Wildlife Service and residents living in areas where the Service reintroduced the predator.[6]

Meanings, then, often are contested. Throughout the chapters that follow, we will see the emergence of different versions of the Hudson River Landscape—different meanings and realities of that Landscape—in the words and deeds of those with whom I spoke. In this time of tension between old, wasteful, destructive ways of living and foresightful, sustainable visions of the future, Landscapes become unsettled places. The Hudson region's reality is very much up for grabs.

When scholars explore meaning, we typically don't address it head on, preferring to come at the concept obliquely. In other words, in my interviews I avoided the most obvious question, What does the Hudson River region mean to you? I did so for a couple of reasons. First, most people don't think directly about meaning and reality very often. They're simply there, effortlessly conveyed in conversation or (re)created through the little things we do each day. Meaning making and reproduction is the most overlooked social taken-for-granted of them all, so such an abstract question would probably have proven to be a conversation stopper—the last thing I wanted to have happen in the middle of an interview!

More tellingly, though, asking directly about meaning would probably have distracted many people from the simple act of telling me their stories. They might have attempted to contort their comments in ways that addressed the region's meaning, when the job of putting their ideas into the Landscape frame was my responsibility, not theirs.

From my analytical perch, as I implied in my Catskill story, I spy a region's Landscape that has been repeatedly written and revised, as it is once again being rewritten today. Numerous activists, business people, elected officials, and organizations are striving to create permanently livable places in the Hudson region. Unlike nearly all of the meaning making that came before, however, today's efforts are intentional: full of focus and vision, compelled by a belief that this special place can be reinvigorated and remade, conceptually and physically, into a sustainable Landscape rich with conscious, conscientious meaning that feeds its people, celebrates its place, welcomes diverse communities, rehabilitates ecosystems, and provides a good life for all.

Sustainability's Challenge

The sustainability revolution that has swept global environmentalism can be traced to the 1987 publication of the Brundtland Report for the United Nations World Commission on Environment and Development,[7] named after the commission's chair, Gro Harlem Brundtland, and later published as *Our Common Future*.[8] The report defined sustainability in the context of "sustainable development," its authors arguing that "sustainable development is not a fixed state of harmony, but rather a process of change in which the exploitation of resources, the direction of investments, the orientation of technological development, and institutional change are made consistent with future as well as present needs."[9]

That definition implies a new rationality that stands opposed to the narrowly economic one predominant back then and tenaciously holding on today. In the old, "rational" actors seek to maximize profit. In contrast, sustainable development's rationality introduces a different logic emphasizing a future in which ecological well-being takes precedence over economic gain. Author Joan Fitzgerald observes that embedded in that shift is "a tacit radicalism—the sustainability agenda is a political critique of the inherent ecological damage and economic inequality created by free-market capitalism."[10]

The Brundtland Report's authors didn't stop there. They also emphasized the importance of social justice to a sustainable future: ending poverty and unequal distribution of wealth and resources.[11] Can our economic system accept environmental quality and social equity standing on-level with profitable gain? This approach has led many scholars to observe that sustainability demands a new accounting, one encompassing equity, the environment, and economics: a "triple bottom line" often referred to as "people, planet, profit."[12]

Sustainability's critique is that we are living life out of balance on multiple dimensions. It espouses a tension between enough and too much, between adequate and excessive. Too many of us use too much energy, too much land in too many wrong ways. We eat too much, and that food comes from too far away. And too many, even in the United States—and certainly in the Hudson region—are left out of today's single bottom-line accounting, their lives, cultures, and politics irrelevant in the face of the dominant constructions of the Landscape.

For the people with whom I spoke, sustainability addresses practical, immediate issues that center on creating livable, equitable communities, protecting ecosystems, and promoting businesses that are deeply "green." It infuses new meaning into work, play, and place. Sustainability is Landscape creation for the long run and for all of us.

Plan of the Book

Before outlining what lies ahead chapter by chapter, a word regarding weaving is in order. Interweaving, actually: in the course of exploring first how the Hudson River region's Landscape emerged and then how different individuals and groups are working to infuse new meaning into our relationship with this place, readers will encounter overlapping characters, organizations, and foci from chapter to chapter. For example, in chapter

3 farmer Paul Arnold discusses the business side of Pleasant Valley Farm, while in chapter 7, on green business, we see the close affinity between a distillery and the local farm that provides its heirloom corn.

Like the intimate interconnections found in functioning ecosystems, the experiences that the region's sustainability advocates shared with me inevitably cross the artificial boundaries of "land use," "energy," "community," and the like. Those interwoven notions are an important part of the joy, optimism, hard work, challenge, and opportunity found in efforts to remake and re-mean the region. In addition, the inclusion of a range of interwoven examples in each chapter helps strengthen the Landscape concept, since any theme that can be identified running through such varied experiences has built-in explanatory insight.

Now for what lies ahead:

A combination of social and economic history, chapter 1, "How We Lost Sustainability," argues that the Hudson region's sustainability challenge is in vital ways rooted in economics and in our past unwillingness to live as if ecology and equity mattered. Critiques of the capitalism-nature-society relationship developed by sociologists and environmental economists provide insight into the emergence of the region's dominant Landscape, and the environment-focused work of historians, geographers, and philosophers helps explain our fraught relationship with this place.

Sustainability's ideal is found in the concept of stable ecosystems: that all of nature's pieces ought to be present as they were at some historical moment—in the Hudson region's case, prior to European arrival—and that they remain that way into the future, gradually evolving on their own. Chapter 2, "A Place under Siege," outlines some of the key ecological obstacles confronting the region's sustainability advocates, from ecosystem health to invasive species to global climate change to, of all things, salt.

Food sustainability, supplying all of a population's nutritional needs using agricultural and transportation methods that can be perpetuated, is fundamental to any conception of a lasting Landscape. In chapter 3, "A Constant Bounty," we see farming as intimately tied to other central topics in *Creating Sustainable Communities*: promoting healthier ecosystems and as a vital part of land use, providing open space, reenvisioning communities, strengthening ties between cities and the land, and farming as the original "green" enterprise.

At best, it seems, the phrase "land use planning" prompts profound drowsiness as visions of late-night planning board discussions over zoning and setbacks come to mind; at worst, land use planning is the favored tool of unscrupulous local growth coalitions comprised of real estate developers and crony politicians. Of course, those powerful interests would not pay attention to land use issues if there was not a great deal of economic and political value in them; indeed, nothing influences Landscape in more lasting ways than land use planning. In chapter 4, "Two Hundred Subdivisions Too Late?" we encounter advocates whose land use visions have remade their towns—even whole counties—in the spirit of sustainability, in the process re-meaning the places nearest to them.

"Community" is a disturbingly vague concept. Not unlike "nature" in its flexibility, at moments community evokes identity and the intensely personal. Yet it also may inhere oppression and conflict. In its variability community may not be among the most "dangerous" words in English, as C. P. Snow once labeled nature, but it is certainly one of the most malleable.[13] That variety emerges in chapter 5, "Remaking Communities," where we examine community's links to sustainability from the personal to the neighborhood and beyond, including its vital ties to environmental justice.

Cities are essential to any credible approach to sustainability. They hold the promise—though rarely the reality—of astounding efficiencies in water and energy use, transportation, and minimizing housing "footprints" (the on-the-ground space used by a given unit of housing). Cities also are often home to local communities that may produce grassroots social transformation, as I discuss in chapter 6, "How It All Adds Up." Such change is desperately needed in the Hudson region, where whole cities such as Newburgh, New York, struggle from decay and neglect. Yet Newburgh, Poughkeepsie, Saratoga Springs, New York City, and numerous other villages, towns, and cities are reinventing their immediate, "micro" Landscapes in ways that will create culturally, economically, ecologically, and socially lasting places.

Perhaps an even greater challenge than ecological sustainability is economic sustainability. Indeed, persuasive scholarship exists insisting that capitalism cannot be sustainable. Our economic system's second fundamental premise, following from the profit motive, has long been that economies must grow forever. Yet that assertion violates multiple ecological laws. Is "sustainable capitalism" a contradiction in terms? Can we even approach it? In chapter 7, "A Complete Disruption," business owners and consultants from the Hudson region insist we can.

To those familiar with American environmentalism's history, only a couple of places in the United States, perhaps Thoreau's Walden Pond and John Muir's Sierra Nevada mountain range, are more closely associated with the environmental movement than is the Hudson region. In chapter 8, "A Landscape to Fight For," advocates argue that this region's Walden Pond is the Hudson River, a thread of life that activists would not let die, and its Sierras are Mount Greylock, the Highlands, the Catskills, and the Adirondacks—with Bob Marshall standing in as their John Muir. But those examples are misleading because they mistakenly elevate the past and ignore the present. From conservation efforts by land trusts to citizen science to creative extensions of the "environmentalism" label, the region's environmental activists have been and remain in the vanguard of shaping the region's Landscapes.

In the concluding chapter, "A Practical Revolution," I argue that if the Hudson River region's experiences tell us anything about sustainability, it is that its ingredients have as much to do with human ingenuity as ecological law. Like the processes that transformed early settlers' agrarian Landscapes into industrial Landscapes characterized by sprawl, overuse, and social inequalities, the promise of newly remade and re-meant Landscapes is very much about choices we make. Especially striking is the intentionality of the region's sustainability advocates. While no single Landscape emerges from their visions, when taken together the storytellers—and their accomplishments—are shaping a new, lasting reality for the Hudson River region.

Chapter 1

How We Lost Sustainability

O nce upon a time, Glens Falls, New York, was among the wealthiest
cities in the United States. Standing on the banks of the Hudson as
the river arcs from its nursery in the nearby Adirondack Mountains, it was
home to numerous sawmills and papermaking plants. Ancient trees cut
from the mountains were floated downriver in huge "rafts" to be processed
into wallpaper and toilet paper, the stuff of prosperity, transforming the
little town above the cave that James Fennimore Cooper made famous in
Last of the Mohicans[1] into the locus of immense wealth.

Today, few of us can locate Glens Falls on a map. Its lone paper
mill employs fewer than six hundred blue collar workers, down from the
"five thousand honest hands" about whom Pete Seeger once rhapsodized.[2]
Between Glens Falls and New York City, two hundred river miles south,
similar stories abound: General Electric's factories dotted the river's shore
but now are all but gone. RCA once built stereos in Albany, and General
Motors manufactured cars in Sleepy Hollow, yet no more. While IBM
remains a presence in Poughkeepsie and Dutchess County, where it long
has made some of its most powerful computers, since the 1990s it has
shed thousands of employees.

Of course, the region's economic story is not completely bleak. Far
from it. New York Harbor—the mouth of the Hudson—was and is home
to massive ports on both the New York and New Jersey sides of the river.
For more than four hundred years the great city first known as New
Amsterdam has been an economic growth machine, and Wall Street—
one of the oldest tracks in Manhattan—is synonymous with capitalism's
potential and its pitfalls.

In this chapter I trace our economic system's role in transforming the region's Landscape over the four centuries since Henry Hudson sailed up the river that would take his name. I then discuss the work of scholars who have implicated business in the creation of the unsustainable social and ecological worlds we know so well—and others who insist that same force can be a driver of sustainability.

My goals here are, first, to demonstrate that Landscape transformation is a historical process. The destruction so many bemoan did not occur overnight; by the same token, the construction of a new Hudson region Landscape is possible . . . and likely will take decades to create. Second, I want to establish the causal foundation for the ecological challenges facing the region that I discuss in chapter 2, some of the community-based social problems that emerge in chapter 5, and even the potential for a planet-friendly capitalism like that advocated for in chapter 7.

Third, it is important to acknowledge the dominant forces that confront sustainability advocates; every individual in the region—to say nothing of the corporations, think tanks, and governments—is invested in our current economic system, making its alteration a challenge fraught with pitfalls. Finally, from Henry Hudson's time this region's Landscape has been in a constant state of flux—change is, after all, endemic to our economic system. Here, I hope to show how, even though this place has been ceaselessly remade, that very renovation process may in the end lead us to a stable Landscape where revision is replaced by simple vision.

A Landscape Overturned

At the heart of our economic system—at least in its classical form, the view that dominates even today—lies exploitation. Trees, soil, oil, minerals, air, water, wildlife, and workers are all used in the creation of profit, and few natural resources were more sought after in the early seventeenth century than beaver.

To say beaver were exploited is to understate the case by a fair bit. As early as the 1500s beaver felt hats were all the rage in Europe, status indicators of such lasting power that, though the styles varied, nations were formed and dissolved, and wars fought, for three centuries beaver remained the choice for headwear among elites on both sides of the Atlantic (Abraham Lincoln's famous stovepipe hats were beaver).[3] So, after their 1609 voyage, when Henry Hudson and his crew reported to their Dutch sponsors that many of the natives they encountered wore furs, it prompted competing trading companies to scramble to stake a claim to this New World territory.

Contemplating the plunder that followed, journalist Robert Boyle wrote, "Of all the mammals of New York, the beaver has the most checkered history. Beavers, of course, were the main object of the Dutch fur trade. They were trapped by the hundreds of thousands and their pelts shipped to Europe for the making of hats."[4] The Dutch did little or no trapping themselves, since beaver were found in the interior, away from the Hudson River, where it was forbidding and even forbidden to them.

That work was left to aboriginal peoples. In his environmental history of New York, David Stradling wrote, "The fur trade gave Native Americans their first exposure to the profit motive and thus initiated a changing relationship with nature. Never before had native peoples hunted so completely for trade."[5] Previously, the first Americans' interactions with other species had been mediated by their strong cultural ties to nonhumans, which required reflective ceremonies and effectively restricted overhunting. Not so with the fur trade.

In asking how it was that acquisitive economics trumped established relations between aboriginal peoples and the beaver, Stradling poses a question that remains relevant today. For those first Americans, perhaps a "spiritual crisis" prompted by increasing disease (transmitted to them, unbeknownst to either group, through contact with the Europeans) compelled them to violate norms that had emerged over millennia living on this continent, or maybe "they simply found the market too alluring, the guns and gunpowder too useful to pass up. For most tribes the fur trade constituted their first prolonged interactions with Europeans, and through increasingly regularized trading, natives purchased a variety of goods, including cloth, tools, and metal pots, all of which they quickly wove into the fabric of their culture."[6]

In 1655, the year of his death, early Dutch settler Adriaen van der Donck's account of life in "New Netherland" was published. Written decades earlier, his memoir recounted a time that was already passing. "We also frequently trade with the Indians," he wrote, "who come more than ten and twenty days' journey from the interior, and who have been farther off to catch beavers, and they know of no limits to the country, and when spoken to on the subject, they deem such enquiries to be strange and singular."[7]

Having all but extirpated beaver on their home continent, Europeans knew from experience that the exploitation could not go on forever, but it was an inconceivable notion to Native Americans. Indeed, by the time van der Donck's book was published, the region's beaver numbers already had crashed. While the fur trade with Europe was over, European economics nevertheless held sway—no other source existed for the goods that native people found so alluring. In Stradling's account, the first great re-meaning of the Hudson region's Landscape occurred rapidly and, in terms of the triple bottom line of ecology, economy, and equality, the new Landscape was complete: ecosystems were fundamentally altered, and powerful dependencies between aboriginal people and capitalism were created.

Graham Hodges, a Colgate University history professor, observes, "It's important for Dutch strategic and diplomatic interests to have a colony along the Atlantic. The English control everything from present-day Maine down to South Carolina. So this is the only point where there is a non-English entryway along the Atlantic coast." Those "strategic" efforts were first and foremost economic. So while the Dutch primarily sought to enrich corporations in the home country, when the British bloodlessly wrested control of the Hudson region in 1664, they were more bent on colonization—control of the land for both political and economic purposes. The British wanted a northern foothold to ward off the French, who controlled Canada south to the Adirondacks (their sweeping presence ran west and farther south, down the Ohio and Mississippi river valleys to the Gulf of Mexico).

The British undertook a subjugation process of land and people that was central to the creation of the continent's third Landscape. The first emerged from native people's manipulation of the ecology after their arrival, most significantly through the use of fire,[8] and the second was the Dutch plunder of fur-bearing animals. In all three, people, ecology, and economy were intimately connected, but the character of those relationships varied in fundamental ways.

The region's native peoples actively observed topography, plant and animal behavior, seasonal signs, and the like—practices long since forgotten. Tom Lake, a New York State naturalist, notes, "Native people employed what we would consider modern concepts of ecology thousands of years ago. . . . They understood that you can control nature in a way, but it's a symbiosis. You're actually helping by fostering new growth and at the same time you're helping yourself because it's going to attract different kinds of animals."

Native people's cosmology, too, contrasted profoundly with today's dominant understandings. For aboriginal Americans "the whole world is alive," observes Vassar College anthropologist Lucille Johnson. "You are in a living universe. You are also a part of that universe, not apart from that universe, as we tend to be. . . . For the Native Americans, people are of the world just as a deer is of the world, just as an ant is of the world, just as an oak tree is of the world."

Those first Hudson peoples invested "natural" entities (their language included no such word as our *nature*) with respect and transcendental importance. The same was true for their fellow tribe members. Most native cultures were highly egalitarian, and when their economies were not entirely subsistence-based (the Lenni Lenape were major traders, and many tribes were known for their special talents in, for example, pottery or canoe building) profit never entered the picture. The people of the region farmed, but one early American estimate was they cleared only about 1 percent of the land, so light was their ecological footprint.[9]

The Dutch Landscape introduced a thoroughly European, anthropocentric understanding of relations between humans and the land in which economics was privileged over all else in social life save, perhaps, religion—although, as Max Weber argued, early Protestantism like that practiced in Holland can be seen as providing higher justification for capitalist business practices.[10] "[F]or all their intensity in pursuit of the pelts given up by the Indians for mere trinkets," writes the eloquent Vernon Benjamin, "the details of this New World, like the trees of the forest, hid an even larger reality that diminished these men and the grand ego of a world they came from. . . . [T]he Europeans who were so intensely focused on the profits of the pelt trade did not see the integrated, natural reality that loomed all around them." He adds, "They were not 'discovering' a New World; they were dismembering an old one."[11] Nature was God's gift for humans to use—not to contemplate, appreciate, live harmoniously with, or worship—creating an unmistakable hierarchy not only of being but of cultures as well. Europeans felt free to break apart nature, whether for profit or science, their outlook privileging their desires over all others'.

In key respects, the particulars of the Landscape imposed by the English differed little from Dutch beliefs and behaviors. Humans continued to be the measure of all things, and under God's direction the land was to be subjugated. However, there were important distinctions between the culture-ecology nexuses created by the two rivals. For one, in their best moments the British respected native people's rights such that London restricted westward expansion of European settlement, something the Dutch, who were almost continuously at war with aboriginal peoples, likely would never have done.

Tragically, the other side of the coin was the British promotion of slavery, including the opening of a slave market in New York City in 1711. To economically and politically powerful New Yorkers—like, before them, Dutch New Amsterdamians—slaves and near-slaves, such as indentured servants and tenant farmers, were necessary for clearing the massive tracts of land that were fundamental to securing British claims to this part of the continent.[12] While native peoples, particularly the Lenni Lenape, had practiced fire-based swidden horticulture in the region for centuries (clearing land using fire, then farming it for two or three years before moving on), the English encouraged extensive land clearing for settled agriculture, a technology practiced on a scale unknown to the natives, remaking the Hudson Landscape on a thoroughly European model. The land was opened for continental animals to graze and European crops to be planted, and those tenant farmers, indentured servants, and outright slaves were compelled to work the land without being allowed to share in their labor's financial fruits.

Industrializing the Hudson River Region

During the summer and fall of 1777, little more than a year after the colonies declared their independence from Great Britain, what many historians consider the turning point of the American Revolution took place in the Hudson region, concluding on the Hudson River shore with the surrender of an entire British army. The battles of Bennington and Saratoga ended an English effort to sever New England from the ostensibly less rebellious colonies to the south, greatly improving the revolutionaries' prospects.

In the early years following independence, economically the United States remained as it had been under the king's rule, agrarian. But the turn of the nineteenth century brought major changes. In 1807, Robert Fulton sailed the world's first viable steamship up the Hudson from Manhattan to Albany and back. And as the years passed, important aspects of American industrialism began and thrived along the Hudson, giving rise to the fourth major Landscape the region has witnessed since *Homo sapiens* arrived on the scene.

Canals constructed by the Dutch in lower Manhattan presaged the Erie Canal, arguably the continent's greatest such system, which ran along the Hudson and Mohawk rivers hundreds of miles west and ultimately out of the Hudson River drainage to Lake Erie. Governor DeWitt Clinton's "ditch," as the Erie Canal was derisively labeled by those who considered it a waste of taxpayer dollars, proved to be more economic boom than boondoggle, and it spurred the arrival of the Industrial Revolution on this continent.

At its peak, the canal floated ten thousand boats and more, and thirty thousand people's livelihoods were directly linked to it.[13] Much of the work was physical, not mechanical, performed by men and horses. Towns and cities sprang up to support first the canal's construction and then its commerce, and what once was three hundred miles of dense forest dotted with the odd clearing for native farms and villages rapidly became a deforested water-borne highway linking one rapidly growing community after another. Farmland worked by thousands of eager settlers spread for tens of miles on either side of the canal, the whites' presence made possible by the ongoing subjugation of the native people, who were killed off, driven westward, pacified, forced onto reservations, or assimilated.

The canal's economic success—in the fifty-eight years it operated as a paying concern, beginning in 1825, revenues exceeded the state's initial $7.5 million investment by roughly fifteen times—prompted the development of others. A privately owned canal, the Delaware and Hudson, was completed in 1828 and allowed massive shipments of comparatively clean-burning coal from Pennsylvania to power the nascent steam-driven industry in New York City and smaller but burgeoning upriver towns such as Newburgh.[14] Soon enough, railroads surpassed the canals as the primary mode of commercial transport in the region, but it was decades before they rendered defunct the canal trade.

Fresh, clean water is as integral to nearly every industry as it is to life, and as mechanization increased, so did pressure on the region's rivers and streams. Some was benign, such as the ice harvesting that enabled city residents to preserve food through the warm months. Perhaps the first industry to dramatically affect stream quality was leather tanning. The Dutch operated a tannery in New Amsterdam as early as 1635, and as the tannin-rich bark of hemlock trees there was used up, the industry moved north.[15] Hemlocks grow tall and graceful, their branches dipping and then sweeping upward as they stretch from their trunks. Living 250 years or more, and growing up to one hundred feet tall, mature hemlock groves block enough sun to create an open forest floor unusual in the Northeast.

It took two hundred years from Henry Hudson's arrival for tanners to find their way to the steep Catskill slopes. In the five decades that followed, up until roughly 1870, they cut down seventy million hemlocks, fundamentally altering the Catskill Landscape. A new economy was introduced to the mountains, a new ecology was carved out of it, and new social inequalities resulted. "Life in a tannery town was tough," wrote forestry professor Hugh O. Canham.

> The work was hard manual labor. Living next to a tannery meant the constant stench of curing leather and stagnant pools of waste material. Streams became heavily polluted as tanning liquors, lime solutions, flesh, and hair were discharged directly into them. Hillsides were stripped of hemlock. On the other hand, the tanneries provided a livelihood, often for immigrants, and gave local farmers a market for the hides of slaughtered animals. Some of the tannery workers owned farms and worked in the tanneries part time or seasonally. Others lived in boardinghouses at the tanneries, where they worked 12-hour days with only Sundays off.[16]

People such as Rufus Palen and Zadock Pratt, whose names live on in the Catskill towns of Palenville and Prattsville (there's also Tannersville), made fortunes off of the devastation and others' labor, leaving those who worked for them to live in squalor amid the blighted, barren hills.

However, the Catskill tanning, and the clearcutting of much of the easily accessible timber in the Hudson River's Adirondack Mountain headwaters for lumber, charcoal, and papermaking at Corinth and Glens Falls, produced a backlash. In retrospect we can see the creation of, first, the New York State Forest Preserve system and, later, state parks in the Catskills and Adirondacks as among the nation's initial acknowledgments that unrestrained ecological destruction for corporate gain could not be permitted. In the limits set on development—such as the famous "Blue Line" demarcating both Adirondack and Catskill state parks—were glimmers of the sustainability ethos blossoming so noticeably in the region today. As well, they foreshadowed the new Landscape that sustainability advocates espouse.

Most of the preservation impetus focused on the Adirondacks, convinced as scientists and policymakers then were that the headwaters of rivers should be protected against development. Then—in the 1870s—as now, economy trumped ecology at nearly every turn. But in this instance the two proved compatible. David Stradling points out that "downstate economic interests . . . argued that despite the growing importance of railroads, New York City's commercial status still relied upon the easy and inexpensive access to interior markets afforded by the Hudson River and the Erie Canal, both of which required the consistent flow of water out of the Adirondacks."[17] Timbering Mt. Marcy, New York's highest peak and the home of the Hudson's source waters, threatened to dry up the mighty river's flow—and the almighty dollar's as well.

After years of squabbling, in 1885 the state legislature was convinced. It set aside 681,000 acres in the Adirondacks, and nearly 34,000 acres in the Catskills, as off limits to logging. Nine years later those lands became constitutionally protected when New York's voters directed, "The lands of the state, now owned or hereafter acquired, constituting the forest preserve as now fixed by law, shall be forever kept as wild forest lands."[18] That "forever wild" clause remains a precious one, particularly because both parks, now totaling 5.86 million acres in the Adirondacks and 707,000 acres in the Catskills, include substantial tracts of privately owned land: 50 and 53 percent, respectively. The parks have long embodied the tension between development and preservation increasingly commonplace throughout the region.

Tanneries were probably the first major source of water pollution, along with the untreated sewage that was dumped into every stream, river, lake, pond, and swamp for centuries. Industrialization increased the quantity and types of pollutants to . . . well, an industrial scale. In his detailed history of the Hudson River published in 1969, Robert Boyle wrote that almost immediately as the river tumbled out of its mountain birthing rounds, it was "greatly despoiled and disfigured by pollution, much of which is from pulp and paper mills grinding up Adirondack wood for greeting cards, stationery, cartons, and, fittingly, toilet paper. . . . At Corinth, a plant of the International Paper Company sucks up eighteen million gallons of river water a day and in return spews raw pulp and paper wastes back into the Hudson through an open ditch and two outfall troughs."[19]

The pollutants built up with each of the 220 miles from Corinth to Manhattan. In The Big Oyster, Mark Kurlansky reflects on the situation at the Hudson's mouth near the turn of the twentieth century, writing, "Sturgeon catches, which had been more than one million pounds a year, giving the fish the nickname Albany beef, started to dramatically drop from pollution, which also ended the caviar industry. Fish trapped in shallow water found themselves suffocated in oil spills. . . . Lobster and bluefish started disappearing. Those that survived, including some oysters, were too contaminated to eat. The sharks stayed off of Sandy Hook to avoid the city's foul waters."[20] Sewage, dye waste, oil, garbage, industrial effluent of all manner: the region's booming economy, spurred by the burgeoning population industrialism attracted, was killing the river.

Boyle paints a chilling picture of the Hudson at mid-century, pre–Clean Water Act. Cities all along the Mohawk—the Hudson's primary tributary—and upper Hudson continued to dump untreated sewage into the rivers, and factories poured unknown chemicals into the mix, creating the "Albany Pool," a thirty to forty mile long stretch of filth so fetid that no dissolved oxygen could be found in the water during hot, dry periods. And, thus, no aquatic organisms could survive there: a riverine dead zone.

Even "clean" uses of the river posed profound challenges to it. Boyle led the opposition to a 1963 Consolidated Edison scheme that would have defaced the 1,380-foot Storm King Mountain to provide power for New York City. Con Ed planned to pump river water to the top of Storm King, the Hudson's most iconic fixture, then release it during times of peak energy demand to turn electricity-producing turbines at the mountain's base. The plan, examined in more detail in chapter 8, would have destroyed a protected state forest and killed untold thousands of organisms daily as pumps sucked them up the mountain or sent the survivors down through the powerhouse, with its spinning turbines and immense pressures. Con Ed pulled its proposal in 1980 under relentless pressure from environmentalists.

Upland, away from the rivers and streams, nineteenth- and twentieth-century industry profoundly affected the look and quality of the land. Early in the industrial era there was the deforesting of the Catskills and Adirondacks, and virtually everywhere in between topsoil erosion was extreme when the land wasn't quickly planted in crops after the forests were felled. Air pollution from coal and wood burning power plants, and from vehicle emissions as the internal combustion engine took hold, fouled the air in cities and towns; one estimate said one and one-half tons of soot was falling on each Manhattan block *each month* in the 1950s.[21]

Industries also polluted soil and groundwater. For instance, daily as I head into work at Skidmore College in Saratoga Springs, New York, I pass a bizarre sight. A couple of old brick structures surrounded by an expanse of asphalt stand behind a high fence, the enclosed area totaling seven acres. It is a Superfund site, by definition one of the most toxic locations in the nation, where, beginning in 1853, coal was processed into gas for streetlamps. The uses changed from gasification to vehicle maintenance over more than ninety years, the contamination building to the point that "coal tar" and a long list of other toxins poisoned the soil and groundwater, posing a threat to ten thousand residents living within a mile of the site.[22] "Cleanup" of the area—including paving over all exposed surfaces—was completed several years ago, but it appears the tourist mecca of Saratoga is permanently scarred.

Even the literal headwaters of the Hudson were tarnished by industrialism. A short walk from the confluence of the aptly named Calamity Brook and Indian Pass Brook (the outflow of dammed Henderson Lake), where cartographers say the Hudson begins, stands an abandoned mine in the ghost town of Tahawus. Deep ponds have filled the huge old pits, and mountainous tailing piles left behind when the mine closed for good in 1989 loom over the infant Hudson. The Adirondack Iron Works mine first shut down in 1857 because the iron was so difficult to separate from impurities. Those contaminants turned out to be the really valuable stuff, and National Lead Industries reopened the mine in 1940 to extract the titanium dioxide, forty million tons all told, for use in warplanes. In 2003, the Open Space Institute purchased ten thousand acres, including the historic mine site, for $8.5 million, and today it jointly oversees the area with the State of New York.

Like the Tahawus Tract, much has changed for the better since Robert Boyle's book was published, thanks to it and to the environmental organization Riverkeeper, which he co-founded. But at times it seems that every positive carries a negative. Some of the worst polluters—the Corinth paper plant among them—have closed down, a good thing for the ecology but a nightmare for dependent one-horse communities.

New laws curb the disposition of industry to treat waterways as dumping grounds, but some businesses were grandfathered into the Clean Water Act, and to this day the Finch, Pruyn paper mill in Glens Falls is the worst Hudson River polluter.[23] The Albany Pool is no more; however, throughout the region "combined sewage overflow," a result of water from streetside gutters being channeled into the same pipes as human waste, finds the river inundated with filth during every rainstorm or snowmelt.

Environmental insults to the region never seem to end, nearly all tied to industrialism. In 1963, around the time that activists started opposing Con Ed's Storm King plans, just upriver it opened Indian Point Nuclear Power Plant. Its reactors supply a quarter of the New York City region's power, using Hudson River water to provide cooling. But in the process, an estimated one billion organisms—"fish and crabs, but mostly larvae"[24]—are killed each year, radioactive elements leak into the Hudson, and radioactive steam is vented into the air around the plant. And as a result of decades of releases of polychlorinated bipheynols (PCBs), in 2002 General Electric accepted responsibility for the largest Superfund site in the nation—all two hundred miles of the Hudson River from Hudson Falls to the Battery in Manhattan (see chapter 2).

Understanding Unsustainability

America's first great painters were landscape artists. Emerging as the group did in the Hudson region, it took the label Hudson River School. Their first works date to 1825, and art historians say the school "closed" fifty years later—a period spanning the early industrialization of the region. Hudson River School artists were known to extoll the promise of industrialism, sometimes portraying the heavy black smoke from factories' stacks as wisps of white. Reflecting the social consensus, in those painters' view industrialism was exhilarating, the potential for economic growth and the resulting social good seemingly endless.

But not all of them accepted the received view of manufacturing as beneficent. Hudson River School painter Samuel Gifford's *Storm King on the Hudson*, for example, depicts a gale lashing the Hudson at the feet of the Highlands.[25] In the foreground, white-capped waves threaten to swamp an old wind-powered Dutch sloop, to the horror of onlookers standing on a hillside. In the far distance a steamship billowing black waste coldly powers away from the tumult. Harshly simple in its rendering, with a rectangle for a hull and another for its smokestack, the "unnatural" steamboat ominously heralds a new era in which nature itself has been conquered.

The region's legacy of unsustainability is a history no different than that endured by most other places in the United States, except the trajectory here was complete—from early, trade-based capitalism to emergent manufacturing to full-scale industrialism and today's "late" capitalism, with its synthetic chemicals and high technologies—while in others industrial capitalism arrived more rapidly or more fully formed. Regardless, a sustainable Hudson region economy was lost as soon as the Dutch began shipping vast numbers of pelts to Europe to stoke the beaver hat craze, fundamentally altering the region's ecology and native peoples' relationship with it.

Now as then, our economic system's obsession with growth breeds dangerous, often tragic outcomes ranging from massive wealth inequality to environmental destruction to the false beliefs that it can all continue forever and that we all will be rich someday. An essential tenet of sustainability holds that economic growth as we have traditionally understood it cannot persist indefinitely: ecologists have never identified a species immune from ecological limits, and there is no evidence *Homo sapiens* is any different from the rest except for our remarkable ability to stave off the inevitable—which may well mean our demise, as it already has that of thousands of other species.

Two divergent social science perspectives are especially helpful as guides for understanding the economy-ecology-society relationships so integral to sustainable futures: critical theory and ecological modernization.

Critical Environmental Theory

Critical environmental theory's roots extend back to Karl Marx's trenchant critiques of capitalism. Its scholars expand the connections he occasionally made between business, labor, and the environment and build on Marx's extensive exploration of the logic of capitalism. Such "ecological socialism," writes James O'Connor, "is concerned, for example, with the health problems of particular groups of workers, pollution problems in certain communities, zoning problems in certain districts, and so on."[26] O'Connor's evaluation of our economic system is direct: "the short answer to the question 'Is sustainable capitalism possible?' is 'No,' while the longer answer is 'Probably not.'"[27]

Why not? John Bellamy Foster argues that, "while we can envision more sustainable forms of technology that would solve much of the environmental problem, the development and implementation of these technologies is blocked by the mode of production—by capitalism and capitalists. Large corporations make the major decisions about the technology we use, and the sole lens that they consider in arriving at their decisions is profitability."[28] Even recycling keeps the "treadmill of production"—the profit-creating process dependent on new technologies and ever-increasing ecological destruction –turning over and over. From a business perspective, its aim is simply to make a profit from others' waste, and doing so inheres yet more wastes, such as water to clean recyclables and pollution-generating energy to transport and process them.[29]

But perhaps capitalism's greatest fault is its unaccountability. It imposes on nature the dual meaning of "source" and "sink": the locus both of raw materials and the dumping ground of that which is no longer usable or needed. Critical theorists insist that businesses never pay the full costs of doing what they do. Drilling for oil, for example, often creates air and water pollution, the price tag for which drilling companies get to ignore; paper companies along the Hudson dump wastes into the river without charge, and the coal-fired power plants along its shores did not have to pay for their carbon emissions until the last few years despite the costs of carbon-induced climate change to society (the Northeast's innovative carbon payment system is discussed in the Conclusion). "Capitalism," summarizes one ecological economist, "must be regarded as an economy of unpaid costs,"[30] the bill ultimately coming due in the form of damaged ecosystems, diseased humans, and the social ills emanating from rampant inequalities.

Critical ecological theory paints a picture of capitalism as an unsustainable economic system fundamentally at odds with both ecosystem health and human equality. Through that filter we see the Hudson region and its people as victimized the moment the Dutch arrived. From fur trapping to PCB contamination, the region's animals, trees, soils, minerals, and waters were stripped or dumped on for profits. Native peoples, and, later, the workers who toiled in tanneries and factories, became unwitting and poorly paid (or unpaid) accomplices in creating an unsustainable, inequitable Landscape.

As for the future, what is inevitable, according to critical ecologists, is social conflict. Following Marx, they argue that powerful business interests and their political allies will not go quietly when confronted by sustainability advocates hell-bent on creating a lasting world. But those advocates, weary though they may be from an economic system that leaps from crisis to crisis and wary of an uncertain ecological future, are increasingly boisterous and demanding. Change is on its way; its extent, and how orderly it will be, is the only question.

Ecological Modernization

One key shortcoming of critical ecology theory is it loses sight of the creativity fostered by capitalism. That's the view of "ecological modernization" scholars. Capitalism's responsiveness to "demand" is one of its great advantages (never mind that it *creates* demand far more often than it responds to it). Ecological modernists argue that the only realistic path to a livable future is through a reformation of our economic system that they insist is already under way, a process of finding a new direction driven by sustainability ideology and not narrowly by the compulsion to make a buck.

Ecological modernization began in the 1980s with a debate over whether policy changes of the sort devised by lawmakers and regulators were capable of adequately addressing environmental ills. "State actors," according to the perspective's foremost advocates, "lacked the knowledge, capacity and legitimacy to intervene in and control market actors and processes."[31] Regulation tends to exacerbate environmental problems, eco-modernists insist, because it puts businesses on the defensive and because regulators do not understand the corporate world.

On their face, arguments like that aren't much different than neo-liberal economists' assertions that virtually all regulation is anathema. But eco-modernists' views are more nuanced. Government needs to be involved in corporate behaviors affecting the environment—unrestrained capitalism creates more problems than it solves—but it doesn't have to exist in conflict with business. "What economic actors want is a more flexible, transparent, predictable, and tailor-made approach to environmental governance," not none at all, explain Gert Spaargaren and Arthur Mol. "Therefore, the state administration should be 'politically modernised' [to promote] more flexible, horizontal, network-like and participatory relationships between state and market actors."[32]

How can corporations be trusted to do right by the environment? Eco-modernists' response to that question is perhaps the most surprising and controversial of all their assumptions: because business, like every other aspect of society, has come to understand the centrality of ecological concerns. In fact, ecology stands on par with economy as essential to social stability, even survival, in our times. Ecological concern has developed "into an autonomous, independent factor which has to be taken into account and to be dealt with in the restructuring of production and consumption"; indeed, "the ecological sphere . . . is no longer 'contained' or 'enclosed' by the economic sphere,"[33] a reversal of the historical relationship between ecology and economy.

Business must respond to this new sphere of influence—this new reality that informs, even directs all else in society. Sustainability, from this perspective, *is* the new Landscape. It is already with us, not simply on the rise; of course it is far from complete, but what's key is there is no turning back. Using economic rationality and market dynamics as a guide, in the short run environmental destruction makes no sense because market share may be lost.

It's the long run that's really important, however. "[A]s nations develop and become technologically sophisticated," explains John P. Hoffmann, "they begin to improve their environmental conditions. . . . Technological sophistication permits more efficient conversion of raw products into finished materials and promotes more efficient use of agricultural, forest, and other types of land."[34] So thoroughgoing is the new ecological mindset that "institutions and social actors attempt to integrate environmental concerns into their everyday functioning, development, and relationships with others, including their relation with the natural world."[35] Business, ecological modernists insist, is rapidly becoming ecology's strongest ally.

Ecological modernization is appealing on multiple levels. Unlike critical ecology theory, it argues that social and ecological change need not be conflict-filled. Nor must change result in social structures—particularly an economic system—radically different from those we know today. And the notion that ecological realities stand on their own as the dominant force to be reckoned with is music to sustainability advocates' ears.

As such, eco-modernization's view of the Hudson region's history acknowledges the extraordinary environmental damage this place has endured at capitalism's hands, but it reads the trajectory of technology, policy, and activism optimistically. The River Observatory Network, a partnership between IBM and the nonprofit environmental advocacy organization Beacon Institute to monitor Hudson River water quality using a network of sensors,[36] and even environmental pariah GE's emphasis on promoting wind power, are indicative of ways that major corporations have begun to take seriously the imperatives of the ecological sphere. Eco-modernists insist there is more in the offing.

A Different Kind of Capitalism

It is not clear whether either of these theoretical perspectives will prove, over time, to be the better at interpreting our era.[37] My own view is that it would be foolish to suggest that we will arrive at sustainability tomorrow by eliminating capitalism. It won't happen, of course, and given the disruption to people's lives that precipitous economic change would prompt, it shouldn't. But our economic system must undergo extensive reform, and soon, if we are to rectify the nightmares of ecological damage and social inequality already with us—nightmares that, in the Hudson River region, began with the arrival of those earliest capitalists, the Dutch, and that have proceeded relentlessly until now. Gus Speth put it well when he wrote of his hope of transforming "the market into a benign and restorative force."[38]

This book is about the pragmatic: real-life people and organizations that are actually doing things differently in their communities, for their cities, on their farms. None of them have walked away from capitalism, and nearly all actively embrace it. But implicit in their words and deeds is that a different kind of capitalist economy is in the making, one skeptical of the endless growth mantra and that takes seriously the need to resolve the human-created tensions between economics, ecology, and one another. Band-Aids and easy-to-swallow solutions won't do.

Like everywhere else, what the Hudson region needs is a serious conversation about its future and a commitment on the part of policymakers, businesses, activists from numerous causes, and the general public to conscientiously pursue a different collective vision for this precious place. Perhaps the stories that follow, which sketch out the next—and perhaps last—Landscape shift in the region, can serve as a starting point for such a discussion.

Chapter 2

A Place under Siege

Ecologists aren't like the rest of us. The Landscapes they construct, reflecting their understanding of the biophysical ones they examine in their research, consist of fragmented remnants, metaphorical "islands" of habitat surrounded by ecological wastelands, "alien" life forms, and whole pieces of the canvas gone missing. Theirs is a scarred construction of nature, one that environmental philosopher Aldo Leopold poignantly gave voice to when he wrote,

> One of the penalties of an ecological education is that one lives alone in a world of wounds. Much of the damage inflicted on land is quite invisible to laymen. An ecologist must either harden his shell and make believe that the consequences of science are none of his business, or he must be the doctor who sees the marks of death in a community that believes itself well and does not want to be told otherwise.[1]

The depth of ecologists' understanding of human-nature connections is not widely shared, nor is the empathy Leopold alludes to, which is why too often "when we talk about ecosystems and ecology, we take ourselves out of it," according to Gary Kleppel.

The "we," in this case, is those of us who don't make a living examining the fractured society-ecosystem relationship that ecologists see—or those who cannot or will not take the time to question what occurs around us. We are blind to their tragic Landscape. Ecologists interpret and analyze what human-created, "anthropogenic" environmental abuse does to local marshes and to the global climate, their role that of planetary psychiatrists, noting with far greater insight than any Freud the blows not to ego but to eco.

Important as ecology is to sustainability, it is tempting to treat its Landscape as *the right* Landscape: to privilege ecology's guidance for understanding and interpreting human-environment interactions as the only perspective that ought to be attended to. After all, ecology has science behind it, and there is no greater authority in a "rational" society. But it is worth keeping in mind that science is a social enterprise. Its standards are human creations born of values; things such as the peer review process, when scholars read others' work and decide if it is worthy of being published, can be highly political. Further, ecology depends on theories and research methods that are debated and ultimately agreed upon by people. Moreover, theories and methods—explanations and means of examination—change over time. And science can produce ambiguous and even conflicting results, as we will see here and there below.

So ecologists infuse Landscapes with meaning just as other social groups do, not truth. But those meanings do carry with them the power and insight of science. They are the result of intense, systematic study, and in the Hudson region they present us with a picture of a place under siege. Home to the largest toxic spill in the United States, land of rampant development, under assault by "invasive" plants and animals, at moments this Landscape's wounds appear to be mortal. Any sensible triage surely would leave it for dead. While the reality is not so glum, ecology's damaged Hudson Landscape provides a necessary foundation for what follows, confronting us as it does with the challenges that must be addressed if the Hudson region is to last be remade intentionally.

After outlining ecology's vision, in this chapter I move on to explore the notion of "ecosystem health" and how ecologists from the mountains to the tidal marshlands assess the Hudson region's environmental status today. One of the most serious classes of threats to that health is "invasive" species, and another is global climate change, the ramifications of which I consider in turn. I conclude by discussing several emerging issues that natural scientists fear will further alter ecosystems and may affect human health as well.

Everything Is Hitched

Gary Kleppel's "we"—the great ecologically disengaged mass of us—is an uncomfortable label for multiple reasons, not least because it points toward a passivity that pervades society. "We become observers," says Kleppel, a State University of New York at Albany ecologist. "Yet humans are the biggest modifiers, the biggest impactors, of environment and of biological communities that has ever lived on earth!"

We inflict seemingly endless blows to the land—"nature"—and then we behave as if society was somehow not responsible for either the resultant bleeding or the stanching of it.

"We are *so* a part of the environment," Kleppel insists, "and the thing that makes us clumsy and bumbling is that we haven't realized (a) we *are* part of the environment and (b) we have not come to grips that we have responsibilities as members of the environment. We believe that there's us and there's the environment. Very few of us think of the environment as our life support system, and it is." To many people Landscape is something "out there." They inhabit houses and cars and lifestyles, but not ecological places, and their responsibilities are largely to family, friends, faith, and workplace—not to watersheds, forests, migratory birds, or the red efts struggling to cross the street in front of their home after a rain.

Overwhelmed by the stresses of everyday life and lured by modernity's escapes from it all in the form of seductive high technology toys, the savory pleasures of ready-made food, and the shopping mall's siren call, we can be forgiven for forgetting that we are biological creatures and that, collectively, our most important relationship is with the planet that sustains us.[2] But Landscape through ecology's eyes reminds us that getting right with the planet is not an option. At the least, we must honor that which sustains us.

More than a century ago, Sierra Club founder John Muir gave voice to the interconnection of society and all else when he wrote, "Whenever we try to pick out anything by itself, we find it hitched to everything else in the universe."[3] Some of those hitches are clear even to the most apathetic of the "we": the link between human food sources and survival, for example. Most other ecological connections are more subtle, tying creature to plant to soil through long chains, such as those between a tomcod swimming in the Hudson and a mink scampering in the Adirondack Mountains.

Exploring those ties that bind all things as one is instructive of the Landscape a society creates: the quality of its interactions with "nature" emerging through an understanding of how a culture treats the plants, animals, waters, rocks, and loam it depends upon. In the Hudson region we find what are, from a sustainability perspective, some of the best and worst examples of Western Landscape creation from the past—and some of the preeminent sources of hope for re-meaning the future human-environment Landscape as well.

Among the tragedies of the past, there were moments in the region's last four hundred years when nearly every tree was shorn from entire mountain ranges, and, in the process of sending the logs to mills downriver, streams were turned into chutes scoured of all life down to the bedrock.[4] Predatory species such as wolves and cougars were killed off, allowing large and small mammal populations to irrupt (a biological eruption), thereby opening the way for, among other things, a rare and potentially debilitating tick-borne virus to become the widespread Lyme disease that we know today. Humans also drove economically valuable species like turkey and beaver to the brink of extinction. Thousands of dams were constructed, blocking fish runs and destroying upriver habitats. Residents were able to tell the color of paint being sprayed onto new vehicles at automobile manufacturing plants by the effluent in their rivers.[5]

The list goes on, each a wound in itself, but there may be no more extreme example of the character of our past Landscapes than PCB contamination. Polychlorinated biphenyls are suspected human carcinogens, and over thirty years, ending in 1977, the General Electric Company (GE) poured approximately 1.3 million pounds of PCBs into the Hudson River from plants in Ft. Edward and Hudson Falls, New York. Even after the dumping ended, PCBs continued to leak from the plants. When the Ft. Edward Dam was removed in 1973, tons of PCB-laden sediment were unknowingly released, eventually spreading all the way to the river's mouth and creating what would become the largest Superfund site in the nation, two hundred miles of contaminated river bottom stretching from Hudson Falls to New York City.

In 1976, New York State's Department of Environmental Conservation (DEC) ended commercial fishing on the Hudson and banned all recreational fishing on the river because of the high concentration of PCBs found in numerous fish species. The ban was lifted in 1995, although today only catch and release fishing is allowed in many areas. As well, PCBs appear to have affected many other wildlife species besides fish,[6] including birds[7] and bats.[8]

After years of court battles and negotiations, the U.S. Environmental Protection Agency, DEC, various environmental and citizens groups, and GE agreed that the company would foot the bill for dredging "hot spots" along forty miles of the upper Hudson where PCB concentrations were particularly high. The work began in 2009 and is expected to continue until at least 2016.[9] While GE has been loath to release cost estimates, the tab for the initial work in 2009 reportedly came to $561 million[10] and Bloomberg pegged the cost through 2013 at "about $1 billion."[11] Ultimately, more than 2.5 million cubic yards of contaminated river sediment will be removed, dried, and shipped to a toxic waste landfill.

How do we read a Landscape where wastes were dumped into or onto it, as has happened to so many places in the United States? In the Hudson's case, when PCBs, excess automobile paint, untreated human sewage, and the like were flushed into the river, the waters were transformed from a life-giving "source," a place from which clean water and food could be taken, to a "sink," where a corporation's or a city's problem was gotten rid of, never to be seen again.[12] The river was where waste was sent as a matter of expediency. It was profaned and treated as if it were lifeless. Water, food, recreation, beauty: those things could be found somewhere else.

Of course, John Muir would remind us that nothing is ever truly gotten rid of. Similarly, Gary Kleppel directs us to the connections between ecology and narrowly human concerns, including quantifiable links in the form of the "ecosystem services"[13] that plants, animals, air, and water provide free of charge. Kleppel explains, "There is a sense among some of us that we do have a responsibility to be receptive to other organisms, even if they are not human, that live in our same place. But I think beyond that what we fail to recognize so often is the amount of services, the amount of things that biodiversity does for us. . . . Just the trees around Atlanta are picking up every year about nineteen million pounds of pollutants from the air. If we were to pay for that service it would cost us forty-seven million dollars a year" in year 2000 dollars. "Ecosystems perform unbelievably important services for us free of charge."

Sometimes *we*—a jurisdiction or a corporation—send problems downstream. Sometimes they are absorbed by trees or by wetlands or great rivers that provide taken-for-granted services, but only when those things are left intact as part of the Landscapes we create. And when oaks and cattails and sucker fish are no longer there, or when our wastes are so excessive or so synthetic that they cannot be cleansed by ecosystems, the remediation may have to occur decades into the future and at an immense financial, social, and public relations cost. In ecology's Landscape nothing simply washes away in space or time. "Away" is always someone or something else's "here" and "now."

Checking the Region's Ecological Pulse

Karin Limburg's love of the Hudson region dates to her days as an environmental activist in the 1970s, when, in the summer between her first two years at Vassar College in Poughkeepsie, she worked for the environmental group Clearwater checking pollution sites on the Hudson River (see chapter 8). Limburg went on to earn her PhD and to become one of the most respected experts on the Hudson River's ecology, literally writing the book on the subject.[14] Although she is technically an ecologist, Limburg is truly an interdisciplinarian, combing dusty archives to gather historical data on American shad and writing articles that combine demographics, history, land use, sociology, ecology; when I spoke with her, she was president of the Society for Ecological Economics.

Limburg has found that "even in the late nineteenth century, those guys knew how degraded not only the fisheries were, but the landscapes that supported them. They knew that the connections between watersheds and the oceans were being disrupted even then." But little was done to repair those rusting links. Succeeding generations accepted degraded ecosystems— polluted, missing certain species, and including new, foreign ones—as givens. Those changes were integral to the industrial Landscape discussed in chapter 1; new meanings of the human-nature relationship evolved, meanings that actually embraced ecological despoliation and excused pollution and destruction as an inevitable part of economic growth.

Individuals and local communities tend to create baseline understandings of reality grounded in their own perceptions, Limburg says, noting that "our sense of what *is* is set early in life." Socialization, personal experience, and community knowledge shape our Landscapes, often resulting in understandings of place that are devoid of history. People forget what once was. Limburg's husband/sometime research partner, Dennis Swaney, comments, "You see change according to human generation time. Unfortunately, things can degrade much longer than that."

We do a poor job of handing down meaning-filled Landscapes from generation to generation, failing to use the past as a metric for the future. In place of such constancy, incessant re-meaning of the society-nature relationship, as when we accept ruined ecosystems as a necessary side effect of "progress," obscures most of the nicks and cuts that we inflict upon the nonhuman world.

Swaney, like Limburg, is a historical ecologist, and that perspective provides him with an understanding of the Hudson Landscape that few grasp. A century ago, he says, extensive agriculture made the region "a completely different place. . . . The forestry activity—lumbering and tanning, especially relatively high in the watershed [in the Adirondack and the Catskill mountains]—must have devastated pristine creeks." Those places today are home to two of the largest state parks in the nation, but,

Swaney notes, history belies their "pristine" aura. Ecologists' Landscapes are complex and convoluted, places full of histories—histories most of us rarely acknowledge.

Assessing Ecosystem Health

Stuart Findlay, an ecologist at the prestigious Cary Institute for Ecosystem Studies, sees much the same picture as Limburg and Swaney. He remarks, "A lot of the big, fundamental changes" to the Hudson region's ecosystems, and to the Hudson River in particular, "have already happened. They're in the past, such as the changes in the connections between the Hudson and elsewhere: the Erie Canal was a major route for invasive species. In part because of [shipping], there was greater need for dredging of the river and stabilization of the shorelines. . . . So these are changes that we're not making anymore. They're not ongoing." They're already part of the dominant Landscape.

Echoing Gary Kleppel, Findlay continues, "But the Hudson that one sees today is very different from what it would have been if these changes had not been imposed in the past." Ecologists were not present to gather data before and after those "big, fundamental changes" took place, but thanks to the historical investigations of Swaney and others, they feel they know enough about habitat history to say with certainty that filling, dredging, dumping, and the like profoundly altered ecosystems that had been in place for thousands of years.[15]

Yet the Landscape constructed by these ecologists isn't all about cuts, bruises, and gashes. Swaney says that the Hudson draws him to it as a person and a professional. "It is an easy river to love," he says almost wistfully. "Driving along the Hudson, it's one of the most beautiful rivers I've ever seen. And it's got a great city at its mouth." Much of his research relies on sophisticated statistical models of the Hudson, giving him the sense that the region is

> a microcosm of pretty much everything going on elsewhere in the world. It's got it all, and it's probably better documented than most other watersheds. To me, it's a beautiful river. It's got history—it was fundamental to the formation of the United States. It was settled first by the Dutch and then by the Brits, so that sort of makes it more of an international river. And it's got every human insult thrown at it that you can throw at it, and in big ways.[16]

The Hudson region that emerges from such a perspective is a place of tensions: tragedy and beauty, shortsightedness and history, insult and embrace.

Limburg and Swaney are among the many scholars whose works emphasize what is variously termed "ecosystem health," "ecosystem status," "ecosystem condition," "ecological report cards," or "environmental quality." In assessing ecosystem health, biologists take into account soil conditions, the oxygen content of streams, biogeochemical cycles, and food chain quality, among numerous variables. The editors of one of the earliest books on ecosystem health linked it to sustainability, writing, "The goal of this dynamic process is to protect the autonomous, self-integrative processes of nature as an essential element in a new ethic of sustainability."[17] Because of ecosystems' complexities, there's nothing like a pulse or a simple blood cholesterol check that researchers can use to easily assess a habitat's health. The almost chaotic mix of species, aquatic and terrestrial components, and other factors in any given ecosystem makes identifying universally applicable measures of ecosystem health a challenge. So advocates are guided by general principles.

Still, almost always one factor—one species—in particular is responsible for a given ecosystem's ill health: *Homo sapiens*. The key question becomes, "How many resources are humans using relative to the regenerative capacity of the biosphere?" Limburg says, "If you play the numbers out, they don't look good. We all can see this. The question is, can we change it?" In this take on the Hudson region's ecological health, human beings become the major players.

But we have to be careful about where we point fingers. Sociology reminds us that not every "player" is equal. General Electric's PCBs, for instance, have the potential to affect marine, riparian, and terrestrial ecologies for generations to come, as do the wastes from Entergy's Indian Point Nuclear Power Plant along the Hudson in Westchester County. By comparison, hikers washing their hands in stream water or the failure of a homeowner's septic system pales to insignificance. The influence of organizations—corporations, governments, and nongovernmental organizations—in ecosystem health is inevitably far greater than that of individuals.

Ecological Traps in the Headwaters

Michale Glennon's approach to assessing ecosystem health goes by the name "biotic integrity." The Adirondack Landscape Science Coordinator for the Wildlife Conservation Society, Glennon grew up in Adirondack State Park and returned to research development's effects on wildlife. The park is so large that Yosemite, Yellowstone, Glacier, Grand Canyon, and Great Smoky Mountains national parks could be nestled inside its borders with room left over.

Glennon's father, Robert C. Glennon, was counsel to the Adirondack Park Agency, the state entity charged with planning in the park, and he went on to become the APA's executive director, serving the agency for twenty years. "I certainly inherited from him a knowledge of Adirondack Park," Michale Glennon says. "Driving down the road, Dad would point out the window at the little DEC signs on the trees. 'See that? *State land*,' like that was the paragon of anything. That certainly had a huge impact on how I saw things." Her childhood was spent canoeing the park's endless waters and hiking its challenging trails, and it shaped her life's mission.

"The experience I distinctly remember" as being formative, Glennon says, "was going with my father to an agency meeting when I was in high school and thinking, 'Wow, this is really interesting to hear the questions that these people have to grapple with for this park' and 'God I would not want to be one of the people who has to make the decision. I'd love to be the scientist who has to go out and study it and frame the information.' " She became that scientist, earning a PhD at the State University of New York's College of Environmental Science and Forestry with an emphasis on wildlife conservation.

Glennon's PhD dissertation used biotic integrity as a lens to examine the status of birds in Adirondack Park. As she explains it, biotic integrity "has to do with the capacity of ecosystems to maintain and renew themselves and to perpetuate over time." It examines the systemic effects of development: how homes, roads, schools, industrial areas, towns, cities, suburbs, exurbs, and megalopolises affect ecosystems. Inherently interdisciplinary, it rests at the intersection of ecology and those large-scale social creations of concern to social scientists. "The tendency," Glennon says, "is for things to get simpler as human beings alter ecosystems," and that simplicity implies fewer species in a given location than before development. Fewer species means less complexity, which equates to damaged ecosystems—damaged because parts are missing, like vandalized portions of a landscape painting's canvas.

Road construction often is the first, and perhaps most important, large-scale blow to forest ecosystems like those in the Adirondacks because roads create open spaces. Glennon explains, "When you create edges and openings, there's a whole host of changes that ecological communities encounter that they would not have encountered had that change not occurred." Some species take advantage of those openings—certain birds, for instance, nest in the denser undergrowth that flourishes when road cuts allow sunlight into a forest. But road rights of way also promote easier travel by predators, creating an "ecological trap" for some of the open space-loving bird species, leaving them more vulnerable to attack. Glennon notes that even hiking trails can create edge effects and the resulting benefits and traps.[18]

As development increases with the construction of buildings, schools, parking lots, more roads, and the like, biotic integrity suffers in many ways, Glennon points out. Domesticated pets—cats, particularly—play a role in reducing ecosystem health when they chase and kill wildlife, potentially in substantial numbers. Even different forms of recreation may have unexpected and differentiated effects. For instance, some animals adapt fairly quickly to things such as noisy snowmobiles, but deer can undergo a great deal of stress when nearly silent cross-country skiers unexpectedly come upon them. Cars on roads kill large numbers of reptiles, amphibians, mammals, and birds, yet homes and businesses can make life easier for raccoons, foxes, and other predators.

Glennon has found the highest biotic integrity in those Adirondack Park wilderness areas that are undeveloped, although biotic integrity was fairly high even in areas where tree cutting had taken place.[19] (It is important to note that large-scale clear-cutting of all trees over many acres is not practiced in the park. So-called select cutting is the sanctioned approach, although the care with which it is undertaken varies greatly depending on the landowner and the logging operator.) At the other end of the scale, the park's hamlets scored lowest on the biotic integrity scale. Why? "It's really roads—how far away you are from a road—that tells you the most about biotic integrity," Glennon says.

She points out that 90 percent of the wildlife species found in the Northeast are present in the Adirondacks, and most species that were in the area prior to 1609 are still there, so in that sense the park's health is good. "What we're missing," Glennon notes, "is some of those large predators. We don't have the wolf anymore. The cougar was probably here in some numbers. The wolverine was probably here in parts of the Adirondacks. Lynx is gone now. So we don't have some of those top-level species, but most everything else is here."

Despite that overall positive picture, Glennon is glum. "I love to think about the wildlife question," says Glennon. "But that's not what anyone cares about. I mean, if there's a deer in their backyard, they think the wildlife's fine. And maybe the deer are fine, but maybe the pine marten or something else is not. The challenge for us as biologists is just to get people to recognize that there is a difference between a bluejay and a scarlet tanager or a deer and a least weasel. Mostly they're interested in the economic question and the sociological question, as they should be. Those are equally, if not more, important."

In that lack of Leopoldian empathy, Glennon is concerned that the scientific data will be ignored until it is too late—until development permanently alters the Adirondacks. "People will be going around and saying, 'This used to be a beautiful woods, and now there's a house every five acres,'" she says. "I don't know how you make those arguments. It's very hard." Such is what is lost when a Landscape lacks a historical memory, a responsibility only humans can fulfill.

Many people, eager to get away from the hustle and bustle of the lowland world, construct homes on those five-acre lots deep in the woods. Low-density backcountry development of that kind affects wildlife in profound ways. Whether it is houses built on steep slopes— a problem I heard people speak about throughout my travels in the park—or irresponsible zoning that fails to compel developers to cluster new houses together and minimize their effects on native species, private land is being poorly managed throughout the upper reaches of the Hudson region. And the APA can do little about it, since it exerts minimal control on development on private lands in the park.

Biological Pollution

As I discuss in chapter 4, development is a serious concern throughout the Hudson region, not only in the Adirondacks. But humans damage ecosystems in other ways as well, and one class of wound that has already altered every ecosystem in the Hudson region goes by any number of ominous names: invasives, aliens, nonnatives, or (a bit less dramatically) introduced species. Whatever the label, these plants and animals arrived in North America thanks to human actions. In some cases, they were intentionally introduced—as was the case with the starling, first released in Central Park by a Shakespeare lover who planned to bring all of the Bard's European birds to this continent.[20] In other instances species have been released by accident, often with tragic consequences for the natives— witness the great blights that killed nearly every chestnut and elm tree in the United States.

Many of us first heard of "invasive" species with mention of kudzu in the South or zebra mussels in the Midwest and North, though, in fact, the ubiquitous dandelion is a European import, as are honeybees. Zebra mussels were especially anxiety producing when they were first noticed in North American waters in 1988. Natives of the Caspian Sea, they began causing problems for Great Lakes cities' water plants and the region's industrial sites soon thereafter as their colonies grew so large that they clogged water intake pipes. In 1991—the same year zebra mussels were first reported in the Hudson River—one biologist said, "Within twenty years the zebra mussel will likely have taken the entire East Coast of the U.S."[21] With predictions like that one, who wouldn't think of them as invaders?

Another well-known invasive in the region—and, increasingly, across North America—is phragmites, a fifteen-foot-tall grass with a flowing head that some compare to a horse's mane. The precise arrival and spread of phragmites is complicated by the fact it has always been here—certain subspecies, anyway. But those endemic varieties are being crowded out by one introduced from Europe, most likely two hundred years ago.[22] Walking through the well-studied phragmites stand at Pier-mont Marsh along the Hudson River shore at the Tappan Zee, where the Hudson widens dramatically into a small "sea" twenty miles north of Manhattan, I was thankful to be on a well-trod path. Had I been dropped into the middle of the marsh, it would have been a struggle to escape, both because of the density of the phragmites canes—going off-trail was like pushing through a forest of skinny corn stalks—and because the plants grew so tall that I could not see the high ground a hundred yards away.

Ecologist Tim Howard bemoans the spread of phragmites. Invasive species generally are "a significant threat to some of the different natural communities," he says, and phragmites is the poster child for those dangers. "Phragmites is moving into many of the lower river marshlands," Howard notes, and as it does so it creates "monocultures" every bit as ecologically barren as a cornfield. Phragmites aggressively crowds out all other plants, singlehandedly reducing diversity; ecologists have long argued that plant and animal species diversity is essential to ecosystem health. Perhaps the greatest threat from invasives such as phragmites is their capacity to destroy that diversity, weakening ecosystems in the process. Since endemic plants and animals did not evolve in interaction with nonnatives, they may be unable to use the newcomers for food or shelter, or they may be unable to avoid predatory new arrivals.

For all its visibility, phragmites is far from the most troubling of the invasives. "Actually," Howard says, "the things that might change our systems the most are the insects. For example, the hemlock wooly adelgid (accidentally imported from Asia in 1924): that's going to really dramatically change our hemlock forests. The emerald ash borer (which arrived in 2002 from Asia) is potentially a big problem as well, and so will be the Asian longhorn beetle (mistakenly introduced in 1996). You and I will never know what a chestnut forest was like, but forests continue to be. There will be some dramatic changes coming in the future from some of these invasive pests."

Once an invasive insect attacks its host species, it can induce sweeping effects. Pointing to one imminent example, Howard says, "Hemlock wooly adelgid will, in the long run, take out all of our mature hemlocks." The hemlock's story is particularly tragic, as I mentioned in chapter 1. Having survived the tanning industry's onslaught, when they are killed off by the wooly adelgid no one knows what will take their place, though an invasive such as the particularly fecund "tree of heaven" (*Ailanthus altissima* or ailanthus)[23] is a prime candidate.

Natural scientists have difficulty specifying how to stop an invasive plant or animal once it has arrived. Hoping that native species will bring it under control usually tops their lists. It is much easier—yet still a huge challenge—to halt nonnative species before they are ever released. David Strayer, of the Carey Institute for Ecosystem Studies, says, "Preventing the unconsidered, unscreened arrival of new alien species is very high on my list of future management concerns for the Hudson." He adds, "In many cases once the alien species is established, it's irreversible."

Stuart Findlay is firm in his assessment of the lack of preventative action, saying, "It's just irresponsible the way we're doing this." Seven new species are found in the Hudson River alone every decade, to say nothing of the new terrestrial arrivals, threats that should not be taken as lightly as they have been by policymakers and regulatory agencies, Findlay insists: "If we let the public find out that we're just randomly dumping a new chemical into the river every year and a half, they'd have a *fit*! Rightly so. But that's more or less what we're doing. Once they're here and established, there's really not a lot we can do about the vast majority of these things. But right now we are not prepared to either find them early or do anything about them early. A few cases, yes, but to a large extent no. We're just not ready."

Strayer notes that management decisions are complicated by the fact that the invasive is almost always something that cannot be anticipated.

Will the new arrival be a crustacean, like the mitten crab from China that was discovered along the Hudson in 2007,[24] which increases shoreline erosion and may thwart the implementation of the state's wetlands management efforts? Will it be another wood-boring beetle, making timber management a challenge? Or perhaps the next invasive species will be a showy ornamental flower that is brought in by homeowners to enliven their gardens, as was the case a century ago with the nonnative "giant hogweed" (*Heracleum mantegazzianum*)—a fourteen-foot-tall plant from the Caucasus whose sap can blind and makes human skin more susceptible to sunburn for years after exposure.[25]

The global economy ensures that nonnative plants and animals will continue to arrive, threatening both the ecological sustainability that is the foundation of life in the Hudson region and ecologists' version of Landscape. Officials have done little planning to discourage the new arrivals. Even obvious solutions, such as requiring that ships exchange ballast water in mid-ocean rather than in port, have been painfully difficult to enact. Scientists know that ballast water, used to stabilize ships, is a major route for the introduction of invasive species globally—it's how zebra mussels arrived, for instance. Ships take on ballast water before they leave a port on one continent and release it at their destination, often thousands of miles away. Thus, animals and even aquatic plants may be imported along with a ship's intended cargo.[26]

The costs of complacency are substantial. As David Strayer puts it, "With invasive species, we're where we were with pollution fifty or a hundred years ago. I don't think you can fault people for polluting when they didn't know it was bad. And fifty years ago with invasives, we didn't understand about ballast water the way we do now. Policy makers need to understand that we're getting this biological pollution coming in, and it has these long-lasting and undesirable effects, and we can do something about it. It's costing big bucks! . . . People just haven't made the connections yet. It's frustrating for us as ecologists because we see the connections."

The broad public conversation about invasive species has hardly begun. Strayer puts the matter starkly: "I would be much happier if we at least had the discussion and the majority of people agreed that in order to have cheap DVD recorders from China we're going to allow all this stuff to happen. But we haven't even had this discussion." Thanks to invasive species, ecologists' dominant understanding of Landscape is in peril, pitted as it often is against economics.

Eric Kiviat often is something of a contrarian when it comes to invasives, proposing a nuanced understanding of the ways new plants and animals fit within existing ecosystems. He notes that many invasive species have been present in the United States for decades or longer (those honeybees and dandelions, for example), have spread widely, yet have not radically altered habitats. Indeed, some may bring benefits with them.

A case in point is none other than phragmites. Kiviat has researched phragmites extensively and says, "One of the values of small phragmites stands is they provide terrific roosting habitat for birds for most of the year." For decades ecologists have acknowledged phragmites' potential benefits. One research group, citing studies dating back to 1994, wrote, "Although historically perceived as a species that alters and eliminates valuable animal habitat, recent evidence suggests that [phragmites] marshes may function as viable wetland habitat . . . by supplying nesting sites for several bird species and food for song sparrows."[27] Those researchers' data came from Piermont Marsh, the same dense cane field I described earlier.

So sometimes our initial anxieties about invasives prove to be overblown. Remember that ominous prediction about zebra mussels overrunning the continent? Well, they're still here and they still cause problems, but in the Hudson River and elsewhere they have experienced population die-offs, in some cases probably from native fish and crabs snacking on the tasty newcomer.[28]

If, in our zeal to wipe out phragmites or other invasives, we fail to consider what else might happen or what might take the invasives' place, that classic bugaboo—the unintended consequence—may rear its ugly head. In the case of phragmites, some of the possible recolonizers of former "phrag" stands are native plants that would be "okay," Kiviat says. But who's to say with certainty what will find a new home in a plowed-under phragmites stand? "Is it going to be phragmites again," Kiviat asks, "or is it going to be purple loosestrife (another invasive), either of which can come into a clearing like that? Or," he adds with the sardonic laugh of an ecologist who respects the complexities of the natural world and the infinite capacity of human beings to mess things up, "is it something else that we don't even know about?"

Kiviat offers an alternative Landscape that resonates with one of ecology's dominant theoretical outlooks, "dynamic equilibrium." The bookend to ecologists' historical perspective on Landscape is the importance of considering the future, particularly when "management efforts"—such as destroying established populations of invasive species—are called for.

"I Think There's Something Here"

Tim Howard is the sort of person whose idea of a "really spectacular" day out is to wade through mud flats looking for rare plant species, work he relishes as Director of Science for the New York State Natural History Program, a collaboration between the New York State Department of Environmental Conservation and the Nature Conservancy. Howard grew up in New Jersey and a Boston suburb, and he frequently visited the Adirondacks while attending Middlebury College in Vermont, just across Lake Champlain. He now works for a program that tracks New York's rare species "plus the great places," Howard says, referring to "the neat forests, the little bogs, and the significant natural communities" from rare grasses to old growth forests.

I spent a day with Howard counting alpine plants on Whiteface Mountain, one of the highest peaks in New York and just a few miles outside of the Hudson River drainage. One side of Whiteface is home to Olympic ski runs, while on the other can be found grasses, wood-stemmed plants, and others that are rarely seen elsewhere. Howard skipped over boulders and expertly perused ten plots, each ten meters square, counting the different species of low-lying plants that struggled to grow in an environment where freezing temperatures occur every month of the year.

"The alpine environment is very stressful," Howard says. "Here in the Northeast it's windblown. Icy in the winter. There's a lot of rime ice buildup, which is from supercooled clouds in the wintertime. The ice immediately freezes on trees and shrubs and rocks, and the wind can" break the plants as a result. "And so the compact alpine environment above tree line here in the Northeast is really a unique natural community." In all of the Adirondacks, only 172 acres are classified as alpine, and they are home to thirty-five rare plants.[29]

But that uniqueness is under siege, and with it ecology's Landscape as well. "Climate is changing," Howard observes. "We have a huge global experiment going on right now. We have warming going on in the Northeast. It's happening as we speak. The places where it may be detected in the natural environment first may be these alpine systems. It may be that these stressful environments where there's a treeline and it's held partially by cold and partially by storms: we may see changes up there before we see changes in the valleys and in the richer forests."

Howard is particularly interested in tracking the changes in those alpine ecosystems. Using a variety of new techniques and taking advantage of transects—fixed, hundred-meter-long lines above the tree line established decades ago for assaying plant life—Howard can follow the changing species composition.

Similarly, he is counting the number of specific rare plants on alpine peaks. That work serves as a baseline for what he fears he will find in the coming years. "Our ecozones might just keep rising up the mountains because climate change is, in part, a warming trend," Howard hypothesizes. "As things get warmer, the species that like the cooler environments will continue to rise up the mountains." Eventually, they will be gone from the Adirondacks.

Doug Burns, a biogeochemist and hydrologist with the U.S. Geological Survey, explains global climate change this way: "It's very clear that we're seeing a warming pattern. That's been almost universally observed. So despite the complexities of climate, we are seeing these patterns that are very consistent with what the modelers are saying should be happening." Computerized models are the predominant way for natural scientists in many fields to explore theories today. The models take into account large numbers of variables and huge numbers of data points. If the modelers are correct about theories of past and future climate behavior, then once they crunch the data their models—their theories—will come close to predicting tomorrow's temperatures, weather patterns, precipitation, drought, and the like.

Models aside, data including evidence from melting glaciers, sea level rise, temperature increases "virtually everywhere"—in the oceans and even below the planet's surface—leave no doubt about the reality of climate change in Burns's mind. "Scientists always look for independent sets of observations," he says, "and if enough independent sets of observations are showing a consistent pattern, then we start to say, 'Geeze, I think there's something here.'"

The "something" in this case is not good for those who prize ecosystem or social stability. In 2014 the United Nations' Intergovernmental Panel on Climate Change affirmed the anthropogenic basis of "global warming" and said those changes pose novel risks that nations of the world are unprepared to meet.[30] Weeks later, the U.S. Global Change Research Program embraced those findings for the United States.[31] The U.S. report's authors wrote that "if not for human activities, global climate would actually have cooled slightly over the past 50 years," thanks to the effects of ash in the atmosphere from recent volcanic eruptions.[32] Instead, the average temperature in the United States is rapidly rising.

The best estimates for the Northeast and New England indicate that average temperatures will increase two to six degrees Celsius over the next century and that sea level will rise roughly one to one and one-half feet. Powerful storms are likely to create surges that travel far up coastal rivers—potentially creating problems a hundred miles or more up the Hudson River, which is tidal for 153 miles, from the river's mouth at the southern tip of Manhattan to Federal Dam in Troy. In research on the Catskill Mountains, Burns found that the climate has warmed one-half degree Centigrade since the 1950s,[33] "significant warming trends," he says, "that led us to wonder if the climate is warming more at high elevation than at low elevation." Of no consolation to Tim Howard, who is looking for evidence of climate change's effects on alpine plant communities, was Burns's observation that "since the nineteen sixties there has been persistent warming" in the Adirondacks.

The bad news goes on and on. "We also found that snowmelt is tending to happen a little bit earlier in the year," Burns notes, paralleling findings from Maine and New Hampshire. Surprisingly, the climate in the Catskills has become wetter—even wetter than the climate change models predicted—thanks to brief, intense rain and snow storms. Bizarrely, those same models indicate longer periods of drought as well, caused by warmer air temperatures. Those unprecedented snow/rain-drought cycles are one reason why the "global climate change" label is more apt than "global warming." The latter hardly hints at the whole story.

Anthropogenic climate change will act back upon us in disturbing ways and for a very long time—into the next millennium, according to one study.[34] Burns notes that its effects on the region may be quite varied. Water use and availability are likely to be affected, for instance. Most notably, New York City depends on eighteen reservoirs, most in the Hudson River watershed, to supply its needs. Higher temperatures are likely to increase evaporation from those massive artificial lakes. Greater demands on the city's water system and the potential for drought may portend water rationing for New York in the future.

Lower Manhattan may be "more susceptible to storm surge (from hurricanes) over time," comments Burns. The city has 520 miles of coastline. Estimates are that over the last century water levels have risen one foot, with another ten-inch rise likely in the next twenty years.

"I've seen projections that it is likely that there will have to be a greater investment in storm barriers and storm walls in Manhattan in coming decades just because of sea level rise," Burns said before 2012's Hurricane Sandy made such investments a fait accompli. "It's not going to be under water twenty years from now, but there is a problem there that is likely to get worse in the future." From the mountains to sea level, climate change will affect every corner of the Hudson region.

Even human health is at risk from climate change. Burns notes that there may be "earlier and longer pollen seasons," which is a comparative "minor annoyance" compared to other likely changes. "The tick season gets longer" with warmer temperatures, Burns observes, "and ticks will be less likely to die off in a mild winter. . . . You can imagine that some insect-borne diseases, if the conditions become more conducive so that they can spread northward or they can persist longer in the year, [will be commonplace]."[35]

Climate change's potential effects won't stop there. The marshes that provide habitat for juvenile fish and that help clean pollution from waters are likely to become inundated, and the region's agriculture industry may undergo significant changes. Grapes, for example, may benefit from warmer temperatures, but apples, which need significant cold spells, are likely to suffer; after Washington State, New York is the nation's largest apple producer. "I think the sugar maple are going to have trouble" if warming is particularly severe, Burns says. "I think people are starting to think, 'What is going to happen to these North Atlantic hardwood forests?' and it looks like they're going to be replaced by forests that you might see in the mid-Atlantic region, like the oak-hickory forests. [Those warm-weather forests will] be better adapted, so they'll start to replace the sugar maple. Just about anything you want to look at, there will be effects."

Ecologist David VanLuven is more blunt regarding the iconic maple's future, saying, "We'll have some catastrophic collapses. The maple syrup industry will have some real trouble." Dairy farms may struggle as cows suffer through extended hot periods in the summer, potentially undermining an industry that is already teetering on the brink of financial collapse.

Wildlife will be affected, too. "The range where brook trout can live will decrease," Burns notes, "because they are a cold-adapted species." Similarly, Eric Kiviat speaks the threat of "a lot of big holes" in the region's ecosystems. Ask a Hudson region ecologist and he or she will give you a litany of likely victims. "There's a plant called the Hudson River water nymph," says VanLuven almost wistfully, as if speaking of a dear friend who is gravely ill. "It lives on fresh water intertidal mud flats. The plant doesn't grow anywhere else on the planet. We'll probably lose that. . . . We'll be able to survive, but I think we'll just lose the richness and depth and quality of life that we have here that makes it so wonderful to be here." Karin Limburg points to similar examples. Rainbow smelt is a once-common fish that was last spotted in the Hudson River in 1995, and Atlantic tomcod is becoming rare; both are likely on the decline because of the warmer waters.

Kiviat says that climate change "is making people rethink everything about tidal marsh ecology. Sea level rise and other aspects of climate change" are potentially that powerful, powerful enough to compel the rewriting of textbooks. Meanwhile, Limburg notes, "there are many, many more tropical strays showing up"—fish from warmer waters that are not expected to be seen in Northeast waters.

And it's not just fish and marshy plants that are threatened. Kiviat points out that the Catskill Mountains "may see the disappearance of some spruce-fir forests and some of their denizens like the Bicknell's thrush," an endangered species. Tim Howard fears the same thing will happen in the Hudson Region's northern reaches, saying, "It's possible that over the next few hundred years the tree line might rise right off the summit, even our higher summits, and we might find that we'll be losing many of these true alpine species here in the Adirondacks."

How do animals "disappear" and tree lines "rise?" Warmer climates allow other species to outcompete the plants and animals that moved in following the last ice age. Even if the tree line does not rise to the mountain summits, something like the "tropical stray" phenomenon that Limburg mentioned may occur in alpine regions, with herbaceous plants (those lacking a woody stem) increasingly prominent on high mountains where they struggle today.

Other scientists note that amateur birders have noticed altered songbird migration timing and numbers, and even historical records of lilac blooms indicate the increasingly early arrival of spring, a sure sign of the warming of the atmosphere. So rapid are climate change's effects that ecologists' physical and cognitive Landscape is being rewritten before their eyes.

The reality is that climate change will affect *everything*. "Ecosystems adapt to their environment, and if the climate changes they'll have trouble," Doug Burns observes. "That's not to say that other ecosystems will not replace what is no longer adapted, but we have industries—fishing guides, the agricultural sector—so if those ecosystems change then these industries, these economies, will have to change as well. Hopefully, it will be gradual enough that we can adapt over time."

Burns is one of a handful of ecologists I spoke with who sees some room for optimism regarding society's willingness and ability to address climate change. An expert in acid rain—technically "acid deposition," since it can fall as snow and even out of a clear blue sky, the acidic nitrogen and sulfur particles attached to bits of dust and ash from coal-fired power plants—Burns says, "In the 1970s, things looked pretty bad in New York. There were reports of fishless lakes, and it was getting worse. The government invested a lot . . . in an acid rain research effort, and in 1990 Congress amended the Clean Air Act such that we've seen improvements in" acid deposition. "That's still ongoing, but there's some hope there."

Climate change will be a "bigger problem than that, bigger in scale," Burns acknowledges. "But I do have some hope. My concern is, do the effects have to become so grave for us to take action that we're so far along in this trajectory that it's going to be harder for us to do something about it?"

Will we act on climate change before it is too late? A lot of things in this book don't depend on action anywhere else; they're about remarkable accomplishments in one corner of one continent. But the "us" and the "we" Burns speaks of once more recalls Gary Kleppel's "we": it is all seven billion human beings, particularly those living in more privileged nations and among them especially the politically and economically powerful. Will we—will *they*, the governments, corporations, and religious and nongovernmental organizations—act before ecology's landscape is completely rewritten?

Emerging Environmental Concerns

PCBs, environmental health, invasive species, global climate change: the list of current environmental challenges facing the Hudson region is impressive and depressing. While those are likely to be the primary concerns in the coming years, others are waiting in the wings. Among them are:

Endocrine Disruptors

"This is something that is very scary," says David Strayer, "and it's unclear whether it's going to be a little tiny thing or a big thing." Endocrine disruptors affect the ability of "certain glands (in humans and other animals) to communicate with various tissues and regulate body functions such as growth, development, and reproduction."[36] They are chemicals, many of them synthetic, that are increasingly found in the environment, particularly in water sources, and common products; PCBs are endocrine disruptors, as are DDT and other pesticides. BPA (bisphenol-A), the plastic additive that was replaced in some products because of its potential effects on infants and children, is another example. Thus, endocrine disruptors may be widely distributed and may have wide-ranging effects on humans and wildlife. Eric Kiviat labeled glyphosate, the active ingredient in the popular herbicide "Roundup," "a sleeper in terms of endocrine disruption."

Salt

Another threat is so prosaic as to be downright shocking: salt. Karin Limburg explains, "In the northeast we salt the roads like crazy. So if you want to look at human activity [and its environmental effects], conductivity is a really good measure," since higher water conductivity indicates higher salt content, and human activity is just about the only source of increased salt content in fresh water. "We found really high conductivity in August," Limburg says. "It's coming out of the ground water." The implication is that salt spread on roads in winter months contaminates subsurface aquifers so extensively that it can be found in some streams year-round. Limburg has not identified the effects of the increased salt, but it is likely that what we in the Northeast think of as a wintertime necessity poses persistent problems for the environment.

Tiny Plastic Beads

In 2014 New York attempted to become the first state to ban the plastic "microbeads" used in beauty products. The *Albany Times Union* reported State University of New York at Fredonia researchers had found that "the Great Lakes contain tens of millions of microbeads—high enough concentrations to rival those found floating in the infamous ocean floating garbage patches." The state's attorney general, Eric Schneiderman, was championing a bill to ban the beads, which cannot be removed from water sources and attract other pollutants, including PCBs, making them toxic vectors that can be bioaccumulated in fish and may pose hazards to human drinking water and food sources.[37]

Unintended Consequences

Even as we look for solutions to environmental problems, we must avoid creating more of the same. For example, many sustainability advocates call for increased passenger rail traffic to get people out of their cars.

Yet Eric Kiviat notes that along the Hudson River's scenic rail route that ferries millions of commuters and tourists each year between cities such as Albany, Poughkeepsie, and New York City, trains emit large amounts of air pollution and kill wildlife (including bald eagles struck while feeding on the tracks next to rivers), and rail companies spray herbicides to maintain the integrity of the rail beds.

In another vein, Stuart Findlay worries about the potential repercussions if environmental remedies fall short of expectations. He notes, "Some members of the general public have been told 'we can fix these things.' For example, 'Removing the PCBs is going to restore the healthy fish stocks.' And I worry a little bit that reality won't be as perfect as it's been presented, and then is there going to be a backlash? . . . A lot of restoration is being sold that way: 'We can do it. Trust us. All will be well.' I don't think that'll really be the case."

Heeding Ecology's Lessons

"A place's ecology" is the foundation of any reasonable answer to the question, "What is to be sustained?" Healthy people, communities, cities, farms, and economies are also essential, and only a misanthropist can get very excited about sustainability that does not include those deeply human components of sustainability. But everything else relies on stable ecologies, lasting ecosystems, which implies that all of nature's pieces are there today and will be into the future, underpinning everything from agriculture to recreation to land use to economy. If sustainability is taken seriously, a given region's ecology will be nurtured and protected by those who live there.

In the chapters that follow, ecology's Landscape emerges at almost every turn. It is a construction of the nonhuman world as endangered by human actions as diverse as toxic pollution, introduced species, and perhaps salt. But ecology isn't simply a natural science. It provides a critical lens on human behavior as well, and on closer inspection ecology's perspective shows us that "nature" is not the only thing threatened by anthropogenic forces. Everything is hitched, after all, and when corporations foul waterways or individuals introduce showy new plants to their gardens that escape into the wider ecosystem, the effects link back to society and to individuals. Time, money, and effort all are spent to right the resulting ecological wrongs. In the meantime, ecology tells us that it is much easier to get it right the first time by better understanding what makes for good environmental health and never forgetting the mindfulness that an ecological education provides.

Chapter 3

A Constant Bounty

When Paul Arnold greets customers at any of the three farmers markets where he sells produce each week, something more than an economic exchange takes place. "I know their names," he says. "I know their kids. We're happy to see each other. I feel like I go and see friends every week. . . . I care a lot about them, and they feel it. I know they care a lot about me," so much so that his customers showed up at his farm to help harvest when Arnold was injured in a farm accident. Farmers markets are not simply commercial venues for Arnold and other small growers. They are community, a place where relationships are created, cemented, and nurtured.

Snow, rain, family tragedy: for more than twenty-five years nothing has kept Arnold from his place at the markets. "With that loyalty, they're also going to be loyal to me, because they know I care about them" the trim, white-haired Arnold says. "And that's what really drives farming systems: that priority of the customer's first." An example of how far Arnold takes that commitment is his year-round presence at the markets, particularly the huge investment he made to purchase two "high tunnels"—essentially, 150-foot-long rounded, plastic-covered greenhouses—that enable him to grow greens even in twenty-below weather.

He explains, "I'm not doing winter markets because I want to make more money. I'm doing winter markets because my customers are almost demanding it of me. . . . I wouldn't want to let them down." "Customer," in the intimate world of sustainable agriculture, is synonymous with "friend" and "neighbor." In the Landscape created and inhabited by Arnold and his customers, the antiseptic, impersonal grocer-consumer interaction taken for granted by many of us becomes a relationship between grower and eater based in friendship, communication, and even trust. Author Michael Pollan calls it " 'relationship marketing,' " arguing that "the only meaningful guarantee of integrity is when buyers and sellers can look one another in the eye, something few of us ever take the trouble to do."[1] Or have the opportunity to do.

In many ways, such relationships are conscious Landscape creations, deliberate nexuses of lifestyle and the land. Agriculture's Landscape is a crossroads where community, farming, economics, and even social justice meet ecology. As it is emerging in the Hudson region, it is also a Landscape full of innovation, surprises, and hope.

The growing season here could be a bit longer, but for the most part the soils—particularly as the Dutch and British found them, but even today—could hardly be richer. Early travelers Jaspar Dankers and Peter Sluyter remarked,

> It is impossible to tell how many peach trees we passed, all laden with fruit to breaking down, and many of them actually broken down. We came to a place surrounded with such trees from which so many had fallen off that the ground could not be discerned, and you could not put your foot down without trampling them; and, notwithstanding such large quantities had fallen off, the trees still were as full as they could bear. The hogs and other animals mostly feed on them.[2]

Over millennia, humus built up the region's soils to the point that they could produce stupendous quantities of food. And produce the region did, in such copious quantities that it led the nation by the start of the Civil War. David Stradling notes, "By 1860, five of the largest vegetable-producing counties in the country were in New York State," including Queens, Kings, and New York counties—all boroughs of modern-day New York City—as well as Albany County, which lies at the center of the Hudson region. "All of these changes revealed the increasingly integrated nature of New York's economy and environment. Growth in cities begat growth in the hinterlands, as production intensified."[3] It was a relationship soon ended, however, and only in recent years have efforts been made to reconnect the region's customers and farmers.

In the comparative blink of an eye, agrarian ways of life died off. As industrialism drew more farmers from the American hinterlands, and more immigrants, to cities in the mid and late 1800s, sprawl ensued.

Then as now, farmers living at the edge of the development zone recognized opportunities to sell dear to eager developers, resulting in the burial beneath streets and houses of those same rich lands that Dankers and Sluyter gushed over.

Author Richard Manning, an irascible Montanan who doesn't mince words when pursuing a truth, poses the problem that emerged more than a century ago and that remains with us: "Agricultural issues are largely ignored by Americans, a factor in the creation of the political vacuum that is the niche of corporate lobbyists. Americans dismiss these issues because they assume only rural areas are affected, and not many of us live there. The assumption, however, is false. Virtually every one of us faces the consequences of our ignorance of agriculture three times a day."

We have a long way to go to educate ourselves, statistics reveal. As Figure 3.1 shows, in the Hudson region's fifteen primary New York counties north of New York City, farm acreage declined 81 percent from 1900 to 2010, from 4.8 million acres to 907,444. Over the same period, the population tripled, from just more than one million to well in excess of three million.

At the county level the numbers are even more disturbing. Bordering New York City, Westchester County today has less than 5 percent of its 1900 farm acreage still in production, as does Putnam County to its north. Across the Hudson, Rockland County has seen 98 percent of its farmland lost to development, although Orange County has managed to hold on to more than 20 percent, and others are in the 20 to 29 percent range. Of the major farming counties in the region, only Warren has close to half of its 1900 farmland still in production; it stands at just less than 45 percent. None of New York's top five counties, in terms of agriculture sales, are in the Hudson region today.[4]

One could be forgiven for reading into such numbers a war on farms and farmers or, more charitably, for interpreting our nonchalance toward the destruction of our sustenance—I refer to the soil—as suicidal. At the least, the statistics reveal a distracted disregard for our most necessary connection with the land.

In his introduction to a volume on transitioning agrarian "landscapes" (by which the editors mean changes on the ground—to farms and the ecosystems in which they are situated), Charles L. Redman says we can understand the effects humans have on ecology as a pattern "of land-use change affecting landscapes, of altered landscapes affecting ecological processes, of both influencing the ways in which humans monitor and respond to their surroundings, and of human responses engendering

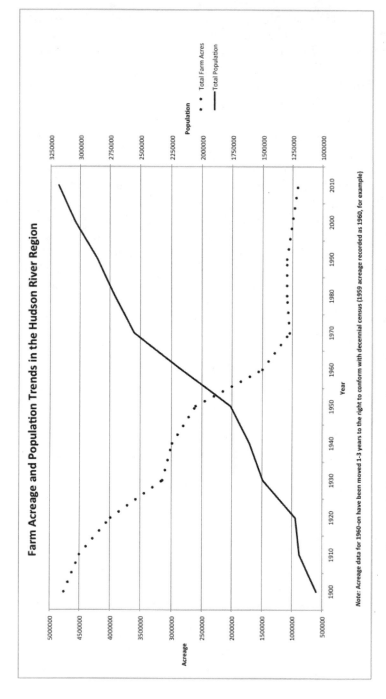

Figure 3.1. Farm Acreage and Population Trends in the Hudson River Region

further cycles of change."[5] The implication of such a perspective is that societies are now playing central roles in creating widespread ecological change through agriculture—and that how we react to those changes will spiral outward in time, creating yet more ecosystemic change.

Stability will only be possible with sustainability. And that stability must include economic and social justice as well. To live sustainably, what we eat, how we obtain our food, who has access to which food, the ways that we prepare it, and the means used to farm it all will have to be sustainable, too. The food and farming Landscape will need to emerge as conscious choices made by individuals, governments, companies, nonprofit organizations: the region as a whole. Some of those kinds of decisions are being made by farmers like Paul Arnold and Ray McEnroe, whom we also meet in this chapter. They are supported as well by agriculture advocates such as Todd Erling and by established food entrepreneurs like GrowNYC, whose efforts I describe in the pages that follow.

"Wonderful Lifestyle"

Paul Arnold's sixty-acre Pleasant Valley Farm is comprised of ridgeland and bottomland nestled among low hills in picturesque Washington County, New York, with another 120 rented acres nearby.[6] However, Arnold, his wife-partner Sandy, and the interns who continuously cycle through the farm only cultivate seven to ten acres. The two high tunnels that allow for winter growing stand at one edge of the farm, just up the way from the spacious home Paul and Sandy keep with their children. Outbuildings include a root cellar, small greenhouse, and a long shed where tractors and other implements are stored. Over the brow of the ridge stand solar panels that generate nearly all of the farm's electricity.

"Our main focus is right here on this farm," says Arnold. "It's to raise vegetables profitably year after year and to show the world that organic farming does work." (While practicing organic methods in every way down to the biodegradable plastic used for row covers, Pleasant Valley Farm is not technically an "organic" operation. Rather, like thousands of other producers, the Arnolds follow "natural" methods, on rare occasions using things such as fungicides to save a tomato crop in a wet year but otherwise following organic standards.)

A popular misconception is that most organic meat and vegetables are produced on small farms, but it's not the case. The *New York Times* reported, "The fact is, organic food has become a wildly lucrative business for Big Food and a premium-price-means-premium-profit section of the grocery store. The industry's image—contented cows grazing on the green hills of family-owned farms—is mostly pure fantasy. Or rather, pure marketing. Big food, it turns out, has spawned what might be called Big Organic."[7] The bias toward large farms notwithstanding, that fantasy is coming true for the Arnolds and many others who operate at the margins of the nation's $283 billion farm industry[8] and who advocate for a local agriculture Landscape where food comes from a friend down the road, not from a corporate behemoth across the continent—or from another continent altogether.

Farm ecologist Conrad Vispo notes that operations such as the Arnolds' are commonly labeled "niche farms," a misleading appellation. "It's not hobby farming," says Vispo. "They're true farms, but they're producing organic or doing grass-raised beef or it's home delivery of milk or heirloom this and that." Todd Erling, a regional farming advocate, echoes those comments, arguing, "I think we need to lose some of the labeling and realize that in the northeast, and in the Hudson Valley specifically, where we work, even the largest farm is typically a family-owned, family-run operation." Even dairy farms of fewer than one hundred head "are making it," Erling adds.

By whatever name, such farms are physically—and often emotionally—close to their customer-neighbors and are part of local communities in ways that transcend economics, even as their owners are making a comfortable living. At a basic level—how land is farmed, where the products from farms are sold, and to whom—farming is returning to its roots. What once was the only way to farm was reduced to a small slice of the massive whole and now is growing in prominence. "Big Organic" is not niche, but little Pleasant Valley Farm is, and its presence affirms the farming Landscape that Vispo and Erling describe: farming families are essential parts of the social and ecological fabric.

In these terms, perhaps what Arnold means is that *comparatively small-scale* organic farming works. It certainly does for his family. He and Sandy took advantage of their lifestyle to homeschool their children, and with them they take six weeks of vacation every year—the family has seen just about every corner of the nation on trips made possible by their lucrative, community-centered little farm.

Neither Paul nor Sandy comes from a farming background. He was raised in nearby South Glens Falls, and after school he went to work for a landscaping company in their nursery greenhouse. There he picked up skills from horticulture to carpentry. Gradually, it occurred to him that he would like to farm. He read everything he could get his hands on, initially raising vegetables on his father's land for two years, then purchasing a corn field where he and Sandy constructed their home and started Pleasant Valley Farm. They never looked back, Paul says, commenting almost wistfully, "For us, it has been a wonderful lifestyle."

It's surprising to hear a farmer say such things. After all, isn't farming about drought and pests and low prices and crops destroyed by late frosts? Isn't the family farm a dying phenomenon? Isn't the Landscape the survivors inhabit one of constant tension, the realization of the classic human-nature conflict from great works of fiction set in a Leninist peasantry-bourgeoisie world? Such does not seem to be the case for Arnold. He and Sandy have made a living from the farm since 1992: more than twenty years with no "off-farm income." Even before the Affordable Health Care Act, they had health insurance. They also fully fund IRAs for themselves and their children each year. They won't be packing up their (nonexistent) broken-down truck and trundling off to California in search of greener pastures any time soon.

No, the major conflict on their farm is with perfecting what they are doing. Paul says he is "always looking: there's got to be a better way. There's got to be a different way, keeping my ear to what my marketing is telling me: my customers—what's important to them." The plot is about pursuing "what's best," not fighting newly arrived pests.

Of course, the farming Landscape is no walk through the lettuce patch. Each season, Paul says, some crop fails—potatoes one year, something else another. When I visited the farm on a bright February day, recent bitter cold had knocked back, but not completely killed off, some Swiss chard in one of Arnold's tunnels. He responds to such challenges by diversifying what he grows: carrots, varieties of lettuce, leeks, onions, and on and on. In the process he creates a Landscape where nature is not something fought against but becomes, almost Taoistly, a force to be met by creative bending instead of resistance to the point of breaking.

The result is a constant bounty. For a summer's day farmers market Arnold picks in the range of three hundred heads of lettuce, fifty to sixty bags of salad mix, 150 pounds of carrots, five hundred pounds of potatoes, and substantial amounts of spinach, onions, leeks, cucumbers, tomatoes, and more. In the winter the quantity may be half of a high-season haul, but it still amounts to a lot of produce. "We have a wide display of items in the wintertime," Arnold says, "probably thirty items. That gets people to say, 'Wow! Let's come. It's worth our while. We'll pick out what we need.' And we're always coming up with something new—broccoli heads, something we find we can store and/or grow. So they're excited about that." The result is that even in the dead of winter Arnold's sales are nearly comparable to those in the summer, thanks to a large root cellar, good planning, those huge growing tunnels, and a comparative lack of competition.

Another key ingredient in the farm's profitability is a Thoreau-like emphasis on *economy*. As Arnold puts it, "What's important to us is that whatever we grow, we sell all of it. We can have trouble during a summer . . . to even have enough to feed two pigs because we've gotten it down to where our waste is miniscule." Ecologists argue that "nature's economy" is a complete one—nothing goes to waste. The Landscape that Arnold creates reflects that view of things, in the process nurturing the land and ensuring that he and his family can afford to continue to live on it.

"Big Organic," Outsized Influence

Tucked in a corner of Dutchess County literally a stone's throw from Connecticut, and straddling the Hudson and Connecticut river regions, McEnroe Organic Farm is Big Organic by the region's standards, though hardly so by national ones.[9] Operated by fourth- and fifth-generation farmers, it sells products throughout the eastern half of the United States, employs dozens, promotes food education, and has grown into a paragon of agricultural entrepreneurship.

Patron Ray McEnroe's farm has been a certified organic operation since the early 1990s. Through Douglas and Suzanna Durst, who eventually would become McEnroe's partners, Ray was exposed to organic methods, and he liked what he saw. At the time, McEnroe had a substantial dairy herd, but, he says, "when they legalized rBGH"—the controversial bovine growth hormone that causes cows to produce artificially high amounts of milk—"I said, 'That's it. I'm bailing out of this, and I'm just going to grow vegetables.' I could see that it was going to destroy the dairy industry, destroy the cows." Such economic bad sense and inhumane animal husbandry was anathema to McEnroe's vision of farming.

That perspective is especially noteworthy because McEnroe Farm's land-community connections are so extensive. McEnroe employs thirty people, most of them full-time, either on the farm, at his farm stand, or at his large composting operation, making McEnroe Farm one of the biggest employers in northeastern Dutchess County. The operation is of such scale and so intimately linked to the community that one employee is tasked with running the Education Department, which hosts school groups that visit as seldom as once a year to as frequently as weekly. Schoolchildren who participate most often learn hands-on all the steps in plant growth and harvesting, and they have been known to go home after their McEnroe Farm experience and demand that their families start an organic garden.

McEnroe's education and outreach also includes a self-guided tour of part of the farm and internships for those seeking to learn the skills they'll need to operate their own farms. Here, Landscape creation is not passive, nor is it proprietary, rarely shared. Rather, it is a practice involving nurturing plants, animals, and the community's awareness of its affinity with the land through food.

McEnroe's commitment to community education grew out of food ignorance. Over the years, he noticed that many people are unaware about where their food comes from and what goes into growing it. "Society is becoming disconnected from its food source," McEnroe says. "You see that in Union Square," the New York City farmers market where McEnroe Farm sells each week. "The greenmarket managers will bring a group of school kids over. You explain how a tomato grows and how it turned red and everything. You feel this moral responsibility to teach these kids where their food is coming from. They have no clue, and they're amazed to hear it." It seems McEnroe is on a mission to inform consumers about their food. In truth, that's just one of his several goals.

When it comes to running a successful farm, "the key to the whole thing is diversification," McEnroe says—diversification in what is raised as well as where it is sold. It is a theme that Paul Arnold mentioned as well, but McEnroe takes it a step farther. Most of the produce from his farm goes to his farm stand or to farmers markets, with some being sold wholesale. There's the Union Square greenmarket in New York City and area grocery stores, particularly natural food stores that specialize in produce—indeed, McEnroe found that he sold more tomatoes through a tiny local health food store than he did at the nearby 45,000 square-foot chain grocery.

"Certain crops," he says, "tomatoes, beets, onions, potatoes—things like that—we'll grow enough of them to wholesale. But we try to limit the very perishable crops and those that are going to command top dollar to just retail. Everybody loves a fresh head of lettuce, but once it goes bad, what are you (the farmer) going to do with it?" Like Pleasant Valley, economy is key, and Ray learned to cut back on his lettuce plantings from fifteen thousand a week twenty years ago to three thousand today. He knows how much to grow to sell out, and he doesn't grow any more.

Including land the McEnroes rent, their farm is more than one thousand acres planted in a variety of crops as well as grain for livestock—another indication of the farm's diversity. There is pastureland and areas where chicken, turkey, beef cattle, and pigs are raised. Whether crops or livestock, everything from the farm is certified organic. It flies in the face of what Wendell Berry, perhaps the foremost proponent of sustainable farming, called the "industrial version of agriculture," with its "products offered for sale by the makers of agri-industrial technology (like the products of the food-processing industry) [that] are not just ready-made solutions; they are ready-made thoughts. And the larger the scale of the technology and the thinking, the harder it is to modify these thoughts by the action of individual intelligence."[10] Berry begs us to break away from the dominant Landscape's grip on our way of understanding food and farming in our lives.

The McEnroe Farm store, much more than a humble farm stand, draws a range of customers. Ray estimates one-third are local, 40 percent are seasonal, and the remainder are passers-by, many of whom have stopped by the store previously on trips to the nearby Berkshire Mountains. It is stocked with the farm's produce, of course, but there is also a large frozen food section and plenty of processed foods of the sort one finds in natural food stores. It resembles a convenience store or bodega for the granola set.

It's not always easy to grow as McEnroe Farm has. Local town officials resisted when McEnroe applied to erect greenhouses behind the farm stand to extend the tomato-growing season. The stand itself had been open and running for three months when officials forced Ray to shut it down. "Too big for a farm stand," he says. "I had all the permits!" Both times, New York State agriculture officials stepped in to smooth the waters.

But the biggest fight was over McEnroe's compost operation. Only 25 percent of the ingredients in the popular, rich, black mixture come from McEnroe Farm. The rest includes manure from horse farms, leaves from Westchester County to the south, and even food waste from New York City restaurants (that's the new "'green wave,' food waste" from restaurants, McEnroe says sardonically; "we've been doing that since Ninety-Two"). It all makes for a major operation. Huge piles of ingredients and curing compost dot a roughly two-acre space in one corner of the farm, the nearby machinery—conveyer belts and large trucks—looking like something more at home in a rock quarry.

And the results are sought after like Carrera marble. "Growers up and down the east coast" buy McEnroe's compost, he says. "It's approved for organic crop production. It's not so much the compost as the potting soil and the like that we create from the compost. We go as far south as Georgia" and west to Tennessee and Missouri. Smaller bags are sold to consumers in garden centers. The compost operation contributes a "substantial" part of the farm's revenue.

That's the situation today, but getting the operation up and running wasn't easy. "They had a lot of fear of the compost operation when it first started, and they all got together to shut it down," Ray says, referring to some neighbors and elected officials. Anxieties ranged from the use of sludge—human waste—to long lines of railroad cars trundling through the rural landscape delivering that mythical sludge. None of those concerns have come to pass, and on the hot early fall day that I spent on the farm, I didn't know the compost operation was one hundred yards up a hill until Ray pointed it out; even standing in the middle of it, there was no smell.

McEnroe Farm is nothing less than an ambassador for a new Hudson region landscape. Its outreach takes many forms, from greenmarket education to training tomorrow's farmers to its massive, lucrative compost operation. Each touches many lives, conveying the potential of the region to be a leader in reminding some, and demonstrating to many, how farming is intertwined with our lives.

Greenmarkets and More

To the casual observer, it is clear that Americans loathe food waste. Just look at the reception Ray McEnroe received from his neighbors in farm country—*farm country*—when he tried to get his compost operation up and running. But as a matter of public policy, food waste is a big deal. In New York City alone, the food waste stream amounts to 1.2 million tons a year,[11] a figure that does not account for what is ground up in disposals and adds to the immense loads handled at the city's sewage treatment facilities, exacerbating environmental injustices, as we will see in chapter 5. The remainder, 17 percent of the city's waste stream, is thrown away and piles up in landfills.

The folks at GrowNYC had a better idea, so they began accepting food waste at their "greenmarkets"—farmers markets to the rest of us.[12] In 2013 alone they collected 1,240,945 pounds. "It's surprising, sometimes, to even us," GrowNYC assistant director Julie Walsh admits. "New Yorkers are usually small-space dwellers"—no one knows for sure, but chances are good the average living space in the city is substantially smaller than most suburban homes—"and (now) people save their food scraps, sometimes in their freezer, sometimes in a compost pail, and they come to the market and drop them off because it's important to them to participate in that kind of sustainable action." The scraps, as well as leaves that locals drop off, are taken to the city's composting facilities. In fact, GrowNYC's program proved to be a catalyst when, in 2012, the city began contracting with various organizations to operate food waste dropoff sites in all five boroughs.

Over the last thirty-five years, GrowNYC's greenmarkets have become a staple of New York City life, not least because of innovations such as the composting program. Found in every borough, the fifty-four markets only offer space to a seller if the products they offer are their own. As Walsh puts it, "We are a one hundred percent produce your own, grow your own market. That is a requirement for participation. What people are bringing to market, whether they're fruits or vegetables or herbs or value-added products that are made from those, the consumer can be assured that they are buying from the person who caught it, baked it, grew it, canned it, foraged it, fished it. . . . Product integrity is how we refer to it." All told, 230 sellers are there at the markets, at least one of which is open every day of the week during warm weather; all are outdoors, and twenty-three are open year-round.

Walsh echoes Paul Arnold when she notes that the markets "build relationships between our consumer and the person who is providing the food that they eat. That's important because I think that's spurred the popularity and growth and the enduring, sustainable nature of the market system." She adds, "That's really exciting for people, and it's a real educational experience. We think that's important, for people to be able to talk to the person who grew and maybe picked that food that very morning, and to ask, 'How did you grow it? What are your agricultural practices? What kind of land management do you practice? How are you growing the food I'm about to eat?'" Given New York's diverse population, more often than in most places consumers can sample new foods and inquire how best to cook them, the education taking on a cultural dimension that subtly connects neighbors and strengthens community members' ties to one another.

Moreover, GrowNYC is aware of the reach of the greenmarkets—specifically, their power to preserve farms and farmers' livelihoods. "We want our farmers to have a profitable outlet so that they have an alternative to selling off the family farm for development because that's the only way to sustain their life," Walsh says. "We want farming, particularly small, family farms, to remain a viable option. It's so important to the health of our environment. This system allows people to make a living at something they love, something they're good at, something that's good for us as consumers, and something that's good for our region."

It's difficult to overestimate the potential benefits to regional farmers from a customer base of eight million. For the creation of a new Landscape, the potential is vast as well. GrowNYC's efforts to link city dwellers with farmers mean that those urban consumers are helping to preserve farms and, therefore, to ensure sustainable Landscapes.

Deeply moved by the first Earth Day in 1970, then-mayor John Lindsey created the Council on the Environment of New York City, a think tank with a clumsy name but an important mission: to lead the city toward what we would now call a sustainable future. That mission broadened over the years to include its flagship program, the greenmarkets, and the name was changed in 2010.

A benign Trojan horse for triple bottom-line sustainability, GrowNYC's greenmarkets began to take Food Stamps—nowadays SNAP (Supplemental Nutrition Assistance Program), which operates using Electronic Benefit Transfer (EBT) cards—in 2005, and today nearly all of their locations do. The availability prompted a thousandfold increase in food assistance program use at the greenmarkets in just eight years: from $1,000 of Food Stamp coupons redeemed in the first year to more than $1 million worth of EBT card use in 2013.

"GrowNYC knows that good food access is not a luxury," Walsh says. "It's a basic human right, and we want to help people to access good, healthy food. It shouldn't be an amenity for a select few. It should be something that everyone has access to."

At the other end of the food chain, GrowNYC has become something of a broker between farmers and others. "In addition to helping farmers with a retail access point," Walsh says, "we're starting to move into wholesale access, Greenmarket Co., which works with small to mid-sized growers, and we link them with end users: restaurants, bodegas, institutions. Last year we had this great success story where a kale chip producer in Brooklyn said, 'I'm looking for someone to dedicate X number of acres to these different kinds of kale and to grow them for me.'" GrowNYC made the match.

"We see that as the next phase of how we can benefit farmers and end users," says Walsh. "We see that as a natural progression where we can increase farmland in production and increase consumption of locally grown items." Once the destroyer of farmland, through programs like GrowNYC's cities may become its savior.

GrowNYC aren't the only ones bridging farms and commercial ventures in the region. In Spring 2014, Capital District Community Gardens (CDCG) created an online marketplace "aimed at wholesale buyers like schools, group homes, hospitals, day-care centers, restaurants, and convenience stores," reported the *Albany Times Union*.[13] CDCG's long-running equity component was expanded as well; its Veggie Mobile, box trucks that run on biodiesel and feature solar panels to power the refrigerators, and Healthy Convenience Store Initiative are aimed at greening inner-city food deserts.[14]

GrowNYC also sponsors textile dropoffs at many greenmarkets (2.6 million pounds of clothes and the like have been donated since 2007, and the annual growth rate is more than 20 percent), promotes gardening at three hundred of the city's 1,700 schools, operates a next-generation farmer training program, and is even experimenting with economic entrepreneurship. "Greenmarket Dirt," for example, is McEnroe Farm's compost branded for sale at the Greenmarkets.

Major customers for that compost are the urban gardeners throughout the city, many of whom participate in GrowNYC's community garden program, which has been around since the organization's inception. "We've helped create seventy significantly sized gardens—some are full-scale urban farms, nineteen thousand square feet," says Walsh. "People come to the garden as members from many different places, but they almost all say the same thing: 'This is the one place that I really feel at home and like it's home. I'm growing something that I grew when I lived in Mexico.' 'I'm growing something that we grew when we were in Africa.' It's this amazing experience for them. This connection to the earth: people want it and need it, and it's universal. It's a way, even in the most urban of places and even if you're far from where you started, to feel that connection."

The urban gardens also promote civil society—opportunities to talk about the issues of the day with others. "Just like a farmer's market," Walsh observes, "that's a place to have a conversation. They're places where people intersect where they might not normally." At the greenmarkets and gardens, people find belonging, community, common ground, and—literally and figuratively—rootedness: the foundation of a new Landscape.

Farming's Ecology

Notwithstanding all the dirt, manure, arachnids, and insects on farms, the tenacious stereotype is that they are ecological wastelands. The picturesque side of our Landscape concept may be present, as may a strong connection to place, but the crucial ecological element of sustainability is missing, the story goes. Indeed, many of us think of the farming Landscape as the first act in wresting place from nature and separating the social from the environment in which it is situated. Visions of corn or soybean monocultures stretching to the horizon, common along highways from coast to coast, only reinforce the taken-for-granted view that ecosystems end at the farm's edge.

But see farming's Landscape through Conrad Vispo's eyes and that bleak picture at least has the potential to be much more complex—and the reality often is. Conrad and his wife, Claudia Knab-Vispo, operate the Farmscape Ecology Program in Columbia County. Trained ecologists, they ask questions such as, What can farmers do to alter the public's sense that farms and farming are antipathetic to healthy ecosystems? The answer has to do with things like planning beneficial crop rotations, the sorts of windbreaks that farmers plant, how they treat seeps from which spring water trickles, and how pastures are grazed as on-farm behaviors mesh with ecological potential to promote native flora and fauna.

And then there are ponds, the watering holes many farmers provide for livestock. "Going onto farms, we realized a lot of these farm ponds were really rich" ecologically, Conrad says. "Naively coming into this I said, 'Oh, all these farm ponds are going to be dead.' No! You've got spotted salamanders, wood frogs. Some of them are really diverse." Accidentally or deliberately, farmers create places rich with potential—often ecological potential that has been met.

Hawthorne Valley Farm in Columbia County serves as a base for Conrad and Claudia's work. The four hundred acre farm has been around for more than forty years and is a hub of agricultural and ecological education for children and adults. Hawthorne Valley sells at three GrowNYC greenmarkets, a couple of hours south, and one nearby in Hudson, New York. It also operates a large farm store that caters to locals and to the weekenders and summer residents who make somewhere else their permanent home. The farm is tied to the local community in many ways, including hosting programs for all of the region's Waldorf schools, some of which involve week-long hands-on farming retreats for students.

Conrad and Claudia's research and consulting is also part of those community connections. They have developed something of a symbiotic relationship with farmers in the county through a research and outreach program that is a retort to natural science's stubborn objectivity. Classically, the natural sciences wanted nothing to do with advocacy. In response, Conrad asks rhetorically, "You've got that information. So what?" When faced with today's challenges, time is too short for science to sit on the sidelines. So the Farmscape Ecology Program has become an act of applied ecology driven by a perspective that asks, in Conrad's words, "How do you present (information) in a diversity of ways that are going to get a variety of people thinking about it?"—people from farmers to history buffs to part-time residents to natives?

Unwilling to limit their focus only to farms, the idea was to "get people thinking of farms as part of a bigger picture," says Conrad. "We wanted to convey that idea of a landscape that includes farms and people and an ecological aspect." They envisioned nothing less than re-meaning farming. Refusing to accept the received wisdom that farms are ecological deserts and that farmers care only about their crops, livestock, and a one-dimensional bottom line, the Farmscape Ecology Program pursued its vision of a new farming Landscape by dividing its work into four components: ecology, agriculture, history, and sociology.

The Vispos' approach is in line with "ecoagriculture," an effort to redirect the ecology-agriculture-rural economy relationships that have developed haphazardly over millennia. With nearly one-third of the planet's landmass under plow, ecoagriculture's advocates note that conscious, careful approaches to those relationships are no longer optional,[15] making the need for farmscape ecology and ecoagriculture dire. Judith D. Soule and Jon K. Piper argue that the dominant "Big Farm" approach to agriculture is tailored "to maximize a single component, yield, while ignoring or disrupting those factors that act to stabilize and maintain biological communities. Many of the links between organisms, the soil, and the physical environment that serve to regulate natural communities have been decoupled. . . . A move toward a sustainable agriculture will involve shifting the dominant goals from industrial productivity and efficiency to goals that acknowledge agriculture as a biological and social process."[16]

Recoupling farming, ecology, and human communities is exactly what the Vispos try to do.

Farmers allow them onto their land to survey for butterflies, birds, fish, plants, and the like. In turn, Conrad and Claudia use their data to help farmers understand better "what they want to do, what they feel they need to do, how that interacts with ecology," Conrad says. But he is careful to add, "It's not our goal to make farms into nature preserves. That's not the point, and I think it would be counterproductive." Instead, the idea is to identify how nondomesticated plants and animals can coexist with, and even enhance, crop and livestock production. The approach is helpful and supportive but not heavy-handed, the guidance subtle, the heeding of it optional, and the point of it all is to inform. "It's really important that people understand where their landscape is placed in history" and in ecology, says Conrad.

Those "people" aren't only farmers, Conrad points out, noting his interest in helping "the average resident to connect to the landscape. Do they have the access to land that they had previously? And not 'public' land necessarily, but the ability to hunt on their neighbor's land or go fishing next door. Has that changed dramatically? And if it has, what does that mean about people caring about the landscape and what does that mean about the future of conservation?"

Implicit in Conrad's questions is the importance of everyone in a community maintaining connections to that place's ecology. When the land is shared, and therefore known experientially, the potential exits for the Landscape's meaning to shift in ways that promote sustainability. Seen through farmscape ecology's lens, sustainability emerges as practices undertaken by people as diverse as farmers, anglers, and weekenders stopping by a roadside stand to purchase a few ears of corn that weave together the contemporary, the historical, and the ecological.

Twenty-First Century Farming

"I feel pretty strongly that we need not romanticize or look back at the good old days" of farming, says Todd Erling. "While we need to take the best of both worlds, where we're going we don't know. To say we need to be back at pre–Nineteen Forty or pre–Nineteen Fifty 'industrial' agriculture is really a false premise in a lot of ways." In other words, to embrace only organic or "natural" farming methods, rejecting what have come to be called "conventional" approaches that freely use artificial herbicides, pesticides, antibiotics, and the like, is a mistake. But it is also a mistake to ignore the lessons that have been learned about conventional farming.

Farming's Landscape is multifaceted and evolving. No one size fits all, and Erling, as the executive director of Hudson Valley AgriBusiness Development Corporation (HVADC), finds himself smack in the middle of the changes. Erling explains, "If you look at post–World War Two, there is where the major shifts started occurring. It happened in degrees, all changes do, and it's going to take degrees to push it in a new direction and the ultimate ends that we want it to be at." Degrees and economics; if sustainable approaches show enough potential to be economically profitable, Erling says, most farmers will follow suit, as Ray McEnroe did. Farming is intensely data driven, with the key datum being the fiscal bottom line.

McEnroe wasn't alone in shifting to sustainable approaches, he and others embodying the transformational role that Erling alludes to. In their assessment of the effects of the sustainable agriculture movement on American farming, Randal S. Beeman and James A. Pritchard write that it "contributed to a general climate of information that encouraged American farmers to experiment with new methods. . . . Ultimately, the connection between ecology and agriculture has helped fuel the development of an environmental ethic in the United States."[17] Environmental ethics, an ecologically aware outlook, and economics have combined to prompt the evolution in American agriculture now underway.

Overall, times haven't been good for "ag" for decades. The number of family farms began to drop off with the Dust Bowl era of the 1930s, falling rapidly from the 1940s through the '80s. Then, Erling says, "from the late eighties through the nineties, you see a leveling off, statistically." More recently, he observes, something strange has been happening: farms have multiplied. "I don't know if it's a change in the reporting or a change in the definition of 'farm,' but we've actually seen an *increase* in some of our counties in the individual numbers of farms."

While Erling, a transplanted Pennsylvanian with college degrees in architecture and urban planning who farms seventy acres in Columbia County with his wife, is unsure whether the latest numbers represent an actual trend, he knows well what is happening around him. Evoking visions of the Arnolds' Pleasant Valley Farm, Erling says, "We're seeing more small-scale, high-value farms. . . . To me it shows the response occurring for CSAs"—consumer-supported agriculture, where customers purchase annual "shares" from farmers, who supply members weekly with fresh produce and other farm products—"and farmers markets: for individuals wanting to know who is growing their food, what is going into that food, what's not going into that food."

That emerging interest in farming-community connections can be found everywhere in the Hudson region, and it's expanding entrepreneurially. For instance, in 2011 an MBA named Donna Williams created Field Goods, a farm-to-consumer subscription service akin to a CSA. But in Field Goods' approach dozens of area farms and food purveyors supply fruits, veggies, breads, pastas, cheeses, and more to Williams's company, which boxes them for distribution to nearly two thousand customers who pick up each week's delivery at work or at a neighborhood location.[18] Greenmarkets, CSAs, farm-to-consumers, wholesaling, value-added processing and packaging: farmers are connecting with consumers in more diverse ways today than ever.

Amazing Ag

United States Department of Agriculture data reveal a huge jump in certified organic farms and acreage in the five Hudson region states (county-level data are not available, making it impossible to estimate what proportion of these farms and acres are in the Hudson region).[19] Between 2000 and 2011, the latest year for which data are available, there was a fourfold increase in organically farmed acreage, and the number of organic farms jumped by 2.5 times. As a percentage of all farmland in the states, organic is tiny: in 2000, less than 1 percent of the regional states' farmland was certified organic; today, however, it is nearly 4 percent. Small as the numbers may be, it's worth noting that at a time when farm acres are shrinking, those planted in organic are increasing.

The region's growing population has led to sprawl in many places, but plenty of towns and counties tenaciously embrace their identity as bucolic settings where farming has been and remains central to the Landscape—witness the "Right to Farm" signs at the thresholds of many jurisdictions, indicating ordinances are in place to safeguard farmers against frivolous lawsuits over things such as smells and noises. In Erling's Columbia County, for example, agriculture is the largest single land use, while the highest return per acre in the region's New York counties is in the "black dirt" region of Orange County. There, the famously rich loam produces high yields, but the county's proximity to New York City means the development pressures are immense.

Perhaps the region is finally responding to the question posed by Blue Neils, Saratoga County's stormwater coordinator, who says, "We tend to think of environmental resources as land. . . . What happens when you've used it all? Then where do you go? . . . There's no paradigmatic or philosophical recognition of the scarcity itself because we don't slow the pace of the development." Somehow, though, even at the edges of New York City, communities are finally putting on the brakes. There, agriculture is thriving. "Ironically," Erling points out, "between Albany and that northern fringe of the City, in the (six Hudson region) counties that we represent there's still an amazing amount of active agriculture happening." Those counties—Columbia, Dutchess, Rensselaer, and Washington on the east side of the Hudson River and Ulster and Orange on the west side— are home to nearly four thousand farms that encompass 655,000 acres.

At least as important in Erling's view is the value of what's produced, more than $400 million worth annually, making farming "second only to tourism and the service sector for our region," he says. In a world of suburbs, shopping malls, and big box stores, farming persists and produces. Under extreme pressure farmers hold on, and with their customer-neighbor allies they not only refuse to let go, they tenaciously and lovingly re-create the farm Landscape as a bastion preserving place and ecology, reinvigorating community and stabilizing economies, the tumult of modern life notwithstanding.

Erling's HVADC is remarkable for precisely those reasons, a Landscape changer akin to a home run hitter's game-altering abilities because of its location in the New York City and Albany exurbs. He speaks directly and comfortably about the "AgriBusiness" part of HVADC's name, a phrase evocative of billion-dollar transnational corporations. Erling notes that "a farmer has to be profitable at the end of the day in order for them to stay in business over the long term. And that's part of sustainability. . . . To me it was very important that we realize that we were not 'Hudson Valley Ag,' that we were not 'Hudson Valley Ag Development,' but that we were 'AgriBusiness Development.' It is truly on a level with manufacturing, with warehousing, with distribution."

Such an approach equates to playing defense by playing offense. If agriculture is going to be respected as a valuable part of a community— and in particular an integral economic force—it must face up to development pressure not only from residential builders but from industries eager to capitalize on cheap land and labor. Agriculture, too, is something to be "developed": supported as a vital economic force and—perish the thought!—encouraged to grow in range and reach. That sort of outlook further enlarges the agricultural Landscape, making it a force for sustainability in the face of competing, almost inevitably unsustainable alternatives.

Maybe 55 Percent

But there is one disturbing truth that the loss of millions of acres to development—and the concomitant paradox of all of those revenues still being generated by the region's farms—cannot hide: the Hudson region cannot feed itself. Referencing current farmland, Erling hypothesizes, "Let's put every square inch of productive land into production for food in New York State. Are we in a leakage or a surplus situation? We're actually in a leakage situation. The numbers vary and 'figures lie, liars figure,' but somewhere between thirty-five, forty, and *maybe* fifty-five to sixty percent is what we *could* produce in New York State to feed our population." Those sobering figures—at best, the large state of New York, with 7.174 million acres of farmland, *cannot* feed the Hudson region's New York State population of approximately 11.3 million—pose a serious challenge to sustainability advocates. What sort of Landscape is it that cannot support the people living there?

"That starts driving it home when we talk about local food," Erling continues, "because we're always so focused on our farmers market. We're always so focused on what we consider local. 'Local' is such a contextual word. Getting back to connections: three times a day everyone depends on a farmer. How do we get the urban-suburban population to understand that there is a direct connection with the foodshed that is allowing them to live in the suburban, urban setting? It's critical to get to that understanding."

GrowNYC is attempting to address that issue, as are farmers such as the Arnolds and McEnroes, but most in the region are unaware of where their food is grown. In some senses we know surprisingly little about the social systems that sustain us. The notion that most of us living in the Hudson region have no choice but to purchase food grown hundreds or thousands of miles away ought to be a wakeup call (though "vertical farming," discussed in chapter 6, may be a useful addition).

Erling's "foodshed" observation brings to mind a bioregional quiz first published in 1981 under the title, "Where You At?"[20] Questions included, "Trace the water you drink from precipitation to tap," "How long is the growing season where you live?" and "Where does your garbage go?" as well as many having more to do with ecology or a mix of ecology and social systems: "Name five grasses in your area. Are any of them native?" and "What are the major plant associations in your region?" Part of the point was to test readers' knowledge—ignorance, for most of us—of what makes their lives possible. Ideally, such knowledge will spur individuals to act.

So where does the region's food come from? Some is grown and sold locally, of course, but most comes from the other side of the continent. Four times each week, Railex trains pull into Rotterdam, New York, less than three hours from New York City, packed with West Coast produce bound for the northeast and New England.[21] Those trains are vital to feeding the region's residents, as is Hunt's Point, the huge fruit, vegetable, meat, and seafood market in the South Bronx. Without them, grocers' produce bins go empty after about three days.

"Those kinds of markets create an opportunity for food to be very cheap," Erling says. "And that's what we're up against, here. What is available and what is affordable to the majority of your population?" he asks rhetorically. "It doesn't do someone a whole lot of good to have a tomato that's grown within three blocks of their house that they can't afford. That's a really important thing to understand." While not enough to feed everyone, locally grown food is available in the region . . . if you can pay for it. Such a class divide challenges the equity portion of sustainability's triple bottom line, and until it is resolved more universally than GrowNYC's acceptance of EBT, it casts a shadow over the farming-community link in the region's emerging Landscape.

Passing It On

Most of the farmers with whom I spoke feel an intense need to share their knowledge with others, and that generational passing of the baton occurs in different ways. One is through socialization—"osmosis," some might say. Kyle McEnroe, Ray's son, is an example. "I've always worked on the farm since we were children and throughout high school and part-time through college," he says. "I started to veer off into landscaping, but I've always had the interest in agriculture. And obviously the family ties to the farm. . . . So, yeah, I guess I've always felt it's been in my blood." McEnroe's undergraduate degree from Cornell is in plant science and agricultural business, and he went on to earn a Master's degree from Cal Tech in landscape architecture.

In an era known for its dwindling family farms, the young McEnroe's commitment to his own, like that of two of his brothers, is heartening. But the fact remains that family farms usually are not handed down generation to generation, though a countertrend is underway: increasing numbers of young people see farming as a viable lifestyle. In New York's fifteen Hudson region counties north of New York City, the total number of farms increased fractionally between 1987 and 2007, from 5,643 to 5,675.[22]

Not only are the McEnroes keeping the farm in the family for another generation, they and Pleasant Valley Farm take on student interns and others, such as participants in World Wide Opportunities in Organic Farms,[23] a global program helping next-generation farmers from around the planet learn the ropes. CRAFT, the Collaborative Regional Alliance for Farmer Training, sponsored by Hudson region farms in New York and Massachusetts, has been in place since 1994,[24] and a "hub farm" to train farmers and farm researchers is being established in the mid-Hudson Valley.[25]

Paul Arnold makes no bones about it; a major goal of his is to "raise a bumper crop of new farmers and mentor as many people as possible and change the world that way." He enjoys working shoulder to shoulder with students from nearby colleges, appreciatively taking their labor and happily imparting his wisdom, reasoning that "they may not go on to be farmers, but at least they're educated about what goes on on farms." Young people have come from as far away as Greece to work on McEnroe Farm, such is the lure of learning from experts at organic agriculture. At times, the Hudson region's farming Landscape extends far beyond its boundaries.

Paul and Sandy Arnold pass along information about farming in other ways, too. They are frequently invited to appear at conferences–so many that they must choose which invitations to accept and which to turn down–particularly to discuss winter growing. The Arnolds also share their wisdom through a regional "Sustainable Farmers Network." The network includes forty farms within about an hour's drive of their home, the members trading information and joining together to buy supplies in bulk, with Sandy Arnold handling much of the coordination and final distribution of items once they arrive at Pleasant Valley.

Each year their farm is a gathering place for the network's two-day conference. "It's all about helping farmers in the area," Paul says. "Some are new and young, some are established." Further supporting the notion that farming's Landscape reaches beyond the region, in recent years word has spread such that farmers from Pennsylvania and New Jersey attend the "pow-wow."

Why be so generous with time, expertise, and even space (everyone crashes at the Arnolds' home)? Paul explains, "As someone said, 'There are no organic growers that are farmers' sons or daughters' (Kyle McEnroe is among the few exceptions to that rule). We didn't grow up in that mindset of, 'You'd better get ahead of your competition.' When we started—there's a group of organic growers that started twenty, twenty-five years ago—there was no information. Someone said we were information poor and land rich.

"Now the kids today are information rich and land poor. But when we started there wasn't any information, because there certainly wasn't any from the land grant" colleges, traditionally supportive of and supported by Big Ag. "We all were talking to each other because you had to for your survival at that point. There still is this propensity to help each other and discuss things because it's always for the good."

Over the years, that circle has grown to the point where the connections are now nationwide. Arnold adds, "When I travel across the United States, there is always someone I can stay and visit with and be uplifted by each other's community and friendship." While the farming Landscape that the Arnolds and their Network neighbors embrace is an expanding one in space and in time—across generations—it is all the more noteworthy because as business-centered as niche farming is, other values clearly are at work as well: sharing, support, generosity, and camaraderie foremost among them.

Ground for Optimism

Sociologists Alan Beardsworth and Teresa Keil ask, "Can we say that the monolith of the modern food system, with its emphasis on large-scale, intensive production and standardized manufacturing, on mass marketing and retailing, is in the process of giving ground to a more diversified and fragmented situation?"[26] We see from the stories in this chapter that individuals, small businesses, and nonprofits are connecting with farms and farmers in ways that grocery stores render impossible. Such approaches to closing the gap between food and the people and places that provide it are a fundamental component of the emerging Hudson region Landscape. The resulting new meaning is an integrative one where agriculture becomes *place,* a locale identified with factors as diverse as community, ecology, and equitability. Perhaps diversification is in the offing after all.

"I feel there's enough people out there to support organic," Ray McEnroe says. "I wouldn't know how to do it any other way. And there's certainly a big push on buying local. That's nationwide. That's going to continue the more educated people become. They aren't there now, but I hope someday they start realizing about their food and where it comes from. And I think being diversified gives me a lot more optimism."

At a personal level, though, there seems to be some uncertainty. Kyle McEnroe says, "It's difficult to stay optimistic about it because it's such hard work for a little amount of money. It's a lot of work. So it's a little difficult to stay optimistic." Yet, in the next breath he adds, "There's definitely a place in the future for me here. I want to stay with it. We just keep developing in different ways. I don't really know where it's going to go, but we keep going." As does agriculture in the region. "We still have a lot of agriculture," says David Church, Orange County's chief planner and an HVADC board member, "but certain sections, dairy in particular, are in trouble. It's pretty common in the Northeast."

"There are real challenges," adds Church, who was raised at the edge of the Hudson region in Williamstown, Massachusetts. "The population's aging—farmers are getting quite older as a demographic. But we've got some smart farmers around who are doing direct marketing, niche marketing, adding value." Also troubling is that agriculture "is still not seen as genuine economic development by some key players," Church adds. "'Farming's dead. Move on. Get a real job. Let's convert this land into something productive' [the critics exclaim]. But there's a lot of understanding that we could be the source of New York City's produce and their milk products, and we need to get smart about that."

As Church alludes, challenges to agriculture, particularly from its pave-and-build detractors, will always be there. Even in Ray McEnroe's bucolic corner of Dutchess County, development is afoot. "The whole area has changed so much from when I was a kid," he says, "and how much farther it can change, I don't know." He is optimistic that current zoning ordinances are an adequate firewall against the loss of more farmland, "but it's just been vast, vast changes in farming around here. You have probably three or four farmers who rent most of the land and farm it, and that's it. It's been bought by city people who want retreats." The farmland is there, but former dairy farms lie fallow. A once-thriving livestock business has dried up to the point where neither of the two old auction houses are still operating. Even where there are no subdivisions, farmland surrounding mini-mansions sits idle, untilled and ungrazed.

Todd Erling observes, " 'It's not farmland without a farmer,' that's one of American Farmland Trust's great bumper sticker slogans. I don't want to break it down simplistically or turn it into a catch phrase, but that's the bottom line. Open space is one thing. Preserving land that may or may not be open is another thing. But without there being active agriculture on it, it really loses the role that it plays in the community, the role that it plays in the economic engine." The peopled side of farming's Landscape becomes clear in these comments, and it stands in sharp relief not only to developers' suburbia but even to wealthy big city expatriates' preference for farmland without the farming.

One of those urban expats who embraces farming, Peter Paden, insists that farming's Landscape does not have to conflict with other Landscape values. Paden, executive director of the Columbia Land Conservancy, says, "I think the (farming) future, potentially, could be very, very rich for a place like Columbia County," and by extension all of the counties in the Hudson region—even the lowlands of the steep, rocky Adirondacks. "I think the potential here to see a rejuvenated agricultural economy" is substantial, Paden insists. It would be "great for the economy," he adds, "but great for conservation and the landscape. Farming done well is good for conservation: good for waterways, good for clean air," for open space and ecosystems, as Conrad and Claudia Vispo have found.

Yet what of equity? Despite the efforts of organizations such as New York City's Just Food,[27] too many inner-city communities struggle to gain access to any fresh fruits and vegetables at all, much less naturally or organically grown ones. Similarly, in economically struggling rural areas food deserts predominate, the old mom and pop groceries long since having closed. What's left in these areas is low quality, highly processed foods that cost little and provide less nutrition. As Michael Pollan wrote, "Whatever its cost to public health and the environment, cheap food has become a pillar of the modern economy that few in government dare to question."[28] Cheap food is low-quality food, Pollan argues.

Along with grassroots activism, he insists that health insurance providers are sustainable agriculture's greatest hope to address inequities (and much more) in the food system, since eating food tainted with pesticides and growth hormones, food raised and grown under unsanitary and inhumane conditions, is dangerous and fundamentally un-nutritious for all, posing health problems for humans and ecosystems.

Surely the solution to food inequality will come in multiple forms. The situation is improving as more and more farmers markets follow the lead of GrowNYC's greenmarkets and accept EBT—those in Saratoga Springs and Troy, New York, and Bennington, Vermont, do so. Along with Pollan's notion of health insurers becoming involved is government support. "Based on average incomes, the United States can afford a more expensive and healthier food system," writes Paul K. Conkin in *A Revolution down on the Farm*, "but with the present income distribution, such higher costs would threaten the livelihoods of those in the lower one-third in terms of income. Thus, a more responsible, environmentally friendly agriculture would require a larger and more costly food aid system."[29] Of course, in an era where government food assistance for the needy is under constant attack, that kind of progressive policy may not be possible.

Another likely ingredient in the food equity pie is urban gardening and farming, an area where, again, GrowNYC is a leader. Echoing Pollan's emphasis on health care, Jennifer Cockrall-King writes, "If we learn to give space in our urban settings to food production and food producers, we'll be healthier, happier, and more connected to the physical realities of our short existence because of it. We've still barely scratched the surface of ballooning healthcare budgets that are directly influenced by our food choices."[30] Some of those same New York City children whom Ray McEnroe mentioned—the ones with no idea where a tomato comes from—are now growing their own tomatoes and learning about food ecology and economics at the same time. But according to GrowNYC, only one-quarter of New York's school children have access to a school garden, and in most urban, suburban, and rural districts few if any students learn about gardening or farming hands-on.

Turning over vacant lots in inner cities and rural communities may be a crucial step in rectifying the wrongs of unequal food distribution, access, and quality that have developed as American society has grown more economically bifurcated. As the New York City Coalition against Hunger has written, "Although 'food deserts' in NYC will not be eliminated by any single solution, the role of 'green' food—food from farmers' markets, CSAs, and community gardens—will compose an important part of any efforts to combat them.

"In addition to the well publicized environmental, social, and economic benefits to the community and local region, green food also can help to encourage health and wellness in communities underserved by the current food environment."[31] Grassroots activism and action as simple as planting an urban garden or as ambitious as demanding that empty lots be handed over to community gardeners and farmers may be instrumental in altering the Hudson region's food and agriculture Landscape.

Chapter 4

Two Hundred Subdivisions Too Late?

Often, local government service begins with a passion. It may be a driving vision for a community's future, unseeable by those in power, that compels someone to run for office. It may be anger about a decision to trim—or add—local services. Or the impetus to put one's name on the ballot may be to give voice to a group that has too long been ignored. For Marirose Blum Bump, it was Red Hook's Landscape.

The little Town of Red Hook—"towns" in the Northeast are autonomous county subdivisions with their own elected officials, highway departments, control over land use, and the like—is tucked in a corner of Dutchess County opposite McEnroe Farm, the Hudson River to its west and Columbia County to the north, just beyond the fringe of the New York City commuter corridor and too far south of Albany for many to make the trip for work. Bard College is in the town; so is lots of farmland.

Bump ran for town supervisor, equivalent to mayor, determined to be a catalyst for changing how Red Hook understood its identity through how it managed development. "My whole impetus for running for office," Bump explains, "was to finally get land use planning to be what is on the agenda all the time. The heart of my whole administration has been land use planning." In a word, she wanted to ground Red Hook's shared sense of self in its sense of place, its version of Landscape.

Before we go too far, let's examine what appears on its face to be an ugly truth: land use planning is the governmental equivalent of household plumbing. Plumbing tends to be hidden, literally but also in our thoughts and casual conversations. If done well, it almost never needs attention.

It's functional, not showy—there's no glamor in Teflon tape and elbow joints. The same is true for things such as comprehensive plans and zoning requirements: except for the initial construction phase, they almost always remain out of sight, thankfully out of mind. Faucets and pretty facades get noticed, not the piping and policy that brings them to life. In a nutshell, unless you're in a place such as Houston, where zoning does not exist, local governments have to have land use planning to avoid chaos. But once in place it's easy to overlook, and it's hardly the stuff of budding political careers.

None of which seems to have concerned Bump. She ignored the yawns and glazed eyes that inevitably accompany any mention of "setbacks" and "settling ponds." Instead, Bump saw in land use a powerful tool for remaking Red Hook, and in 2003 she won election as the only Democrat on the town board, constructing her platform with that land use tool as her hammer. Before she left office after her first term to spend time with her ill husband, she succeeded in changing not only Red Hook's direction, but its demeanor as well.

Land use decisions are so important to sustainability because they enact Landscape, often in the legislative sense but always because land use decisions influence, even determine Landscapes. Virginia H. Dale, Rebecca A. Efroymson, and Keith L. Kline write, "Cumulatively, the ways in which people transform and use the land represent the most significant human modifications to the planet. . . . Human occupation has direct effects on the land it occupies and has both direct and indirect down-slope, down-stream, and downwind ecological effects."[1] Land use is where vision meets reality and a community's future is determined.

This chapter takes us from one end of the Hudson region to the other. It begins in the Hudson estuary, the area where the greatest population growth is found and where Marirose Blum Bump pursued her vision, then moves to a general discussion of the need for sustainable land use. The lower Hudson region is in dire need of global climate change adaptation strategies—essential land use changes—of the sort that we discuss next. We then move north and west of Red Hook, into the heart of Rip Van Winkle country, to tell the story of a land use advocate who never seems to sleep, René VanSchaack. Following that, we head to the High Peaks region of Adirondack Park, where the land use challenges are unique in the region. We also discuss the efforts at creating subregional solutions to land use sustainability, and we conclude by noting some of the lingering difficulties that confront planning in the Hudson region.

Making Red Hook Red Hook

Before her election as supervisor, Bump was steeped in Red Hook's land use issues. Her involvement began in 1986, when she joined the town's master plan committee. The group worked on writing a comprehensive plan that would guide land use for decades to come. And worked. And worked. Finally, six years after their toils began, the committee presented its plan. It was adopted . . . but it was never implemented. The enabling ordinances were never approved. The plan just sat there.

"What did that master plan say?" Bump asks. "Well, it really did cover land use. It covered naming and then protecting your riverfront. Naming and protecting your water supply, your aquifer. Naming, locating the oldest forests. Which roads are scenic? How will development happen? Back then the idea of the conservation easement, it was real—it was put in there. A very, very visionary, forward-thinking document that took land use planning" into the twenty-first century—or could have, if only it had been made law.

That plan asked and answered a question steeped in the notion of Landscape found throughout this book: "What is Red Hook?" the committee inquired. "What do you want your community to look like in twenty years?" It was an introspective document intended to infuse Red Hook with rich meaning, a communal statement of what that place is all about, that would be rendered visible in the ways that streets are laid out, how business storefronts look, and where farms, forests, and trails are located. It would first affirm Red Hook's identity and then transform the town by putting that identity into practice. Land use planning is the ideal vehicle for that work: the creation of Landscape.

"What is Red Hook?" was a question that Bump, a New York City native transplanted to the town as a teenager, had actually had most of her life to consider. Bump's parents moved the family to Tivoli, a Red Hook riverfront village. "You'd trek the woods," she recalls. "Back then there was nothing to do except hike around and ride your bike, explore the woods. My mother would say, 'You have to go to the dentist,' and you'd have to ride your bike to the village of Red Hook. So you'd go eight or ten miles on your bike, taking shortcuts through fields or woods. You can't do that today."

I asked if there were factors other than security that would keep a parent from saying the same thing to a child today. Bump replied, "It isn't really security at all. It's built. There's somebody's fence or yard or house."

The old paths no longer exist. The fields and forests of Bump's childhood are subdivisions and roads.

Clearly, Red Hook is not what it used to be. Historically, the riverfront was dotted with estates and industrial sites, an odd but not uncommon juxtaposition made both possible and essential by the Hudson: its beauty and its potential as a commercial highway attracted industrialists who sought escape and others who wanted inexpensive transportation. Two incorporated villages, Red Hook and Tivoli, were the town's commercial centers, while smaller concentrations of homes—hamlets like Upper Red Hook, Barrytown, and Annandale—enjoyed their own identity. The rest was farms and woodlots.

The latter continue to characterize the Town of Red Hook's sense of self, even if there are fewer of them. Bump says, "When you do a survey, the answers come back, 'We want to keep our town a rural town, but we want to encourage growth in our villages. We want our villages to thrive.'"

Without the implementation of the new master plan, the only controls over development were zoning ordinances enacted in the 1960s. Those laws required roads to be constructed as wide as the New York Thruway, the interstate highway that runs between New York City and Buffalo. Provisions such as that one came as a shock to Bump. "We have this little rural town and little rural villages and we had little dirt roads and we had scenic roads—the best scenic roads," she says. "But as soon as the county or the state or the town came in and did something to those roads, it was suddenly like the Thruway." That approach was a "military-minded Cold War script," Bump adds. "So you're losing the identity that people reported that they wanted," losing it because of outdated land use requirements.

According to David Kooris, Red Hook's experience is not unusual. Kooris, a former a vice president at the nonprofit Regional Plan Association, explains that communities all across the United States "often create comprehensive plans that embody a vision we have for our communities and our neighborhoods, but we don't always translate that vision into the tools that will actually achieve it"—in particular, zoning laws. What's found in comprehensive plans "is often significantly more sustainable than the zoning," Kooris says, "which is typically a holdover from the advent of zoning in the middle of the twentieth century." Red Hook, then, was prototypical. But Bump was not.

Once she took over the supervisor's chair, she quickly turned to implementing the master plan that had languished for the better part of a decade. Bump was committed to a democratic process to making it happen. "We had at least ten community meetings, with input from everyone," she recalls. "We invited everyone to the table, from the most classic builder and developer to the most environmentalist/conservationist/preservationist (individual) and everyone in between." Others insist Bump's approach is the way planning must proceed if it is to enjoy legitimacy among the broader public and if it is to have the sustainability effects that are needed today. Melissa Everett, executive director of Sustainable Hudson Valley, advocates "a new way of going at planning and development. First of all, high-participation, whole-system planning rather than just land use. Second, localization and green industry clusters. And we've helped to figure out, with the communities that are taking their own initiatives around climate change, how to marry that with economic development."

Following similar steps, Bump and her constituents arrived at "our vision, which is: We'd like to keep Red Hook rural. We'd like to have the riverfront dealt with, know what's going on there." Under the plan, the town's two villages will indeed be where future development will occur, preserving farmland and promoting the concentration of economic growth rather than sprawl and its attendant costs, such as road maintenance, police and fire services, and schools.

The result, in a set of enabling ordinances enacted under Bump's leadership, is a clear message to developers, she says. Bump, who worked for two decades with her husband in their custom home construction business, explains, "You're no longer going to be able to build on our farmlands willy-nilly because it's easy. Hey, eventually the farmlands will be used up and you will have to learn to build on less-prime places. So now's the time to do that." She adds, "We want to keep Red Hook Red Hook." In the "Centers and Greenspaces Plan" that the town implemented, the villages will grow but "the old 1960s planning" is no more, Bump says.[2] Village, hamlet, and rural character will be preserved, creating a Landscape that embodies Red Hook's character: a remaking and re-meaning of the town.[3]

"Centers and Greenspaces" is an example of "smart growth." An increasingly commonplace term, smart growth is less often actually practiced than it is talked about, although in 2010 New York State instituted the "Smart Growth Public Infrastructure Policy Act," mandating that state-funded infrastructure projects be reviewed according to smart growth principles.[4] Author Matthias Ruth writes, "Smart growth . . . focuses on changes in land use and transportation in order to improve the quality of life of local populations within the broader contexts of social, economic, and environmental change."[5] The Smart Growth Online Web site claims,

"Growth is 'smart' when it gives us great communities with more choices and personal freedom, good return on public investment, greater opportunity across the community, a thriving natural environment, and a legacy we can be proud to leave our children and grandchildren."[6]

Smart growth emphasizes the avoidance of sprawl by "in-filling" (building where road, water, sewage, and other forms of infrastructure already exist), creating mixed-use developments (such as multistory buildings with businesses on the lower floors and residences higher up), providing public transportation, creating a range of housing choices (including for low-income persons), and more, all of which help preserve open space and agriculture and reduce the environmental costs of development, including those associated with global climate change.[7] As Ned Sullivan, executive director of Scenic Hudson, puts it, with smart growth "projects are downtown-oriented, use green building practices, and take into account climate change."

Another success that Bump is particularly proud of is Red Hook's community preservation fund. Supported by a 2 percent fee on that portion of real estate transactions that exceed the *county's* median sale price (about $350,000 at the time it was enacted) and paid for by purchasers, the fund was adopted by referendum in 2007, when, out of more than 2,600 ballots cast, the proposal passed by thirty-one votes. Red Hook became only the seventh municipality in New York to enact such an ordinance.

The intense resistance to the tax on the part of those whose property values skyrocketed in the years before the law was passed and then wanted to sell their homes was shortsighted, Bump insists. "It's only the kind of community that emphasizes preservation and keeping its rural character and its beauty *and* encourages growth in a certain way that allows for that profit to happen," Bump says proudly.

Supporting Sustainable Land Use

Localities like Red Hook are not alone as they plan for their futures. Among the greatest resources available to those in the lower Hudson Valley—the counties just north of New York City—is the Regional Plan Association. RPA provides planning assistance to Ulster, Orange, Rockland, Westchester, Putnam, and Dutchess counties, as well as New York City and areas outside the Hudson region in New York, New Jersey, and Connecticut. Since the 1929 release of its first plan for the New York metropolitan area, RPA has worked on projects to bring together cities and towns to coordinate land use protection and transportation needs, and it also promotes larger discussions about the future of the greater New York area, as reflected in its involvement in the New York-Connecticut Sustainable Communities project.[8]

"Buildout analyses" of municipalities' zoning ordinances are one tool that RPA uses to support better land use. They "demonstrate how that growth which is coming to the Hudson Valley would occur, given (a municipality's) current regulations," David Kooris says.

> In enabling stakeholders to see which portions of the landscape that are currently forested or farmland would be consumed by development, how that development would be laid out, which roads would be impacted because the vast majority of the traffic is funneled into a handful of arterials: it's a much more tangible future for people to respond to.
>
> We find that communities and civic participants are able to understand the threats or potential threats posed by a two-hundred-unit subdivision. But when it comes to the cumulative impact of the dozens of five- to ten-unit subdivisions, it takes a much more robust visualization and graphic articulation of what that means to begin to have a discussion about an alternative scenario.

RPA presents different possible development outcomes to communities, scenarios that enable them to explore what they get with a "business as usual" approach and a range of alternatives. Often those alternative futures better "reflect the visions laid out in their own comprehensive plans" than do existing zoning laws, Kooris notes.

The outcome of RPA's work with local communities can be seen in places such as Woodbury, New York, which "recognized the opportunity for some new housing around their train station that would provide an opportunity for their seniors to downsize from their homes when they desire to do so and for their children to move out of the house without leaving the community," Kooris says. Another example he cites is the town of Blooming Grove in Orange County, which "recognized the opportunity to stitch together all of the open spaces that they were mandating as a component of development so that they add up to a regional trail network and open space system that was greater than just a collection of independent pocket parks scattered across the town." As with Red Hook, careful land use planning became an expression of a community's Landscape aspirations.

Esteemed environmentalist Gus Speth notes, "Each year, the United States is losing about two million acres of open space—six thousand acres a day—and about 1.2 million acres of farmland, with prime farmland disappearing 30 percent faster than average."[9] Aspirational Landscapes, the shared containers of a community's vision of itself and its relationship to place, are of little import when actual Landscapes exist only as concrete and shopping malls.

Ecologist Gary Kleppel advocates taking an approach similar to RPA's and applying it to the whole Hudson Valley. Although his purpose is to explore the effects of development on invertebrates in streams, his musings are instructive. After historical and contemporary land use data are plugged into a computer model, scenario creation for the region becomes possible. "What if," Kleppel suggests, "we did nothing" to alter the current course of development?—akin to RPA's buildout analysis scenario. "We can project what the landscape would look like." The same can be done under a different scenario, for instance one in which development becomes concentrated, à la Red Hook's "Centers and Greenspaces" plan.

"Instead of building sprawling suburbs," Kleppel posits, "we're building little villages. When we build little villages, all the roads change back to little country roads," minimizing impervious road surfaces, thence reducing runoff, and, therefore, likely improving life for invertebrates in streams, stream health generally, ecosystem health more broadly—and creating sustainable human-ecological Landscapes.

Other benefits accrue from land use decisions informed by a sustainability ethos. For example, communities are likely to be cooled even as climate change increases temperatures globally thanks to the absence of all that blacktop and the presence of shade trees that have been left standing. Such social-ecological benefits are what Andreas R. Edwards has in mind when he writes of "regenerative development," explaining that it "improves the health of habitats, the strength of social networks and the depth of a community's historical roots. This perspective is the essence of thriveability: enhancing natural systems and supporting flourishing social networks."[10]

Thoughtful land use isn't only about concentrating development where communities want it or creating cool pockets instead of heat islands. It's also a matter of social equity, regenerating connections severed by social class differences. Some of the most intense land use pressures in the Hudson region are along the Hudson's riverbanks, places that have historically been attractive for recreation, especially among the poor, but can be difficult to gain access to. Alex Matthiessen, former president of the environmental group Riverkeeper, observes, "In rushing down to the waterfront to redevelop these beautiful waterfront parcels, developers are essentially replacing the old industrial sites, the old factories that were preventing access for the public to the river, with these massive condominium and mixed-use complexes that are also going to prevent the public from getting access to the river," swapping an old problem of equitable access for a new version of that same old problem.

"What we need to be doing," Matthiessen argues, "is approaching the waterfront with a much more balanced view. Let's use the waterfronts to revitalize some of these blighted communities that have been struggling for many years, but let's also make sure that we take this opportunity to preserve open space, to create public access so that the people can get back down to the river" as they used to.

Everyone needs to be able to "get down and feel the river directly," Matthiessen insists, "to boat on it, to fish on it, to picnic by it, to swim in it, to observe the magnificent wildlife that is coming back to the Hudson. As long as they can do that, they'll remain stakeholders and they'll remain invested in our collective effort to restore this magnificent waterway."

According to Edwards, such approaches are essential if sustainability is to fulfill its potential. He goes a step farther, endorsing a principle that "'[h]abitats shall be equally accessible across economic classes . . . providing affordable housing for everyone'" and promoting the "creation of places that bring people from the neighborhood together."[11] Without people interacting with rivers, forests, and the like, those places lose meaning, and therefore relevance. When residents don't interact across social boundaries such as class and race, shared Landscapes are rendered impossible.

Adapting to Climate Change

There's another problem with those rehabilitated-for-condos riverside fortresses Matthiessen decries: in a few years parts of them may be under water. Ecologist David VanLuven advocates that local governments "integrate climate change considerations into their land use decision making and permitting so that we don't have situations where we're doing a lot of construction right on the water and in fifty years the water has risen

X number of feet, combined with major floods and storm surge. All of a sudden we're looking at really ugly situations where people's very valuable properties and investments are being imperiled because they shouldn't have been built there in the first place." The solution, VanLuven says, is "adapting" to the effects of climate change, the ecological ramifications of which were discussed in chapter 2.

Adaptation does little to address carbon emissions, the primary cause of climate change and the attention grabber in the media. VanLuven acknowledges the importance of emissions reduction, but he points out that the benefits of such policies—assuming they are ever adopted on a wide scale—"are not going to hit for another forty years. . . . If we *radically* reduce our emissions, in seventy years the climate in New York is going to be like Virginia (today). We need to start thinking now about how to adapt to those coming changes so that they don't catch us completely off guard."

Adaptation's purpose is more immediate: to protect human and ecological communities alike from climate change's ravages. And, VanLuven adds, with a nod toward Matthiessen's social justice concerns, "We've got to be thinking about people and the Hudson at the same time. We need to be worried about poverty. We need to be worried about homes being flooded." Adaptation, then, is about addressing equity, ecology, and economics within the context of climate change.

Among the eighty adaptation strategies that came out of the Nature Conservancy's "Rising Waters" project,[12] for which VanLuven was a driving force, were several approaches that involved effectively communicating information about climate change's effects and about adaptation options. Among the latter were ideas as diverse as encouraging or requiring rain gardens to slow runoff; appropriating state funds to purchase floodplain lands and to "restore, reconnect, and protect riparian corridors"; requiring permeable surfaces (for new roads, parking lots, sidewalks, and the like); and a host of emergency and disaster preparedness initiatives.[13]

The list is a sobering reminder of how unsure even the experts are regarding the best adaptation strategies, how far the region is from agreeing on which strategies to implement, and how much adaptation will cost. New York State takes climate change seriously, but neither it nor the vast majority of local government entities were considering adaptation as rigorously as VanLuven or the Nature Conservancy would like even before the Great Recession. In its aftermath, both the will and the means appear to be lacking.

But acting on adaptation today carries with it distinct advantages, including that it helps avoid long-term ecological and economic costs. Gary Kleppel points out that society has an opportunity to address "three inseparables: climate change, energy, and land use." Cheap energy is the driving force. It has indirectly altered land use in ways that contribute to climate change, making the suburb and the exurb possible, allowing persons to live great distances from where they work, go to school, recreate, and the like. As a result, the effects of climate change are exacerbated.

Kleppel notes one example with multiple ramifications: sprawl. "All the forest and permeable substrate"—land cover capable of absorbing water, including soils and plant roots—"is being replaced by hard substrate that doesn't hold water. There's a very simple question: What happens to the water? Well, it goes away. It goes into our streams, washes through the streams very quickly, disrupting the animal communities, especially the invertebrates that live there." Invertebrates are essential for stream life, since they eat tiny plants and are themselves eaten by larger animals. Without invertebrates, stream health suffers, creating cascading effects throughout ecosystems. And without permeable surfaces, aquifers do not recharge. The solution to that cascade of problems is to pave with permeable asphalt.

The benefits of such adaptations can be immense. For example, in Rockland County, New York, which borders New Jersey and is a bedroom community for New York City, "the demand for water has gone up a great deal" because of the county's rapid population increase over the last forty years, explains Doug Burns. "They get most of their water from subsurface supplies." Without permeable surfaces, "What might have been a mild drought at one time in Rockland County has become a more severe drought because they live on the edge in terms of their water needs," says Burns, noting that climate change will increase the likelihood of severe drought and, thus, inadequate aquifer recharge. "There is an interaction between human development, water use, and climate."

Permeable surfaces, rainwater catchment, and similar adaptive strategies could save Rockland millions of dollars over a proposed desalinization plant.[14] Practical strategies such as these show that conceiving and creating sustainable Landscapes are far from pie-in-the-sky exercises; they hold the promise of economic savings and will help avoid future social conflicts. Imagine being a Rockland County decision maker confronted with questions of how water should be distributed during a drought. Paving with permeable materials may help avoid such wrenching discussions altogether.

Greening Greene County

Across the Hudson River and a little north of Marirose Blum Bump's Town of Red Hook lies Greene County, home to a man who frames land use issues a lot like Bump does. "The fact of the matter," says René VanSchaack, "is if you want to maintain rural quality of life, you've got to make hard decisions to save land when you consume land. It's got to be balanced fair and equitably." That observation is a difficult one for developers and sustainability advocates alike to hear. Many developers resent "regulation," seeing nothing in zoning and environmental protections for themselves while, quite often, others just want to draw a line in the sand, to declare all development ended—after all, so much has already been lost to subdivisions and shopping malls.

But in many areas of the nation, social and political will won't allow the extreme ends of either of those sides to prevail. Moreover, our economic system cannot contemplate an absolutist preservationist attitude. So the playing field is effectively tilted in the developers' favor. VanSchaack's approach evens things out a bit.

And he has some powerful allies, among them ecologist Karin Limburg. She cut her teeth fighting the worst excesses of development and rampant pollution. But hard-learned realism wins the day. "To have a good environment," Limburg says, "you have to develop your way through. You have to actually destroy a lot, build your wealth, and then you can take care of your environment. If you look at the history of the European colonists in the Hudson Valley, that's probably the case."

In nation after nation, widespread environmental destruction has resulted from the adoption of industrial capitalism as an economic system, and restrictions on that destruction have been dependent on enough wealth being generated that environmental preservation can gain a toehold without significantly impeding economic growth. In our political and economic calculus, Landscape means loss: loss to gain.

VanSchaack's Greene County is home to most of the Catskill Mountains, visible from the state capital in Albany. It was here that America's first great visual works of art were produced, the luminescent landscape paintings of the Hudson River School, and it was the Catskills that Rip Van Winkle stumbled out of after a twenty-year slumber to discover a changed world.

When I spoke with VanSchaack, he was Greene County's Soil and Water Conservation District executive director—not a position one associates with community catalysts. But he had assumed a different role in his birth county. VanSchaack had become a one-person sustainable land use powerhouse.

Now in his fifties, VanSchaack was born in the village of Catskill, and he traces his Dutch lineage back to some of the region's earliest settlers. After a stint in the military he eventually returned home and ended up at Soil and Water, where he grew the agency and made a name for himself as someone whose word could be trusted and who would get a job done. The bulk of the district's work is performed under contract for New York City, which relies on reservoirs in the Catskills for a large portion of its drinking water needs. But VanSchaack's reputation has little to do with reservoirs and aqueducts. Rather, it is his hard-nosed approach to balancing development and conservation that has won him accolades.

Conservation through Development

In a sense, VanSchaack is an advocate for only one thing: his way of doing things. "My position is that I draw the line and I don't budge off the line," he says, hardly sounding like a deal maker. "And I set it so high that there's not going to be any credible hole. . . . And it better darned well have integrated this guy's idea and this guy's idea." In other words, he forges a compromise position early in the negotiating process and insists that it be what's adopted, trusting his sense of fairness and community need to guide him. It's reverse mediation: VanSchaak makes the decision and brings the stakeholders to it.

And, indeed, when he applies his approach to contentious land use issues, he almost always does win. He takes into account equitability, rationality, data right up front—all of it, everything that the public policy process ought to do but often does not. He is an arbiter who has no stake in a negotiation aside from balance and the headlong pursuit of his version of Landscape. But he's no tyrant. VanSchaak's approach has everything to do with transparency and efficiency. Everyone's cards must be on the table, he insists, and no one's time, money, or reputation should be wasted in fights over the future of a given piece of property.

VanSchaack's view is that most environmental advocates naively insist that they can stop development, and on occasion they can. But the majority fail to acknowledge the forces arrayed against them: a regulatory system that was created through a compromise process that allowed developers the loudest voice, the politicians who created and continue to endorse those policies, and the big-money business interests whose sole focus is profit—the rest, including any rich notion of democracy, be damned.[15] Instead of denying development and fighting battles that will be lost more often than not, VanSchaack insists what activists ought to be doing is directing development, looking to make deals to pursue their interests and insightfully understanding what matters most to those they oppose.

VanSchaack's approach is a proven winner, but he finds it difficult to grasp that he is one of the few who, first, attempts the sort of mediation he does and, second, won't allow posturing, bullying, or even refusal to participate in a negotiation to stop him from advocating for environmental preservation through development. "At the end of the day," he says, "it always amazes me that more people don't see how this all fits together. I see it very simplistically. It's not simple, but it is simplistic"—simplistic in the sense that it is an approach to negotiation that is open and honest.

Everyone involved in VanSchaack's version of poker comes to the table stripped to their underwear. With nothing to hide, and with trust in the dealer, the game almost becomes cooperative rather than confrontational. Almost.

Seeing the Landscape

What has VanSchaack accomplished? Building on the connections he made throughout Greene County over fifteen years with the Soil and Water Conservation District, VanSchaack offered to work as a consultant—one of his several Soil and Water hats—to the county Industrial Development Agency in 2001 to help facilitate discussions with local environmentalists as the IDA sought to create shovel-ready business parks: tracts where permitting and other complicating factors had already been addressed before a developer even knew the land existed. VanSchaack notes that it is resistance on environmental grounds that typically slows development; in most cases compromise comes about only after a drawn-out battle in which attorneys, consultants, and engineers walk away happy but everyone else leaves embittered.

Intially, VanSchaack recalls, the IDA administrator's attitude was "no thanks" when the Soil and Water man offered to serve as go-between. "We'll call you when we need the B-team," was the message in so many words, VanSchaack says. Two years later, the first site was not permitted and a local environmentalist—a friend of VanSchaack's—had filed a lawsuit to halt the project. Then the IDA hired a new executive director, Sandy Mathis, a local who, knowing VanSchaack's reputation for problem solving, asked for a meeting. When they spoke, Mathis asked

VanSchaack to attend a public hearing on the project two days later. Van-Schaack arrived to a packed house. "The place was loaded with very irate people," VanSchaack recalls. "They were very antidevelopment. They didn't understand what was going on, but they already had it ingrained in their mind that they didn't want this. Keep in mind, this community has one of the lower per capita incomes in the Hudson Valley. We don't have a lot of rich people hanging around here in Coxsackie," implying that the stereotypical groups that resist development were not to be found, but the locals were certain nevertheless that the business park would bring disaster to their community.

In a meeting with the IDA's board of directors afterward, VanSchaack insisted that "every single person" who objected in writing to the IDA's environmental impact statement for the business park be placed on an advisory committee. VanSchaack knew many of them, including a former state Department of Environmental Conservation wildlife expert, a birding guidebook illustrator, "several other credible people," plus the person who sued to stop the project. "You gotta have some faith in me," Van-Schaack told the board, uttering his mantra. The board, its back against a wall, had little choice but to follow VanSchaack's "simplistic" approach.

His next move was to visit each potential advisory committee member—all of the opponents of the plan—to invite them to join. They all said yes. "As a result of that, we started the Greene County Habitat Advisory Committee," VanSchaack says—now the Greene County Habitat Conservation Partnership.[16] The committee had a substantial voice in reenvisioning the business park proposal, and ultimately it was constructed.

What was in it for the conservationists? An acre and a half of land was set aside for every acre that was developed, and "we worked on more of a landscape scale," VanSchaack points out, situating the project in the context of the county's long-term socioecological future. "We knew there were other vacant lands here and here, and they're going to come into the picture sometime. When they do, how does this fit with that?" VanSchaack's Landscape perspective began to take shape, one in which Greene County would take on a new meaning: economically viable beyond the odd ski resort town, community focused, and environmentally sophisticated.

He explains his approach to the county's Landscape as if he were composing a landscape painting—or at least filling one in: "When you start to talk about things from a landscape perspective, on a landscape scale, it's not really a question of seeing it or thinking about it. . . . It may be five hundred acres that I'm working on, and those paint-by-numbers colors are kind of small." *All* the colors, the various pieces of the conservation picture, have to be seen, he insists, even when the momentary focus is on a small piece.

It's easy to become overwhelmed by the big picture, and when that happens "you don't get a lot of paint on the paper," VanSchaack says. "Things happen at that smaller scale, but you've got to be cognizant of the big scale." Maintaining focus on the little bit in front of him—*this* project and its unique opportunities—is essential, he says, even as he keeps in mind the whole canvas: ecosystem-level goals can only be achieved through painstaking attention to each part of the painting.

Numerous state and local officials have praised VanSchaack's artistry. One admirer, Karin Limburg, simply says, "René is very good."

The sequel to the initial business park followed almost immediately. VanSchaack argued that his landscape-scale vision, intended to fulfill Greene County's conservation needs and address business development pressures decades into the future, should be what guided the environmental assessment process for the park. He met with resistance from traditionalists who demanded that every development project be opposed piecemeal, on its own with no attention to the landscape and to the gains that clever compromise might yield. VanSchaack recalls responding in his usual no-nonsense way: "You know it's going to get developed. It's a big, flat field on a state highway a half-mile from a Thruway exit. It's gonna get developed. That's reality."

I write that VanSchaack "met with resistance"; as he is wont to do, he literally met with opposition groups to hear their concerns. "We didn't wait to go to planning boards when we had a full plan," VanSchaack recalls. Instead, he and the IDA gathered with relevant stakeholders before the plan was publicly announced. Historical preservation groups, the Habitat Advisory Committee, even elected officials from nearby towns that, under the state's home rule law (see "Getting to Regionalism," below), had no legal say in the process: VanSchaack estimates that he has participated in hundreds of conversations with groups large and small, "always taking the time to sell the message," a process reminiscent of Marirose Blum Bump's approach to enacting Red Hook's comprehensive plan. When it comes to successful land use planning, communication is key.

If anything, VanSchaack's results have been even better than those in Red Hook. The second business park's environmental impact statement—a moment when many developments encounter substantial resistance from stakeholders who have played no part in the discussion to that point because they were not invited to the table—was virtually unopposed. For a third project, VanSchaack and the IDA promised a two-to-one conservation set-aside that preserved 750 acres. Some of the preserved land was under consideration for landfill sites and had caused consternation in the hamlet of New Baltimore. Other plots were prime habitat for the Northern Harrier Hawk, a threatened species in New York. More than one-third of the acreage was protected by conservation easements, which means it stays on the tax rolls.

In time, VanSchaack's tough love approach has yielded substantial ecological savings. The environmental community and state regulators "started to say, 'Okay, maybe we can let you think ahead on some kind of conservation in anticipation of what future growth might be,'" VanSchaack recalls. He responded, his comments dripping with sarcasm, "Well, it's nice that you privileged me with this right, but this is what we should be doing. This is what your textbooks say. Your Army Corps (of Engineers) wetland mitigation manuals say in the first paragraph that you should think on a landscape or a wetlands scale. That's what it looks like when you really do it. The problem is, you've never seen it done before. It means having trust up front and making compromises," the foundations of his Landscape vision. It's a vision echoed by others in the region. Stormwater management professional Blue Neils says land use "is always a compromise. It's always a compromise."

Some of these stories may give readers the perception that VanSchaack is somehow "pro-business." It is true that he moved on to join the IDA, but he is as hard-nosed with intransigent developers as he is with stubborn environmentalists, and he insists that his outlook "balances" development and conservation. His commitment to conservation is clear in how he seeks to implement his Landscape vision. "We should use the power of the economics at the time they come in"—from the time developers initiate their proposals—"to secure the long-term conservation that's needed," he says. "Time in and time out again," VanSchaack adds, "all up and down this Hudson Valley, these communities have said, 'Oh, wait a minute. We need to think about saving some of this.' Well, you know what? They're about two hundred subdivisions too late. They're about five shopping centers too late. They're about two industrial parks too late. . . . We've been satisfied with 'we got the little green medians and we're gonna do some trees in them. And you know what, beyond the loading dock we'll leave a half acre. And when you add it all up': Add it all up? There's no value when you add it all up!"

It's time to do things differently. Piecemeal approaches do little for conservation. Resistance to development absent a broad vision creates entrenched enemies. What about turning the adversarial project on its head, placing "simplicity" front and center, thoughtfully channeling development, preserving habitat, and promoting a new Landscape?

The work, VanSchaack admits, "is an obsession," adding, "I could make much greater money, but that's never been in my blood." When with the Soil and Water Conservation District he often worked sixty-plus hour weeks, personally covering twice the value of his contract in billable work. His personality is big, and he is anxious that he comes across as bombastic or arrogant. More fairly, VanSchaack is self-assured and self-mocking, once remarking to me, "God, I've got a big head!" He is also so humble that he avoids appearing on the dais with high-level elected officials and has to be tricked into showing up at awards dinners when he is the guest of honor. Embarrassed that "his" stories put him too much in the spotlight, he insists, "It's not me, me, me, look at me. It's more me, me, me: I can do it, you can do it. It's a passion."

Playground for the Rich?

"On one hand," says lifelong Hudson Valley resident John Mylod as he considers land preservation in the region he loves, "we're under tremendous pressure right now. On the other hand, a lot has been saved over time. We have a huge legacy of important parkland in the valley. The Taconic Park system, the federal park system, the Adirondacks. It could be so much worse." The railroads that line both banks of the river were actually responsible for significant amounts of land preservation, Mylod notes, since the railroad companies controlled almost all the property on the river side of the tracks and rarely agreed to let anyone build on it. In other cases, open space preservation occurred when estate-owning families such as the Roosevelts, Goulds, Millses, and Vanderbilts transferred their land to government or religious control, protecting ecologically and scenically valuable areas from development.

While it could be worse, development pressures in the Hudson Valley are nonetheless substantial, with populations increasing and sprawl seemingly never-ending in places where there are no Bumps or VanSchaacks. Ecologist Eric Kiviat observes that development "has a lot of direct and indirect effects on the Hudson, the direct effects being people building on these marvelous bluffs and islands along the Hudson. They're going to clear the vegetation and cause erosion and visual and auditory disturbance and use pesticides and fertilizers and change runoff. Indirect effects: changes to streams, changes to outdoor recreation, things like that. . . . I think communities are really struggling with that, now."

Indeed they are, and one can be forgiven for thinking that the huge, remote, seemingly pristine Adirondack State Park is exempt from such concerns. It is not. There was a time when few but the very rich could afford the time or money to visit the park. "In the Gilded Age," Robert Boyle wrote, "opulent camps followed one upon the other. Not all the 'camps' were within the Hudson watershed, but the most lavish was— Fox-Lair," which was situated on 1,200 acres owned by a New York businessman and included "an enormous chateau, 215 feet long," as well as stables, servants' quarters, and a golf course.[17] As I discussed in chapter 2, researchers have found that development's effects on wildlife begin with the smallest, simplest form of development—a trail through the woods, and there are plenty of them in the Adirondacks—and extend from there all the way to suburbs and concrete wasteland cities. The "great camps" had great effects.

Michale Glennon notes that ecologists studying heavily forested areas like the Adirondacks struggle to identify the cumulative impacts on wildlife from different forms of development. "Sort of the blessing and the curse for the Adirondacks is that you can go to the top of any mountain around here and it looks green for miles and miles," Glennon says. "It looks beautiful," but roads and power line corridors and cabins in the forest "all add up." While the effects of those and other forms of development are not easily computed, there are sound scientific reasons to argue that widespread human alterations to sensitive ecosystems harm ecosystem health.

Glennon is gathering data on the effectiveness of one proposed approach to concentrating those alterations, clustered development, wherein homes that otherwise might be located far from each other are sited closer together: each still on its own plot of land but near enough to one another to avoid the ecological effects typical of dispersed development.[18]

"The idea," Glennon says, "is that we can keep our influence contained and the rest of a subdivision area can be communal forest or whatever. It's a really big thing to think about because so often the argument is, 'Well, it's a six–hundred-acre area, but we're only having a five-acre footprint around each house and ninety-nine percent of it is going to stay forest.' Well, yes, from a simple area standpoint that's true. But a forest with long roads through it and long driveways going to houses is a different forest than one that didn't have those things beforehand." Wildlife has its own needs, and they are rarely self-evident to humans. Fleeting disturbances—doors slamming or lawn mowers roaring—may be enough to chase off certain species, altering ecosystems in the process.

In the upper reaches of the Hudson region, the pressures on forests are particularly intense, Glennon explains. Like any land use planning organization, the Adirondack Park Agency looks at projects one by one, "and nothing ever looks that bad," she says, echoing David Kooris's observations regarding the cumulative effects of development at the other end of the Hudson region. "It's just one project. But when you add it to the other eight hundred that (are approved) this year and the other eight hundred that are going to happen next year and the year after that, then it starts to become something that we have to think about. . . . How do we think about where we want to be in fifty or a hundred years?" The Adirondacks need a unified Landscape vision if its tenuous ecosystems are to be preserved.[19]

The park is under intense pressure from a version of unsustainability exportation. Mark Roseland writes that unsustainability is exported when "the production or extraction of natural resources in distant parts of the world . . . causes serious problems of environmental degradation there."[20] In the case of the Adirondacks, what is being exported is housing—second houses, quite often—roads, the secondary effects of those things, and the ecological destruction that accompanies them. In the process, the park's Landscape becomes something very different from what Glennon and others have in mind. Its constitutionally protected "forever wild" characteristics are threatened or lost as it effectively becomes chopped up into a crazy quilt of habitat fragments, the Hudson headwaters' meaning and reality muddied in the process.

Glennon's long-term prognosis for the huge park's ecosystems is not optimistic. "I think certainly we're going to see a lot more exurban development or backcountry development" in the Adirondacks, she says. "Exurban" development occurs in previously rural areas beyond even the farthest suburb.[21] Glennon adds, "I think the forces driving that aren't going away. People have a lot of wealth in this country, and the Adirondacks have absentee ownership from every state but one. So I don't see any reason to believe that those trends are going to change." As global climate change's effects become more pronounced and make life uncomfortable for many more people, the cool mountains with their abundant shade and seemingly endless waters will become even more attractive, only adding to development pressures in the Catskills, Adirondacks, and similar areas across the country.

Directing development in ways that will reduce its effects on wild-life and wild lands "will take a lot of effort on the local scale and on the landscape scale (Adirondack Park as a whole), because I don't think the pressure is going to lessen very much," Glennon says. "Somebody said a couple of weeks ago, 'Well, you know, isn't that just the foregone conclusion that the Adirondacks are going to get developed? Isn't it just a playground for the rich, and we can't do anything about that, can we?' I don't want to think that. . . . Maybe we can plan it the right way."

The Adirondacks are one of the rare mountainous areas fortunate to have the *potential* for effective planning already in place, thanks in part to Glennon's research. Whether the APA and the park's towns and villages will take advantage of that potential is a question vital to continued human enjoyment and to ecosystem survival alike.

Getting to Regionalism

One challenge, perhaps a unique one, that northeastern and New England states face in pursuing sweeping sustainability strategies is "home rule," the devolution of substantial amounts of power to comparatively small jurisdictions, towns, which dates back to colonial times. Under home rule, places such as Red Hook control their land use destiny. Neither the county nor the state can mandate zoning standards, for example, nor can towns or counties be compelled to cooperate with others regarding proposed development, transportation, economic, or other decisions.

To hear some speak of home rule is to be reminded of a time when feudal city-states controlled Europe and each noble answered to no higher authority. René VanSchaack says such local decision making "only works when you're willing to make decisions at the local level. Having the power to rule only works when you have the *cojones* to sit on the throne." He claims that home rule is used by some to avoid having to make difficult decisions, an observation that David Church concurs with. Church, who heads one of the busiest planning offices in New York, Orange County's, says home rule is "too dominated too often by personalities and 'common sense'—but your common sense is not my common sense. It still works at many levels in many ways, but we do have to somehow get better regional functionality on these issues. It's the only economical way to do it."

Home rule enables the sort of parochialism, self-serving, and retrenchment that is anathema to sustainability advocates, who often call for "holism" and "cooperation" because they recognize that many problems extend across jurisdictional lines, as must their solutions. However, the evidence that I saw indicates that home rule is more flexible than its anxious critics give it credit for, and it appears that cooperation across jurisdictional boundaries—"regionalism"—is an emerging reality. Although he wrote about national-level cooperation, Simon Dresner gives voice to the importance of regionalism as well. He observed, "Attempting to achieve sustainability in one country is almost useless if other countries continue to act unsustainably. Sustainability seems to demand global agreements about the use of the environmental space."[22]

David Kooris argues that "the key to regionalism is identifying those few things that are best dealt with at the regional scale. Not trying to replace municipal government with regional government. Not trying to force activity at the regional scale for something that is economically and efficiently dealt with at the local scale. But identifying that handful of things that literally cannot be managed at the municipal scale and continuing to make the case that this is not removal of authority from the local scale. It's actually an addition of authority because you're tackling the challenge at the scale in which you can have an impact on it."

Cross-border transportation issues are examples of the sort of "regional" approach that Kooris and others advocate. For example, automobile commuters passing through multiple jurisdictions create problems all along their routes. Mass transit is an obvious solution to such issues, but few small jurisdictions can foot the bill for those costly systems, nor should they, since improved bus or rail service is likely to benefit every municipality it serves.

Regionalism, David Church insists, is essential. "The market is regional," he points out. "The infrastructure is regional. I don't know if that means county or multi-counties or a new definition of region. . . . The Hudson Valley has this sense of connectivity, but we've never been able to get it to institutionally resonate." In the vacuum created by home rule, Church points out, numerous regional bodies have been developed for specific purposes. Some are state entities, such as the Hudson River Valley Greenway, which was founded in 1991 to promote historical and environmental preservation while supporting economic development.[23] Others are nonprofits, such as the Hudson River Watershed Alliance, whose mission is to promote research and education efforts pertaining to the Hudson and its tributaries.[24]

David Kooris suggests a flexible response to regionalism, saying that it "can be as formalized as a memorandum of understanding or a compact between municipalities to jointly work on an issue, or it can be just an informal conversation. Much of the work that we've done in the Hudson Valley on regionalism has been less formal interactions between municipalities where we have worked with clusters of a half dozen to a dozen municipalities." Even in a Balkanized political structure, Landscape doesn't have to be lost.

Lingering Land Use Challenges

Dennis Swaney, who wears an environmental historian's hat as well as an ecologist's, observes that over the last four hundred years the Hudson region has experienced "land use change probably unrivaled in the States." That continued change will be a reality for decades to come is not in question. What's not clear is the form it will take. The Hudson region is home to exciting examples of smart growth and exceptionally thoughtful land use planning. It is also fortunate to have natural scientists, social scientists, government officials, and NGOs that point out the dangers and opportunities ahead.

Of course, development is likely to remain a grave challenge to the region's sustainability. When pondering the problems that concern him most, ecologist Eric Kiviat says that "land use change, absolutely, is higher on my list than climate change because it's happening faster and it's going to be harder doing anything about." David VanLuven shares Kiviat's concern but links the two issues, observing, "We've got this wave of development sweeping north up the Hudson. The Hudson River is clean, now. You can swim in it. You can eat the fish out of it. Blue crabs from the Hudson are being shipped south to make Maryland crab cakes! People want to live on the Hudson, now. We could trash it in the process or we could do something really good, and climate change may be the overarching threat that sparks some action."

Connections such as those are vital to effectively addressing future land use *and* environmental problems. Landscapes, René VanSchaack would be quick to remind us, are wholes, and even as one focuses on one topic, connections to others cannot be ignored.

If development as we know it is to be successfully challenged, it will likely take the form of smart growth—and if smart growth is to be taken seriously, it must occur in larger towns and cities. However, as David Church points out, "we've had a real challenge with the cities (in the Hudson Valley)—Newburgh, Middletown, Kingston, Poughkeepsie,

Beacon. Those places have had a rough go, and we need to be much smarter about that. I think we need to go to extraordinary effort, provide extraordinary resources to help these places get fully healthy."

Those cities struggle with high poverty, homelessness, and unemployment rates, problems that less-developed towns and rural areas have largely avoided. Even in the city of Hudson, whose rebirth has been acclaimed by many, the new growth has not been smart—not *socially* smart. The main street is dotted with expensive restaurants and entertainment venues, Church observes, "but what about a block away? That's the issue for some people in Hudson. All you have to do is round the corner. Tell me how that neighborhood benefitted from forty antique shops?"

New York's cities are hampered in what they can accomplish because of local government's reliance on property taxes rather than equitable distributions from state and federal governments. Church explains, "You get a lot of local decisions being made merely by how to increase the tax base, and that's a real challenge. I want [a new housing development] to be in a different neighborhood and a different design, near a bus route and within walking distance of a school, and I'm told, 'We can't do that. If we start asking those kinds of questions, this development will go away to another town, another county, another state.' So managing (development) remains a real challenge underlain by this need to get the property tax base up." Regressive property tax systems are unlikely to ever help struggling small cities out of poverty, and without the smart redevelopment of cities and villages, the Hudson region's Landscape can never be a sustainable one.

Chapter 5

Remaking Communities

WITH JESSICA ALEMAN, MARY RYNASKO,
AND KATARRA PETERSON

W e invoke "community" often and casually. Frequently, it connotes
a group defined by emotional closeness emphasizing well-being
beyond the individual with intense personal ties among group members.
Sometimes, community is synonymous with "neighborhood." But, thanks
to our hyperconnected world, it increasingly implies connections with
others beyond spatial proximity and temporal immediacy.

In nearly all senses, however, community invokes something shared:
it may be faith or philosophy, place or patriotism, even distinction and
difference from others, but in some way community unites people. Not
unlike "nature" in its flexibility,[1] community's evocation of identity and the
intensely personal emerged in a number of my conversations with sustainability advocates in the Hudson region. While there may have been some
variability in the meanings they ascribed to community, one commonality
was its immediacy and its importance to individuals' lives.

Ajax Greene, who co-created a large and growing support network
for local businesses in the Hudson Valley, insists that community got lost
along the way and that people want it back. "I think we've had a lot of
changes in American society," he says, "and I think people are hungry
for connection and community," something he first found working with
New York City athletic clubs, where the workout was only part of why

folks showed up. As we will see, problems often are felt—lived—at the community level, and there, too, is where Greene and others argue they can and should be resolved.

Authors Chris Maser and Christine Kirk quote noted conservationist Wendell Berry as writing, "That will-o'-the-wisp of the large-scale solution to the large-scale problem, so dear to governments and universities and corporations, serves mostly to distract people from the small, private problems that they may in fact have the power to solve. The problems, if we describe them accurately, are all private and small. Or they are so initially." Maser and Kirk add, "It is thus imperative that we address the fundamental causes of our problems at their roots—our thinking and behavior at the local community level—or we will always be dealing with symptoms and band-aid solutions that compound the problem by denying the cure."[2] From this perspective, new Landscape meaning must be grounded in community. Implicitly, it is only as communities adopt and pursue new understandings of the people-place connection that those meanings can spread in earnest, and with them solutions to Landscape ills.

Many have identified community's essential ties to the environment. Hudson region historian David Stradling writes, "In late 1969 Ada Louise Huxtable, architecture critic of the *New York Times*, described a 'crisis of the environment' composed of threats to both the country's natural assets and its communities, as bulldozers tore through the countryside and urban neighborhoods alike. . . . Huxtable argued that, given the environmental crisis, 'the question is survival.'"[3] For Huxtable, communities were the collective canary in the coal mine; as their relationship with the environments in which they are situated, and on which they depend, goes, so go us all.

In the intervening decades little has changed except, perhaps, our disengagement from our communities. That increasingly inward focus on self and family is not the result of a contagion sweeping the populace. Rather, a host of factors have brought it about, few of which have much to do with individual choice. Sprawl, long work and commute hours, the need to work two jobs, and the resulting lack of time to participate in public life have all pulled us back from our communities—and, in the process, have left them at least as vulnerable as they were in Huxtable's day.

Moreover, ecologists commonly refer to "communities" of plants and animals, species whose survival is bound to that of others, yet humans often fail to see ourselves as members of ecological communities. "The vast majority of people are not connected to the community in which they live," says environmentalist Tom Lake. "They know what time the mall opens on Saturday, but do they know when certain flowers bloom? Do they know when certain animals are migrating? No. If you were a native person living here five hundred years ago, your life depended on knowing those things. Those were very important bits of information that you passed on. Today we have lost a lot of that basic knowledge."

Lake notes that pre-Hudsonian native peoples "understood the concept that you can control nature in a way, but it's a symbiosis. You're actually helping it by fostering new growth, and at the same time you're helping yourself because it's going to attract different kinds of animals. These are fairly sophisticated concepts of ecology that escaped us for the last three hundred years until recently."

The symbiosis that Lake speaks of is "mutualism"—when species benefit one another. Some argue that another form of symbiosis, "parasitism," more closely describes humanity's Landscape relationships in the Hudson region and, indeed, throughout the developed world. When societies behave parasitically, they fail to recognize the intimacy of their connections to the ecological communities around them. Philosophers such as Henry David Thoreau and activists like radical environmentalists have asserted for more than a century that nature is important in and of itself, wholly apart from any value we may try to draw from it.

Such "ecocentric" arguments—even though today they are based not on ethics but in science—tend to fall on deaf ears, prompting ecologists and others to adopt the "ecosystem services" notion, introduced in chapter 2, to reinforce the social-environmental connections that humans seem bent on severing. Ecologist Gary Kleppel comments,

> One number that always impresses me is that just the trees around Atlanta are picking up every year about nineteen million pounds of pollutants out of the air. If we were to pay for that service, it would cost us forty-seven million dollars a year in year two thousand dollars. That's a big number.
>
> Robert Costanza, who is a professor of ecological economics at the University of Vermont, in a paper in *Science* in Nineteen Ninety-Seven suggested that the world's ecosystems perform thirty-three trillion dollars' worth of services for us each year at no charge. The gross domestic product of our ecosystems in North America is eighteen trillion dollars. Just in my little town of Knox (New York), I estimated that if we took the wetlands and put them together, they have the capacity to

process as much raw sewage as a four-million-gallon-per-day sewage treatment plant. That's just in my little town of Knox.

Sometimes, connections to ecological communities, and to ecosystem services, are right under our noses—or in our front yards. Consider the efforts by Westchester County to promote leaf mulching. Many communities in the Northeast and New England spend hundreds of thousands, even millions of dollars each year on leaf pickup. Some allow residents to rake or blow the leaves to the curb, where huge vacuum trucks pick up the leaf "litter," a process reminiscent of garbage pickup. Others require residents to purchase decomposable brown paper bags and line the street with the leaf-filled sacks. The leaves and bags are hauled off to be composted, for instance by McEnroe Farm, as mentioned in chapter 3.

There was a time when leaf mulching seemed progressive, "green." Before then, leaves were treated like trash and hauled to the dump or perhaps burned. But in some communities today municipal composting is as out of date as landfilling leaves was twenty-five years ago. Westchester, Orange, and other counties encourage residents to leave those leaves right in place. "It's utterly insane to be driving tractor-trailers ninety miles away," a *New York Times* article quoted a local landscaper as saying. "My feeling is that if I'm taking away your leaves, I'm stealing your property."[4] That purloined property is packed with nutrients. An inexpensive special mulching blade attached to a lawn mower—the "mulch" setting found on many mowers doesn't do the trick without the blade—shears leaves into "confetti" that quickly decomposes.

The result for lawns is lots of nutrients that don't have to be replaced by fertilizers, saving homeowners money, time, and effort: multiple ecosystem services in one. And by keeping leaves in place, we service ecosystems. When it rains, the nutrients running off from curbside leaf piles flow into ponds and streams that already are choking on nitrogen and phosphorous; mulching retains those nutrients in front yards. Emissions from two-stroke leaf blowers, vacuums, and leaf-hauling vehicles are eliminated as well. Do no harm is one thing. Doing good is something else. Homeowners who use mulching blades insist their grass looks great, and they water less in dry periods. What comes from the land stays on the land, saving homeowners money, an example of ecosystems services waiting right outside your door.

∿

In the pages that follow, we first consider some parameters of sustainable community design. Then we meet activists who are leading the fight for environmental justice in the Hudson region, in the process bringing the "equity" portion of sustainability's triple bottom line to the fore. We also explore the community-based work of an innovative sustainability education center that aims to address problems as Maser and Kirk suggest: literally at their roots. Finally, we examine the challenge of developing "complete," inclusive communities.

Sustainable Community Design

Gary Kleppel says he is reminded of a lifeboat when he thinks about community. "That is really what a lifeboat is," he muses. "It is a community of people who are working together to save themselves because you cannot save yourself without a community." Community, Kleppel insists, is essential to individual and collective survival. Unless we find ways to unite our disparate communities, and the large number of us who are disaffected and adrift from any community, hope for creating new Landscapes will be lost.

"I think sustainable community design involves thinking about the community in ways that we already know—in fact, in ways that we have known for thousands of years," Kleppel says. "We know the scale of communities." By "scale," Kleppel is not only referring to community size—in fact, simple geographic size may not be terribly important. No, scale has much more to do with the connections individuals create with one another. So many communities today are limited—we refer to them as "bedroom communities" for a reason, after all. Thanks to suburbanization, the automobile and all that is entailed in "auto-centered" culture,[5] and political and economic systems that reward unsustainable practices such as lengthy commutes, the deep ties that bind complex communities where diverse, meaningful, face-to-face interactions can take place have been severed.

Kleppel's concept of scale, then, serves as a metric for community—not a uniform standard, but one that situates human groups and their behaviors within an ecological framework—and when listening to him speak it becomes clear that on multiple dimensions we have exceeded community's rightful scale.

"Why should that guy who's making milk in New Scotland, New York, have to send it to Vermont to be made into cheese?" asks Kleppel.

"Why don't we have a cheese factory right here and let him sell his wonderful product to us in our town? Suddenly we have an economy, and there are tools, such as the transfer of development rights, that allow the person who lives on that landscape to be assured of the value of their land, at least as assured as the market allows for any other homeowner or property owner. . . . That's what I mean by sustainable community."

Rather than extensive communities of the sort that so many of us take for granted, where great distances divide nearly everything that we do, Kleppel and others embrace intensive ones characterized by localization. The cheesemaker not only buys and sells locally, they employ their neighbors. Economic and social loops become closed, and life becomes more fulfilling.

In places, Hudson region residents are ahead of the game. Artist Leslie Reed lives in the tiny Greene County community of Athens, her home just steps from the Hudson River. She told me that "there is so much more emphasis on local here than anywhere else I've lived that it's great to feel like you're living in a community that understands what's important to you. . . . We're lucky to live in an area where it's easy for us to eat local." Reed's community is defined, in part, by that easy availability of locally produced food. She tells a story of her mother endlessly searching for items that Reed can find a short distance from home.

And community is about even more than food and buying what we eat and drink locally, important and meaningful as being a "locavore" is. Things like recreation matter, too—witness New York City's Central Park and Newburgh, New York's, Downing Park, places in the heart of their respective cities that draw people to run, skate, sled, paddle, relax, attend plays and concerts . . . the list goes on and on.

René VanSchaack describes a park planned for the Green County town of Coxsackie. It anchors a walking/biking trail system to enable locals to commute without ever starting their cars. "You'll be able to bike out of the village," VanSchaack says, "connect to the YMCA, the first business park, the technology part of the first business park, the second business park, the third business park—so all of these will eventually be connected by this trail system."

Such a trail, located not at the edge of town but in the heart of it, holds the potential for reinvigorating community as it combines non-motorized recreation with commuting and a host of other activities. The community concept is grounded in other things, too, all of which are, ideally, nearby: places of worship, civic spaces where everything from casual conversation to protest takes place, schools, and workplaces.

In these observations—making milk locally, buying food from one's neighbors, getting to work and school using trails that wind through parks, relaxing and recreating in those parks—is the promise of a Landscape that connects us to one another through multiple networks: agriculture, economy, work, play, education, faith, family, friends. In such aptly scaled places meaning easily threads through all that we do. There is the potential to affirm a shared people-place reality wherever we go; such communities are lively, invigorating, spatially and temporally scaled at a level that works for people and place.

In contrast to that promise, in the unsustainable communities of which nearly all of us are a part, the Landscape is, first, fragmented and, second, incoherent. The fragmentation occurs when we enact each piece of our lives in a separate space disconnected from the others. Often the only commonalty in that fragmentation is our auto-centric culture: we drive to the grocery store, drive to the gym, drive to the play or concert. Kleppel, Reed, and VanSchaack's implied vision is of the gym workout being replaced by the walk, run, or bike ride to the farmers market, where perhaps musicians or a theater group perform and where we meet and interact with friends and get to know acquaintances better. Their antidote to fragmentation is integration—Landscapes where the distinct networks of our lives meld into one.

Unsustainable communities are incoherent in the sense that everything is from somewhere else, and those other places often are not known to us. Where does your cheese, milk, broccoli, or whiskey (see chapter 7) come from? Who makes them? Who are the actors on your stage or the musicians at your local concert? The incoherency emerges because so many things, from food provenance to the players at the theater, are far removed from our communities.

A tremendous amount of energy goes into providing us with our incoherent lives. Nearly everyone in the world participates in a far-flung economic empire dependent on inexpensive, ecologically destructive oil, natural gas, nuclear, and hydroelectric energy to provide nearly everything we eat, wear, and use. In the process of pursuing our incoherent lives, we exacerbate global climate change, ecological destruction, and environmental injustices. As integration is the counter to fragmentation, so localization is the response to incoherency.

In the next section, we will see that to get to the point where integration and localization can take place, some communities have had to fight their own city governments. Yet those grassroots struggles have galvanized citizens, in the process politicizing them, empowering them to be their own scientists, policymakers, and sustainability advocates, and emboldening them to demand that even the poorest communities receive environmentally just, equitable treatment.

Struggling for Environmental Justice

If the "equity" portion of sustainability's triple bottom line is to be accomplished, communities will be where we will notice it most clearly. How racially diverse will our neighborhoods, schools, and workplaces be? What sorts of jobs and incomes will those living on our streets have? What will be the ethnic background of the representatives we elect? How willing will we be to ensure that immense gaps in income, education, and opportunity are a thing of the past?

Columbia University economist Elliott Sclar, a lifelong New York City resident, says, "The notion is that the value of a city comes about because of all the people who come together in it, which means they have to have access, which means you have to have ways of getting them together that's affordable to all of them.

"There's this notion that runs around in economics that equity and efficiency are tradeoffs, that the market may be efficient even if it is not equitable. But I've come to the conclusion that equity is long-run efficiency: if we do the equitable thing, we in fact do the most efficient thing." He adds, "Equity makes for a more robust and healthy society. . . . We really ought to see it as the essence of what a good society is for everybody."

It's not only economists who insist equity will somehow harm someone; our political leaders often claim that the small things government does to promote equity—providing food and medical care for the needy and elderly, unemployment insurance for those who can't find work in a depressed economy, or establishing a living wage for working people— are somehow misguided, yet the evidence shows public benefits and fair wages *spur* local economies as recipients and blue collar workers spend what they earn and use their benefits. If we understand "efficiency" as both avoiding negatives such as crime and civil strife and promoting healthier, happier individuals and communities, then the positive correlation that Sclar draws between equity and efficiency makes good sense.

The U.S. Constitution ensures equality of opportunity, but sustainability's understanding of social *equity* is a more expansive and complete notion. Nowhere is that push for community equity, and toward eliminating the "inefficiencies" that permeate too many people's lives, clearer than in the environmental justice movement. It got its start more than a quarter-century ago, when sociologist Robert Bullard's wife, Linda McKeever Bullard, asked for his help. Browning Ferris Industries had located a garbage dump in a predominantly black, middle-class neighborhood in Houston, where Bob taught and Linda practiced law. Residents of the neighborhood approached Linda about filing a lawsuit opposing the dump, which was within sight—and smell—of the local high school.

Houston has no zoning; almost any land use can take place anywhere. Bob and his students investigated landfill sites in the city, revealing that *all* of its landfills, and six of eight garbage incinerators then operating, were located in predominantly black neighborhoods; going back to the 1920s, nearly every waste disposal facility had been similarly situated.[6] Convinced that something more than coincidence was at work, Bob set out to examine what he soon realized was a phenomenon reaching far beyond Houston, one that had long existed but never before been labeled: environmental racism.

Over time, other studies indicated that, under some circumstances, social class was a more important factor than race in the siting of LULUs[7]—locally unwanted land uses—and other environment-related discriminatory behaviors, so "environmental justice" became the commonly used phrase for the observation that "[t]he costs of environmental degradation are inequitably distributed in this country across the lines of both class and race," Valerie Gunter and Steve Kroll-Smith note. "Poor and working-class communities in general, as well as poor, working-class, and middle-class communities of people of color, are more likely to host polluting and/or hazardous facilities than are white middle-class communities or any community higher on the socioeconomic scale."[8] Depending on factors such as public policy and the type of facility, researchers have found that race, class, or the combination of the two nearly always play key explanatory roles in where LULUs and the like occur.

Chris Maser writes, "The concept of environmental justice . . . asserts that we owe something to every other person sharing the planet with us, both those present and those yet unborn."[9] Such a morally grounded, environmentally secure future is hardly in hand. It is a measure of the pervasiveness of environmental injustices that not only does their investigation support a small army of scholars, but the U.S. Environmental Protection Agency and, in the Hudson region, the Connecticut Department of Energy and Environmental Protection, New Jersey Department of Environmental Protection, New York Department of Environmental Conservation, and the Massachusetts Executive Office of Energy and

Environmental Affairs—representing all of the Hudson region states save Vermont—all have a substantial environmental justice presence.

Remaking Harlem's Landscape

Environmental justice is both a scholarly endeavor and a social movement, and one of the nation's first environmental justice activists was Harlem's Peggy Shepard. Shepard grew up in Washington, D.C., and Trenton, New Jersey, the daughter of an MD and a homemaker. She attended a prestigious boarding school and dreamed of attending either Russell Sage or Lake Forest for college. Neither would allow black students in the dorms, however, so she enrolled in her parents' alma mater, Howard University.

After graduating she married and moved to Indianapolis, where she wrote for the *Indianapolis News* in the "women's section," the English major landing the job based only on some poems she'd written. Shepard recalls reporting on stories such as the women's versus men's lunch lines at a local cafeteria, where "the men got in an expedited line because they were businessmen, but even though they were working women, you had to stand in line with the shoppers." It was the start of a life of challenging taken-for-granteds and inequalities.

A move to New York and exposure to the city's political world whetted her appetite for social change, and in short order she found herself working for Jesse Jackson's 1984 presidential campaign. There, Shepard says she began to get a sense of "the difference of neighborhood resources and capacity" in the city, observations that would inform her later activism. Some areas of New York were privileged, others dumping grounds.

The first community struggle she got involved with was over the North River Wastewater Treatment Plant, a massive sewage treatment facility that handles 125 million gallons of waste a day from the entirety of the west (Hudson) side of Manhattan north of Greenwich Village. When the plant was proposed, "people thought the idea was jobs, and they came to me and said, 'Can you help organize to get this community jobs at this plant?'" says Shepard, who had been elected Democratic District Leader in West Harlem, an unpaid but powerful position advocating for the interests of the predominantly black community there.

Soon after the plant opened in 1986—a landmark moment, since it was the first time in New York City's history that raw sewage was not being dumped into the Hudson River—Shepard and everyone else living in or passing through West Harlem understood that the real issues had little to do with who got jobs. "The emissions started making people sick," Shepard recalls. "The whole place smelled." North River was indeed a LULU.

Gunter and Kroll-Smith write that "environments and communities are often unwitting actors in what are contemporary social dramas: vivid, emotional, and conflicting portrayals of villains, victims, sacrifices, and, sometimes, redemptions."[10] In the end, the North River plant struggle followed that trajectory. But no one could have anticipated what occurred along the way.

In the early months after the plant opened, community leaders, Shepard included, took to the radio and other public venues to voice their anger and disgust at the olfactory and health assaults the West Harlem community was enduring. When city officials did not respond to their pleas, "we developed a civil disobedience strategy," Shepard recalls with a wry smile. "In 1988, on Martin Luther King Day, we organized people to hold up traffic on the West Side Highway at seven in the morning on a workday, and on Riverside Drive. . . . Seven of us got arrested." Shepard and the others became known as the "Sewage Seven," and for the first time the local press paid attention to the fight against North River.

That same year Shepard cofounded West Harlem Environmental Action—WE ACT—and in 1992 WE ACT won its lawsuit against the city over the sewage plant, including securing a $1.1 million fund to benefit West Harlem. WE ACT knew it wasn't going to shut down the plant, Shepard says, but residents were convinced they didn't have to live with the oppressive stench, a constant reminder that they were being dumped on by their own city.

Over time, the city retrofitted the plant with a $106 million odor control system, including monitoring sites in West Harlem. New York State followed through with plans to construct a twenty-eight-acre park atop the plant, complete with a swimming pool and football field. (In his generally insightful book *Green Metropolis*, David Owen praises the park, handily overlooking the incongruity of its location; more disappointing, he does not mention the injustices that accompanied North River's siting, creation, or implementation. For that matter, in his sweeping examination of sustainable cities he never mentions environmental justice at all.)[11]

Out of necessity, WE ACT's eight years of protests against North River were a grassroots effort. "Having no scientific data on the relationship between community health and the plant," writes Kelly Moore, residents "relied on their own local, often personal knowledge about the plant's effects on them and their families."[12] However, in time residents got the data. "People take things on themselves" when they are part of a community-based movement, Shepard says.

> Some people had a little technical expertise, so they agreed to do the research on the engineering, and somebody else was doing research on how the plant got here. By the time you're in two years, you've got fifty or sixty people who know as much about that plant and about the city planning commission and the whole process of getting it here as someone who worked for the city. That level of accountability that residents can get from government is so important, and it's energizing and it's empowering.

People researched the plant on their own and bombarded officials with countless questions. Just asking questions changed them. Using the answers, they changed Harlem.

Reflecting on the journey that their struggle took them on, Shepard says, "Once you've been through that kind of process—and all of this is happening with the community," not simply the handiwork of a bunch of hired experts, "you've really got an educated, empowered segment. And once you're able to ask the government questions like that, you're able to ask them questions on a number of other issues."

Shut out of politics for decades, even centuries, Harlem—historically, the home of most of Manhattan's persons of color and infamously poor and poorly educated—became a savvy, dynamic political entity through the North River struggle. For the first time residents took charge of their Landscape.

Gunter and Kroll-Smith have observed that communities are where grassroots political change is found. In neighborhoods one finds "the awakening of a political consciousness as people encounter the duplicity of corporations and government agencies. Citizens become moral entrepreneurs, posing questions about the distribution of justice and fairness to the ecological and political conundrums of environmental controversies."[13]

Such was certainly the case in West Harlem. "What the North River plant issue allowed us to see," Shepard says, "was that the whole community was being used as a dumping ground. You know, when you really become alert to one or two key environmental issues, obviously just the research on that leads you to have a broader understanding of sustainability and the kinds of impacts that happen in an urban community. You begin to see things for what they are."

West Harlem residents rejected the dominant Landscape imposed on them and their community by city, state, and federal officials. Its meaning became one of oppression. It smacked of the old days when persons of color were essentially powerless, even in the eyes of city leaders. North River was the catalyst in West Harlem residents reclaiming their right to create a Landscape of their own.

Once that fight was over, however, WE ACT's work was hardly done. Indeed, even as the struggle against North River continued, word came that the Metropolitan Transit Authority, which operates the city's bus and rail systems, planned to construct a second West Harlem bus depot. It would be the larger Harlem community's sixth depot—six of the eight then in existence on the island of Manhattan. All those buses idling, leaving, and returning through the day means such depots localize intense ground-level air pollution associated with childhood asthma, but the issue was not one that interested the big environmental interest groups. Shepard says with a weary smile, "The mainstream enviros don't deal with hot spots. They deal with federal clean air regulations that should make things better for everyone, right? But, then, there is a neighborhood community level that the large enviros don't deal with. If things aren't working there, then perhaps overall regulations aren't working the way they need to."

For eighteen years WE ACT kept the pressure on the MTA, which insisted the depots were located uptown because that's where the riders were—a notion so preposterous that Shepard laughs as she says the words. Through a lawsuit, public hearings, press conferences, public health studies—even bus shelter advertisements—WE ACT campaigned for, and eventually won, cleaner running buses for New York's 5,600 vehicle fleet.

Afterward, Shepard, who sat on Mayor Michael Bloomberg's Sustainability Advisory Board, took the fight for clean air and lower asthma rates downtown, to fashionable Park Avenue, where many of the city's dirtiest oil-fired boilers (used to provide heat and hot water in high rises), are still found.[14] WE ACT also has successfully advocated for community-directed planning that resulted in a new park along the Hudson where once there was a parking lot, and it is a voice for locally grown food in schools, fresh food availability in corner bodegas, transit equity, and more. Out of sewage has grown a great force for just Landscapes.

Sustainable South Bronx: Filling a Void

Miquela Craytor insists that what the South Bronx needs is "a new paradigm for an area that believes it deserves a better one. I've had conversations with folks here, and there's fear about the positive change. There's

Remaking Communities / 121

fear—I've heard this time and time again: 'These things are not meant for us.' There's fear of the positive. 'It's obviously meant for someone else.'" And then the kicker: " 'It's obviously meant to gentrify and push us out.'"

The notion that this neighborhood, which straddles the Hudson and East River watersheds and is home to the poorest congressional district in the United States, is next on the list of New York neighborhoods to be "discovered" by the wealthy, resulting in soaring home prices and the gradual squeezing out of its current residents, is one of the key hurdles that Sustainable South Bronx has to overcome as it seeks to improve the lives of the predominantly Hispanic and black residents who call the area home.

Craytor, now the former executive director of Sustainable South Bronx, relates another comment, this one even more poignant: " 'I'd rather not breathe than not be able to afford to live in my neighborhood.' I believe everyone can breathe *and* afford their neighborhood," she says, "no matter what their reality is. I look forward to the day when people are not afraid to have the quality of life they deserve."

There is something perverse about a community fearing the arrival of the sorts of things Sustainable South Bronx hopes to bring—clean air, safe and beautiful parks, good paying local jobs—yet that is the anxiety many there live with. "I often go back to the psychology of an area like the South Bronx," Craytor says, "where in many ways it was a war zone. The drugs. The burning of buildings. The City of New York tearing down huge blocks of land for urban renewal. When you have all these outside influences dismantling what you thought you could trust, why should you put the energy or effort into planning something?"

Add to those blows repeated broken promises by elected officials and an anomic void develops. Why cling to hope, much less envision a better day, when for decades a whole community has been treated as expendable to the point that it has given up on itself? South Bronx residents can be forgiven for asking, "Where is there a place for us in this Landscape?"

Combatting such pessimism and cynicism has proven to be a lesson in patience for Sustainable South Bronx, which was founded by charismatic native daughter Majora Carter in 2001 and is perhaps the nation's best-known environmental justice organization. Craytor insists that "you need to build trust, and these projects take a long time. We've been working on our Greenway project for over ten years, and we only started construction [in 2010]. When it started to happen, I think a lot of people were shocked. They thought it was just another promise that was empty."

When completed, the South Bronx Greenway project will include 1.5 miles of riverside walks and 8.5 miles of "green streets" to link areas well away from the river to numerous new and existing parks, including twelve acres of rehabilitated waterfront along the Bronx River. The *New York Times* praised the early steps of the multiphase project, writing, "For years one of the most blighted, abused waterways in the country, the southern end of the Bronx River has been slowly coming back and with it the shoreline that meanders through the South Bronx. . . .

"[C]ompared with the headline-making projects in Manhattan and Brooklyn, the unexpected renaissance under way along the south end of the Bronx River flies largely below the radar. Park by park a patchwork of green spaces has been taking shape, the consequence of decades of grinding, grass-roots, community-driven efforts."[15]

Like WE ACT, Sustainable South Bronx is making a difference from the ground up, as Maser and Kirk urged us to do, remaking and re-meaning its community through citizen involvement. In the process it is filling the emptiness of vacant lots and broken promises not only with parks but with jobs, thanks to BEST, its Bronx Environmental Stewardship Academy, which trains residents for green jobs. Academy graduates participate in other Sustainable South Bronx initiatives, such as its energy efficiency and SmartRoofs programs, designed to save neighborhood businesses and residents money and to cool the city—an ideal version of sustainability's triple bottom line.

Putting a Number on Environmental Injustice

"You begin to see things for what they are," Peggy Shepard said of the illuminating investigation of environmental injustices that West Harlem residents undertook. Based on my research, "what they are" is chilling.

In response to a request by the Hudson Sloop Clearwater environmental group (but operating independently of them), students Jessica Aleman, Mary Rynasko, and Katarra Peterson joined me in statistically examining environmental injustices in the fifteen New York counties with substantial areas within the Hudson River's watershed (these counties lie north of New York City on the east side of the Hudson and north of the New Jersey state line on the west side).[16] Our results make clear that even hundreds of miles from West Harlem, facilities very different from the North River plant are dumping on persons of color and the poor.

The New York Department of Environmental Conservation (DEC) provided us with the locations for fourteen types of permitted pollution facilities—two thousand in all. Those facility types fall under four broad headings—air polluters, water polluters, solid waste facilities, and hazardous waste facilities—as well as Superfund sites (typically abandoned manufacturing facilities, Superfund sites are the nation's most poisoned places).

Using geographic information system (GIS) software, my students combined the DEC-supplied facility location information with data on twelve demographic characteristics from the 2000 U.S. Census. The GIS software allowed Jessica, Mary, and Katarra to compare the "neighborhoods" within one mile of each facility with the rest of the region to see what, if any, differences there were.[17]

Our findings were disappointingly in line with West Harlem's experience and the expectations of environmental justice scholars. They include:

- The neighborhoods around major air pollution facilities, such as coal-fired power plants, were home to a far higher proportion of persons of color than the rest of the region; they were economically less well off; residents were less well educated; they held fewer white-collar and more blue-collar jobs; and housing values were lower. Indeed, for most of the demographic variables, our results resonate with environmental justice scholars' expectations that facility neighborhoods will disproportionately be home to persons of color and the poor.

  For instance, in the neighborhoods near those major air polluters, the population was 21.7 percent black; outside those neighborhoods in the fifteen-county region, blacks comprised 6.7 percent of the population. All told, nearly 37 percent of the facility neighborhood population was non-white, whereas nonwhites made up less than 14 percent of the remainder of the region's population. Hispanics were 8.7 percent of the neighborhood population, compared to 9 percent elsewhere in the region. Almost a quarter of the neighborhood population had no high school degree, and less than a quarter had completed college—figures respectively ten percentage points higher and ten points lower than the rest of the region. Finally, mean housing values for areas of the region a mile or more away from a major air pollution facility were 20 percent higher than in facility neighborhoods.

- Around large, but not "major," air pollution facilities (such as many industrial sites), the story was similar: blacks comprised three times more of the population, the proportion of families receiving public assistance was three times greater, and mean household income was $14,875 less than in the rest of the region. The only variable to diverge from the environmental justice hypothesis was the percentage of blue-collar workers living near these facilities: it was 17.9 compared to 18.1 elsewhere.

- We found comparable results around industrial surface water polluters, such as pulp and paper-making plants that dump wastes into rivers and streams. On a percentage basis, neighborhoods near those facilities were home to two and one-half times more persons of color than the rest of the region, the poverty rate was 11 percent versus 6.3 percent, the unemployment rate was nearly 50 percent higher, and neighborhood residents were comparatively less well educated. However, mean housing values were more than 10 percent higher, and fewer blue-collar workers lived near the facilities.

- The areas near sewage treatment plants exhibited similar characteristics. It was almost 50 percent more likely that a person of color lived near those facilities than elsewhere in the region; household income in the plants' neighborhoods was more than $19,000 less; the poverty, unemployment, and public assistance rates were all higher; neighbors tended to hold less prestigious jobs; and their homes were valued almost $52,000 less than those living well away from wastewater treatment locations.

We found similar results near garbage dumps, facilities on the U.S. Environmental Protection Agency's Toxic Release Inventory of toxic air polluters, and facilities where hazardous waste was created, handled, stored, or disposed of. Neighborhoods surrounding these locations tended to be home to nonwhites and the poor, with disproportionately high numbers of residents living in poverty and, unsurprisingly, fewer who had earned high school or college diplomas. They earned less and their homes were valued lower. The only exceptions were municipal facilities that discharge waste into groundwater and Superfund sites, many of which (such as the one in Saratoga Springs that I mention in chapter 1) are older and around which middle-class, largely white neighborhoods grew before the sites' contamination was known.

The consistency of our findings surprised and disappointed all of us who worked on this project. Overwhelmingly, the demographic characteristics of those living in the region away from one of these facility types were substantially different from those of the neighborhoods near these facilities.

Environmental justice scholars struggle over whether race or class is more strongly associated with environmental injustices; our findings do little to resolve that debate, since both persons of color and the poor of all races live near noxious facilities in the region. What our results make plain is that the Hudson region's Landscape is an unfair one. Not everyone is equally likely to be exposed to the sights, smells, or unseen dangers emanating from plants, factories, dumps, landfills, and other LULUs.

A variety of sustainability-related concerns emerged from our study. For instance, Robin Saha and Paul Mohai, the scholars who outlined the methodology we used, have noted that the location of objectionable facilities often follows a "path of least resistance"—Robert Bullard's term for when "new facilities [are] deflected or directed to minority and low-income neighborhoods and communities, which [are] seen as the paths of least resistance due to their need for jobs and their political vulnerability associated with limited access to resources and allies in government."[18]

The South Bronx experienced such treatment when major expressways were constructed through the heart of the community decades ago, and, of course, one can imagine that the North River plant and all those bus depots were destined for Harlem based on the assumption that resistance to them would be minimal.

The environmental justice movement, however, is forcing a change in that calculus. Its concept of Landscape places a premium on an equitable environment: thriving, livable communities where no one bears the burdens of ecologically harmful practices more than others—and where we eliminate those practices to begin with in favor of those that are responsive to local economic need and environmental health.

Regenerating Community

If one were to look for how a community can best be separated from what sustains and even justifies it, Scott Kellogg says we need venture no farther than New York's capital city. "Albany's a great example of what *not* to do," says Kellogg. "We had a bunch of really short-sighted megaprojects in the nineteen sixties and seventies that devastated the landscape of the city of Albany. The Empire Plaza is a perfect example and [Interstate] 787: we built an interstate *parallel* to the Hudson River, physically severing our access to this water body, which is the only reason ecologically or economically that this city even exists in the first place.

"When you cut off your ties and your history like that, it's like pinching the city's artery, and it starts to die a slow death." In contrast, Kellogg's work with the Radix Ecological Sustainability Center is all about rebirth: bringing new life to urban communities in particular.

Every bit the sustainability entrepreneur, Kellogg's first major foray into community sustainability was in Austin, Texas, where he and his wife, Stacy Pettigrew, founded the Rhizome Collective. In 2009, they shifted their attention back to New York's Capital Region, near Stacy's hometown of Saratoga Springs, and began what proved to be the laborious work of establishing Radix. The city's bureaucracy proved infuriating at times, but eventually they received the green light to locate the nonprofit at the site of a former gas station. They completed a two-story, twenty-by-sixty-foot greenhouse on the site in 2011, added large chicken coops and rabbit hutches, and began reaching out to the locals to educate them about creating sustainable communities in an urban context.

Kellogg says that when he asks people to identify an ecosystem,

> most people describe a rainforest or desert or coral reef—
> something, typically, where humans are absent. It's interesting
> that we don't see ourselves as components of ecosystems or
> anthropogenically dominated environments as being parts of
> ecosystems. But cities, of course, are ecosystems: a community
> of organisms interacting with the living and nonliving aspects
> of their environment. . . . It doesn't mean that they are neces-
> sarily healthy or high-functioning ecosystems, but once we've
> identified them as such, we can ask the question, How can
> they be transformed? How can we meet human needs while
> simultaneously regenerating damaged ecosystems?

Sustainability is Radix's reason for being—Kellogg points out that *radix* is Latin for "root," and returning to what grounds communities is at the heart of the center's goals.

Kellogg wants to help his neighbors learn how to "close the loop" in city ecosystems so that they are "producing more of our food, water, and energy within city limits, and processing our waste internally as well. I'm not necessarily of the belief that we need to be growing one hundred percent of our food inside the city, but twenty percent? That's very doable." Kellogg adds, "I think it's really important, if we're going to be having conversations about transitioning into sustainability as a society and a culture, that we look at these environments and see how they can be redesigned, how they can be made capable of providing their residents with more of their needs, whether it be food, water, waste management, energy production."

The aim, Kellogg admits, is as ambitious as anything one can imagine. "My loftiest of goals would be to transform the global culture, global society, and try to steer us in a different direction completely," he says, explicitly envisioning a regional—even global—Landscape rooted in triple bottom line sustainability. "I don't expect, realistically, to do that in my lifetime, but I'll do what I can as long as I'm around."

So how does Radix pursue those dreams? The center practices education through demonstration. On its half-acre lot stands the greenhouse—warm and humid on the clear, bitterly cold February day when I visited—and chicken coops; raised beds for gardening line one side of the property, and more will be constructed as soon as the old asphalt can be dug up.

Inside, under the huge sloping polycarbonate roof, nasturtiums—a California flower whose mustardy petals are delicious—grow in trays, as do pea sprouts, lettuce, and more. Water cycles through a bed of watercress that Kellogg invites visitors to sample, then into a large tank housing carp, thence into one with water-cleansing snails, and then back around. A black plastic tank holding 1,500 gallons of rainwater collected on site stands out of the way against the back wall, which is also lined with trays of oyster mushrooms growing in coffee grounds. More mushrooms, shiitakes, hang on thick tree branches that had been inoculated with the spawn.

Kellogg insists that the point is not that everyone should construct a massive greenhouse and start raising their own chickens for the eggs and protein. Quite the opposite, the goal of Radix is to serve as a community resource to show the "scalability of everything we have here," he says. "It can be scaled down, or even up, according to the space they have access to. That may just be a south-facing window. When you have that, there's a whole lot you can do. Growing microgreens. You can grow sprouts in your kitchen and you don't need any light. You can grow mushrooms in all sorts of marginal spaces because, unlike plants, they don't require sunlight for photosynthesis." A ten-gallon aquarium is enough room to raise your own fish, and a worm bin for composting can sit atop a refrigerator (the finished compost then can be used to grow those microgreens). "If somebody has a back yard, that opens a whole other world of possibility," Kellogg adds.

Sales of the mushrooms, watercress, and microgreens through a membership-driven "community-supported education" venture (akin to farmers' CSAs) provide revenue, with more coming from a compostable food waste pickup service. Together, they are examples of what Kellogg calls "ecologically regenerative microindustries, where we can take sustainable practices and couple them with an economic engine, then use the byproducts of those industries to promote the regeneration of damaged urban ecosystems." After, for example, mushrooms are harvested, the substrate on which they grew can be spread over lots contaminated by spilled petroleum products. The enzymes left by the mushrooms will break down the hydrocarbons, helping restore the soil.

Paid tours of the facility for schools and colleges with the funds to contribute also help Radix pay the bills (free tours are offered to poorer schools and monthly to the public), as do Regenerative Urban Sustainability Training (RUST) workshops held several times a year. The tours for school children—Kellogg calls them "chicken education"—are particularly important. Touching on the sort of food ignorance that Ray McEnroe and Julie Walsh mentioned in chapter 3, Kellogg says that many children have "never seen or interacted with a chicken in their life. They understand that 'chicken' is a food and 'chicken' is an animal, but there's not necessarily a connection between the two of them. Just teaching that kind of ecological literacy, having a connection with your food and where it's coming from," is missing in most children's lives but can be a vital first step in grasping sustainability.

Compost from Radix's for-fee residential and restaurant food scrap pickup program is finished at the center and used in the raised beds, something Kellogg says helps the planet and community alike. "By diverting it from the landfill, intercepting this organic matter and composting it aerobically on the surface of the planet, we can be building deep, rich, fertile garden beds to grow nutrient-dense food for our urban populations and at the same time be building a new biological skin on the surface of the city," says Kellogg. "One of the biggest limiting factors to growing food in the cities is the fact that soils are damaged or nonexistent or contaminated. The remedy in any of those situations is to apply as much compost as you possibly can."

Compared to sending food waste to landfills, composting it cuts methane emissions, a greenhouse gas twenty times more potent than carbon dioxide, and has the potential to heal, feed, and—thanks to the jobs composting operations create—employ those living in blighted communities.

Kellogg shares those sorts of lessons with attendees at the RUST workshops. Packed into a weekend is an immense amount of information. Conversations begin at the nearby Albany Free School, then the scene shifts to the center. There, attendees receive education about, and hands-on experience in, aquaponics, microlivestock (raising chickens, ducks, rabbits), raised-bed gardening, vertical food production, mushroom growing, composting, rainwater collection, soil toxicity/bioremediation, and more.

Along the way, ties are made to oceanic fisheries, the Hudson River, estuaries, creating closer communities, climate change, alternative vehicle and cooking fuels, and public policy. More than seven hundred people attended the workshops, which are capped at fifty participants, in the first seven years they were offered. Tuition is on a sliding scale, allowing scholarships to be offered to promote race and class diversity, and a "worktrade" option lowers the cost in exchange for six hours of work at Radix before the class begins.

The Radix Center's Landscape envisions an intimate tie between communities and place, notwithstanding that place is in an urban setting. Scott Kellogg insists that, through creative use of biology and simple technologies, city dwellers can nurture their immediate environments, play important roles in curbing global climate change, live healthier and more meaningful lives, and promote local economies. What's particularly exciting is that he treats Radix as a laboratory. The center explores new ways of linking communities and ecologies, allowing the RUST workshops to offer guidance that is tried and true.

Constructing Complete Communities

Environmental justice challenges us to make our notion of community more inclusive, prompting us to take seriously the equity expectations in sustainability's triple bottom line. Consumed by race, class, and other forms of status—or trapped by those same phenomena—we effectively wall ourselves off or find others keeping us out. Social tragedies are made of such in- and out-group behavior.[19] Environmental justice advocates compel us to think seriously about those "natural" differences that we know aren't natural at all. They ask, How do we unite communities?

To be clear, communities are divided along many lines, not only those of race or class. For example, Columbia Land Conservancy Executive Director Peter Paden notes that in Columbia County communities split themselves up in numerous ways. "In Pine Plains they read the newspaper from Dutchess County," Paden says. "That's their point of reference. It makes it a little fragmented. It makes it hard to work on the county as a community. The people along the river, they think of themselves as on the Hudson River. Whatever happens a little inland seems *over there*. . . . There's never been anything to really bring it together." In places, jurisdictional boundaries are viewed as arbitrary, even meaningless, because people find identity and a sense of belonging elsewhere. However frustrating to some, Landscape, a place where a group's meaning and identity is grounded, does not necessarily correspond to lines on a map.

For Jeff Golden, the key to community-based Landscape is bringing people together. Golden is co-founder of Common Fire, a pair of intentional communities—communes in the region devoted to sustainability and social change. He says, "We look at communities—the places where people are actually living and working intentionally, from the ground up, building something different—because we've seen that people working in isolation can have a brilliant sense of what's happening in the world (but what individuals need is) an environment that allows them to actually manifest change."

In my conversation with Golden I found insights for how we might bridge the gulfs that divide the vast majority of Hudson region residents who will never be part of a commune. Describing the importance of intentional communities, Golden said, "When we come together with other people in an environment that we intentionally create to be sustainable and thoughtful and to have the conversations, that is when we've actually got a solid place that we can stand on and start to make the broader changes in our larger communities." As I've mentioned, remaking and re-meaning Landscape involves precisely such conscious choices about the sort of relationship a community has with its environment and community members with one another.

At the regional scale, the sort of unanimous mutual understanding of ideology, purpose, and goals that is essential for small-scale communal living is impossible, of course. However, large numbers of us manage to agree on a great many things, and thanks to our democracy (including the uber-democratic town meeting system found in three of the five states in the Hudson region) we have the opportunity to unite behind sustainability-oriented policies and policymakers. "Long-term social/environmental sustainability is a consciously directed process within the democratic system," argue Chris Maser and Christine Kirk. "It is the development phase of a sustainable community."[20]

How might we pursue those policies and identify those policymaker-candidates? For Golden, communication among community members is key. Why can't the conversations that Common Fire envisions take place in our neighborhoods, develop into dialogs among communities along the lines of those promoted by the environmental organization Clearwater (see chapter 8), and spread throughout the Hudson (or any other) region? Such a grassroots approach was how WE ACT and Sustainable South Bronx accomplished much that they have. By spreading the word locally and coming together to act in common, meaningful, lasting change can occur.

An understandable response to such simple, seemingly simplistic solutions for long-running social problems such as environmental inequalities is that many people just don't care enough to bother participating in conversations about their communal future. Jeff Golden's riposte comes from experience, and it amounts to, Hey, people will surprise you. Common Fire "has lots of people who have a job as a sales person or running some kind of business that doesn't exactly jibe with most people's sense of environmental sustainability or justice," he says.

> And yet, when it comes down to it they've thought a lot about the world and their place in it and how they want to make a difference. We let them tell their story, and then we figure out how that fits with the other stories in the community and how we can support each other.
>
> There's not a checklist: "Have you tied yourself to a tree?" "Do you have a car that runs on cow crap?" or these other things. It allows for the diversity and wholeness of each of our human experiences and where we find joy to emerge and be part of the solution.

If given the chance to meaningfully act to better their future, people will do so. Moreover, Common Fire builds diversity and difference into the fabric of the community. What if all communities did the same? What if the dialog about the future of the Hudson region's Landscape began where people are—differences and similarities alike—not where anyone imagines they ought to be, and went from there?

Such a thing is happening at Hawthorne Valley Farm. In recent years the organic operation has actively sought to make deeper connections with its rural Columbia County neighbors, with increasing success, exemplifying the integration-localization concept mentioned at the beginning of this chapter. Executive Director Martin Ping and Director of Farm Operations Steffen Schneider "have been more outgoing and willing to meet other people where they are and not come on as if 'We've got this special project and we're doing everything right' or anything like that," says Conrad Vispo. "It's always just, 'Well, this is what we're doing. We're doing some things right. We're doing some things wrong.' Because of that, there's an increasing connection between this place and the rest of the county." Through interacting with others and sharing notions of what this Landscape is and what it can be, community members can find common ground for mutual action. In that sense, Landscape becomes that which unites us.

Connection, after all, is integral to community. But a community along a three hundred-mile-long corridor such as the Hudson River region? Environmental advocate David VanLuven sees the possibility of uniting far-flung places through, of all things, global climate change:

> The things that we need to do to address climate change—both in the short term through adaptation and in the long term through emissions reduction—are the same whether you are concerned about biological diversity in the upper reaches of the estuary or you're worried about heat island effects in the urban core in Harlem.
>
> Environmental justice and biodiversity conservation and clean water conservation: those are three areas of the environmental movement where we're lumped together but we don't usually work together. But this is the kind of thing that may actually get us working together. It's the universal threat that may get a lot of folks who are working on completely unrelated things suddenly starting to think together.

Perhaps the greatest environmental challenge humanity has ever confronted can become the basis of a new solidarity. Authors Maser and Kirk observe that "a community's world view"—its meaning-filled filter for all that occurs there—"defines its collective values, which in turn determines how it treats its surrounding landscape. As the landscape is altered through wise use or through abuse, so are the community's options altered in like measure."[21] The threat we collectively face may prove to be the thread that prompts conversation and, ultimately, connection, as we seek to create the community so integral to the emergence of an integrated Landscape.

Chapter 6

How It All Adds Up

It's reasonable to argue that cities are the antithesis of sustainable places. All the evidence is there: their construction destroys ecosystems
instead of protecting them. They are huge, and almost all of them east
of, say, Kansas City, cover some of the nation's most fertile farmland with
their sprawl. Like their food, virtually everything their residents consume
comes from somewhere else, and all those folks consume a lot: from
smart phones to steel skyscraper girders to automobiles to the pavement
those vehicles drive on and the fuel that powers them, cities are where we
find the consumers and the consumed . . . and the pollution and other
wastes that result.

Moreover, those consumers consume largely cut off from one another. It's no accident that Edward Hopper chose New York City to locate
Nighthawks, his painting of a diner with its mute, lonely, and alone denizens: four people, including one couple, apparently disconnected from
one another even in the small space of a corner restaurant.[1]

Is there even an environment for cities to sustain? As Gertrude
Stein said of her hometown city, Oakland, "there is no there there."[2] Cities
destroy place and ecology. They separate not only individuals but whole
groups of people from one another. There is no there there because *there*
is a place of meaning, and cityscapes are devoid of the kind of intimate
connections between people and place—community—essential to Landscape. Oakland was nowhere for Stein; Paris, however, was another matter.
Regardless, does anyone feel an affinity for concrete, steel, and asphalt akin
to that of a sweeping mountain view or a stark desert relief?

Nighthawks is the artistic embodiment of this criticism, depicting cityscape as a place as far from Landscape as one can imagine: no trees or sky or water to be seen, no people engaged with one another in ways that represent the place's meaning, the air itself seeming to have been sucked out of the setting.

At their worst, cities are like that. Impersonal. Blighted. Unecological. Utterly artificial. Devoid of meaning in any important way, at the least devoid of any hope for too many, they may lack culture and may segregate and oppress the majority, providing distinct advantage to but a few. Abandoned by all who could get out, late-twentieth-century urban flight saw the best minds and the best jobs leave cities such as Detroit, Cleveland, and Oakland, to be replaced by destitution and, some have argued, cultures of poverty.[3]

Most cities, however, bear little resemblance to that picture, and some would insist it's a caricature. Of course, the great city standing at the southern end of the Hudson River region has never existed without problems, but New York City is also atypical in its commitment to sustainability. The lesson for other cities to draw from its experience is how it addresses the challenges it faces.

Many experts view New York as a mature mega-city, both the city and the entire metropolitan region. In its massive, multidimensional reach, it provides an example of a range of problems, opportunities, and shifting landscapes. A hundred years ago, for instance, visionaries did things like construct subway lines running miles from Manhattan's core out into farm fields. By the same token, fifty years ago city leaders built highways that bisected neighborhoods, and created a host of environmental and social injustices. Urban studies scholars recognize that New York is full of mistakes and successes. Perhaps plowing a subway line into a field wasn't smart, but creating sustainable landscapes wasn't an issue on many people's minds a century ago.

Today, however, urban sustainability is a must. Economist Elliott Sclar notes that "as of Two Thousand Seven, more than half of the world's population lived in areas classified as urban. By the middle of the century, that figure will rise to somewhere between two-thirds and three-quarters. Three out of four people will be in urban places." Sclar sees tremendous potential in that concentration of humanity. Cities are where we ought to be. He says,

> When you think about it, almost everything we do, we in fact do more efficiently in urban places because of access. The only

thing you leave out is mining, maybe. I used to leave out agriculture, but increasingly, with hydroponics and other things, urban agriculture is going to play a larger and larger role in the food supply. When you think about it, there is no global problem, including sustainability, that we're going to solve if we don't deal with it as an urban issue.

Echoing Sclar, others insist that cities need to be seen as part of the solutions to some of the great challenges confronting society. Many city dwellers are already there. Julie Walsh, assistant director of GrowNYC, says, "I'm always amazed at how New Yorkers, by dint of necessity, lead fairly low-impact lives. They live in small spaces. . . . I think on the face of it sometimes people think, 'Ugh, urban! What's it got to do with environment?' or 'Urban environment—it's a paradox.' But it's not. . . . They're really passionate. The people of this city want a clean and green and sustainable place to live and to work. We know how much people are willing to do to achieve it."

New York City residents consume less space and energy than most of us. They drive less and walk more. Those behaviors come about because of the way the city is structured. Its physical form and its economic realities promote, even compel, the low-impact living Walsh referred to. David Owen of *The New Yorker* argues the point this way: "The crucial fact about sustainability is it is not a micro phenomenon: there can be no such thing as a 'sustainable' house, office building, or household appliance. . . . Sustainability is a context, not a gadget or a technology. This is the reason that dense cities set such a critical example: they prove that it's possible to arrange human populations in ways that are inherently less wasteful and destructive."[4]

Owen overstates the argument only a bit. Absent extreme changes in our population, culture, and economy, we won't get to sustainability without better and different technologies of many sorts. But the truth is that sustainability will only be achieved with major, macrolevel developments, new economies and pointed government regulations chief among them.

Here, we explore both that context and some of those technologies, with an emphasis on New York City. In this chapter's first section we consider what it is that makes New York the vibrant, dynamic city that it is. Then we turn to arguments by historic preservationists about the need to pursue sustainability by renovating, rather than destroying old buildings. Next, we consider the role of landscape architecture in creating new, sustainable Landscapes. We examine a radical proposal to bring farming into cities, vertical agriculture, then discuss the importance of transportation alternatives to automobiles and of creating vehicle-free zones in cities.

High Density

Elliott Sclar directs Columbia University's Center for Sustainable Urban Development, and he knows New York City in the deep, complete way that only a native can. At our interview site in his Upper West Side office he quips, "I was born on One Hundred Fifty-Fifth Street—they say I haven't gotten far in life." Always "an intuitively city person," Sclar confesses, "I totally love riding subways. Sometimes it gets a little uncomfortable when it's crowded, but I love it then anyway." He adds, "I love the notion of what New York is. I love the fact that it's a city that almost reinvents itself every twenty years with a new group of people, and that's what makes it so vital."

That "notion" or "reinvention" is a far different one than former mayor Michael Bloomberg's unsustainable vision of churning through one-fifth of the city's architecture every twenty years. Sclar says the city doesn't have to have new buildings to remake itself, only new people and new ideas. Recent arrivals, many of them immigrants, "live in buildings my grandparents lived in," he says with a professor's passion for his core subject matter, "but they see completely different things. They see different opportunities differently. They use the streets differently. They design transportation systems for themselves that are different. Any city that can absorb diversity is going to do well."

Sclar's reinvention is a human one, implying that a city is, first and foremost, its people and that as those people go—culturally, temperamentally—so goes the city. It's a wonderful point, reminding us that a city's reality, reflected in its meaning, is in our hands. It is not given but is made and remade over time.

A generalist, as one might suspect from Sclar's love of subways, his particular passion within cities is transportation. Noting that transportation is responsible for 30 to 40 percent of greenhouse gas emissions, and that a substantial portion of that figure results from trips in urban areas, Sclar reminds us that automobile culture was not always thus. "In the nineteenth and early twentieth centuries, we had cities that we were building around rail and around public transportation. We—in the middle of the twentieth century—transformed our older cities, retrofitted them, to the automobile," thanks in part to "visionaries" such as Robert

Moses, whose classist and racist approaches to landscape design altered life in New York City and beyond.[5] "What we have essentially done is make mobility an end in itself," a terrible mistake that misses the point, Sclar insists. "The essence of what a great city is, the essence of urban life, is access. Mobility is a way to get access, but access is what everybody wants."

That access is to jobs, cultural opportunities, parks and recreation, schools. Disproportionately, urban locales add those features to a region's Landscape—in New York City's case, of course, it comes with some of the best of those things any place has to offer. But cities such as Albany and Poughkeepsie, and even small towns and villages like Hudson and Woodstock, contribute to the social and economic richness of the Landscape in outsized ways.

Sclar and his students study global urban sustainability, with an emphasis on "both the notion of sustainability as an environmental challenge and as a social justice challenge," he says. "Equity is an important piece of what we do." The lessons Sclar has drawn concerning the transportation-equity nexus boil down to a few simple factors: "Cities should be mixed-use so that people can walk," allowing workplaces, housing, schooling, and parks to be located near each other; "for longer distances, but reasonably short, nonmotorized transport should be safe—bicycles"; then comes public transport, with automobiles a distant and last choice for getting around. Using those guides as a metric, in many ways Manhattan is a model for the equity side of sustainability. When transportation is affordable, as it usually is in dense cities, the poor don't pay disproportionately to get around. As a result, from jobs to cultural opportunities the barriers to access are lower.

In *Green Metropolis*, David Owen writes that "dense urban centers offer one of the few plausible remedies for some of the world's most discouraging environmental ills, including global climate change."[6] Sclar affirms that view, observing, "Density works fine when you have good public services. When you have police, fire, and good schools and water and sanitation: when you have all those things working, people can live at high density very efficiently. Manhattan is probably the premier example." Other cities—Sclar mentions Nairobi, Kenya—stand as polar opposites. "The real issue is, if we want to preserve open space, if we want to preserve farmland, we've got to start talking about land use patterns that allow urban life at high density," observes Sclar. "It works well at high density. People love it. The issue is that all of the incentives built into our public policy have been to sprawl."

New York sprawls, too, of course. The same subway lines that once stretched to potato fields now barely reach the suburbs, to say nothing of the exurbs. Thousands of commuters take one-hour to ninety-minute train rides (and even car trips) to the city from far out on Long Island, New Jersey, Connecticut, or from as far up the Hudson as Poughkeepsie; I once rode a train into New York with an actor who boarded in the city of Hudson, nearly two hours away.

And let's not forget New York City's water supply, exemplary of a form of sprawl that often gets overlooked: infrastructure sprawl. Though not nearly as excessive as Los Angeles' or San Francisco's water wanderlust, New York's carried it to the far side of the Catskill Mountains, where reservoirs 120 miles from the city catch water otherwise destined for the Delaware River. More than half of the city's 1.2 *billion* gallon daily demand is satisfied by a massive tunnel system, sending waters that would have flowed past Philadelphia and into Chesapeake Bay over into the Hudson drainage, under the Hudson River, and into holding reservoirs. Thence it flows to the taps and toilets of city residents and businesses. One of three tunnels carrying water from the Delaware Aqueduct System is leaking approximately 1 billion gallons of water a month; the city hopes to bypass the leaky section with a new tunnel slated for completion in 2020.

In many ways the city's five boroughs may be a model of sustainability, but it isn't perfect. Dense as it is, New York nevertheless casts a wide net, drawing in not only 278,000 "super commuters" each day who travel more than three hours, round trip,[7] but sucking water from a neighboring watershed and food from across the continent. Such may be the reality for any "sustainable" city; compromises will have to be made.

For these reasons, some will question New York City's identification as a hub of sustainability. In recent years, for example, other cities have been rated higher on various sustainability scales.[8] The question for New York, and all other large urban areas, is, how do they minimize—and perhaps someday reverse—the negative effects of those compromises and rehabilitate the ecosystem and social damage created in the course of compromising?

New York City provides some of those answers, its consumers purchasing huge amounts of produce and more from hundreds of regional farmers, as we saw in chapter 3. And, to avoid a multibillion dollar water filtration plant investment, in the 1990s it began a mere $1.5 billion project to purchase lands adjacent to and near its Catskill Mountain reservoirs, ensuring the waters' purity while permanently protecting forests that may have been felled for development. Dennis D. Hirsch writes, "In this way, forests, wetlands, and riparian lands serve as 'living filters' that remove sediments, metals, oils, excess nutrients, and other contaminants from the water supply."[9]

New York's reach is so great that it affects the region's Landscape in complex ways, some beneficial and some destructive. Indeed, in many instances what appears to be short-term destruction ends up promoting sustainability decades later—a rare phenomenon in the suburbs.

Preserving What's Left

New York is always being rebuilt, insist some experts. In this telling, the physical city is perpetually unfinished. In the last few years one of the greatest building booms ever took place, giving some the sense that the city is always creating opportunities for itself to recast its future in steel and concrete. It is a city that is "continually becoming," so much so that, as noted earlier, even sustainability champion Michael Bloomberg envisioned 20 percent of the city's building's being replaced over twenty years. The city that never sleeps always builds.

Such an observation could be bad news to preservationists such as Françoise Bollack. She notes that part of the "promise of the green movement is that people would become again aware of their surroundings so that they could live a fuller life. It's just that simple. Because I think you have one life to live, and if you live it like a zombie, it's kind of a half-life." She, like so many, sees immense opportunities for living a full, rich, engaged life in even the largest of cities—*especially* in such places. "I think that's part of trying to design a better life for ourselves," Bollack explains.

As an architect, design is very much on her mind, while as an advocate—she was the first female president of New York's Historic Districts Council, which watches over thousands of older buildings throughout Manhattan—Bollack's emphasis is the antithesis of creating the new by wiping out the old. In her view, there is inspirational wisdom in what was. "Old buildings are very well built," this connoisseur says, "so you get to really learn construction methods and construction technologies that you don't learn in school. The buildings are wonderful teachers. They make you a better architect."

And what has Bollack, a Paris-trained émigré to New York in 1970, learned at the feet of these master buildings? For one, she has found that in old structures "people know how to behave. They know what to expect when they pass the door. The building doesn't brutalize them.

The building is operating in an order that has enough history behind it that people are not surprised, in general, by old buildings. . . . There is a sense of familiarity that allows you to operate comfortably." Early modern buildings work at an archetypal level, as if they anticipate our movements through them thanks to a shared DNA. Even "the new thing," when introduced into an old building, "acquires immediate authority because it situates itself in a well-known context," Bollack observes.

"There is a saying in historic preservation that the most sustainable building is an existing building," says Bollack, who teaches at Columbia in addition to running her own architecture firm. "The greenest building is an existing building." Based on energy expenditures alone, it makes no sense to tear down a salvageable construction and start all over. There was the energy used to make and transport the bricks, for example, and to create and install the water, sewer, electrical, sidewalk, and road infrastructure. "An old building is, in and of itself, as an object, green," Bollack says.

> If you had to demolish it you would engage in a very non-green operation. You would be destroying something that you've made. You'd spend energy destroying it, so it's wasted, and the third piece of waste is that you will have to rebuild it. It's going to be rebuilt less well, and you're going to have to spend energy rebuilding it. So it's an absurd construction.
>
> The other aspect of sustainability of old buildings is that old buildings were built before the modern methods we have invented to not deal with nature, such as air conditioning.

Air flow and intelligent siting do a lot to curb the need for air conditioning in the first place. "So old buildings—the way they're built and conceived—makes them green and sustainable."

Bollack knows whereof she speaks. "I live in an un-air-conditioned apartment, and at a maximum I would say we're miserable two weeks a year," she says. "We live in a prewar apartment, so it's cross-ventilated, the ceilings are rather high, it has shading, all of those things, and most of the time it's comfortable."

Just as keeping an older car in good working order rather than buying a new one is almost always the more environmentally responsible choice, Bollack insists old buildings and their characteristics, particularly their built-in energy efficiency, need to be preserved. Refurbishing them in ways that maintain their structure, beauty, and comfort makes far more sense than pulling them down and replacing them, even with new "green" structures.

Data support her argument, as will be seen in a moment. But let's begin by making a strong case for a new building over against renovating an old one. The old apartment building in this thought experiment is structurally sound but not particularly attractive. It dates from before World War II, so it possesses the characteristics Bollack describes, although it is not otherwise historically significant. It's a good old building, nothing more.

Alternatively, consider a new condominium building. It will be constructed to the U.S. Green Building Council's high LEED standards: energy efficient, built to conserve water and promote clean air indoors, it uses sustainable building materials and is minimally wasteful.

By the data, which is preferable? A 2011 study by the National Trust for Historic Preservation argues that for multifamily residential buildings such as these, renovating the old building is the more sustainable route on each of four metrics: climate change, resource depletion, human health, and ecosystem quality.[10] The study considered seven types of structures, from single-family homes to large office buildings, and examined the environmental effects of renovation compared to new construction in four climatologically distinct cities: Atlanta, Chicago, Phoenix, and Portland, Oregon. With the exception of some aspects of converting an old warehouse—just one of the seven building types—to a multifamily dwelling rather than tearing it down and starting again, the data indicate the way to go is reno.

Such observations beg the question: When we sacrifice old buildings, what else do we lose along with the energy investment, historical relevance, and landfill space? I think we lose meaning. Replacing an old building with a new one does introduce new meaning—everything means *something*, after all. But that act of painting over the brick and mortar of a building's construction on a Landscape's canvas and beginning anew tells us something about ourselves and our approach to both the cityscape and the Landscape.

The scholar in me insists there is no single, correct version of that story: a developer will infuse the new structure with a quite different meaning than will Françoise Bollack, and the opposite is true if she wins her struggle to resuscitate an old building. But the sustainability advocate in me reads the "text" of redevelopment in a different light. I have to wonder what it says about towns, cities, and society broadly when we blithely bias new against old. How can developers, planning boards, and elected officials be so eager to clear the canvas? Where is the moral responsibility to the present and the future—and a little bit to the past—to do all we can both to honor what was and to leave behind a livable planet? Thanks to reports like the National Trust's, we even have data indicating that knee-jerk redevelopment is de-development: destruction not only of the structure but of the building's legacy, its educational content, and the sustainability potential lost to the bulldozer. Their report notes that even with a high LEED-rated structure, it can take ten to eighty years to bring the energy savings ledger into balance once the wrecking ball does its damage.

As organizations such as New York's Landmark West! have long insisted, we need to reflect on what our actions tell us about us. Few other cultures display a more dismissive view of the built past than ours, and many that we admire—Europe, in particular, but regions of Africa and Asia, too—treat the old and rehabilitatable structures in their cities as precious things. They refuse to allow moneyed interests to trample history and environmental good sense.

Taking from the Ground . . . and Putting It Back

Sometimes, though, when the old gives way to the new it is up to Mark Morrison and Leonard Hopper to salvage what they can. Landscape architects, they inhabit a world where sustainability has been a practice since the profession was founded, and today their work can be found at its cutting edge. "People are flocking to it now," says Hopper, "but when you look at what (Central Park designer Frederick Law) Olmstead did, he was a promoter not only of landscape but of environmental justice and (rectifying) social inequalities: Central Park was as much a social experiment as it was an ecological, environmental experiment."

Sustainability, Hopper adds, "is not fringe any more as it might have been in the sixties or the seventies. It's become mainstream because there are so many far-reaching, wide-reaching benefits to so many people in so many ways." A key difference from a couple of decades ago, Morrison and Hopper insist, is that policymakers and developers realize that sustainable landscape design responds to public needs, such as foresightful planning and keeping taxes low, and it's appealing to the traditional single bottom line because buildings and grounds both look and perform better.

In New York City, elected officials and builders are less and less at odds over building design requirements. Why? Part of the answer lies in what *Green Metropolis* author David Owen identifies as the four "accidents" that encouraged population density and thereby allowed New York City to stumble into the twenty-first century as a model for sustainability.[11] First, as an island New York could only grow outward so much; the sprawl that characterizes auto-intensive cities such as Atlanta and Phoenix wasn't possible there, so it grew upward (true for Manhattan, if not for the metropolitan area as a whole); verticality promotes density, encouraging more sustainability. Second, the city's grid pattern of streets, designed in the second decade of the nineteenth century, enhances that density. Third, the city has always been home to what we today call "smart growth," a worthy fad sweeping every city and town with any pretense of a sustainability ethos. But in New York it has never been new or different to mix ground-level stores and offices with upper-floor residences. Finally, it is fortuitous that nearly all city blocks were filled in before the automobile's arrival so that the temptation—realized in the suburbs—to create life around the automobile (wide streets feeding multilane arterials, massive surface-level parking lots, great distances between home and everything else) was never fulfilled.

In a dense, mixed-use, automobile-unfriendly place such as Manhattan, it didn't take much for city officials and builders to make the initial sustainability leap into green buildings. The city was primed for takeoff and well ahead of many other places. One thing that helped move city policymakers along was crisis, particularly CSO: combined sewer overflow. The lack of separate sewage and street runoff systems means that sewage treatment plants are overwhelmed when snow melts or heavy rains hit. That combined flood is diverted into the Hudson River, returning it to the disgusting days of yore when it resembled an open sewer. When city officials accepted CSO as a serious problem, they soon identified green buildings and green infrastructure as ways to address the problem.

Surprisingly, the green infrastructure requirements the city instituted for new construction often don't add to construction costs. In fact, Morrison says, "if it's being designed in the right way, especially if it's new construction, they should be *saving* money or at least breaking even. . . . As developers do, they're trying to make money. If they can make it by being green, why not?"

On a small, property-by-property basis, making thoughtful, deliberate choices about what we want our Landscapes to be like and how we want to live in them is at the heart of landscape architecture. When added up, those little bits have the potential to make big differences when guided by intelligent macrolevel policies. One example that Hopper and Morrison mention was the work they did on a new wing at Lawrence Hospital in Bronxville, New York, just north of New York City. "When you look at hospital patients," Hopper says, "when they have access to an outdoor space, or even a view of an outdoor space, they heal faster. Their hospital stays are shorter." Trees, flowers, a snowy lawn: our Landscape connections are so profound that human health is tied to them in shockingly simple ways.

Often called in to help others work out "unresolvable" landscape problems, Morrison says the issue this time was the seeming necessity of cutting down several large, old trees to make way for underground tanks needed to catch runoff before it washed down drains.

A "green roof" proved to be the answer—and to more than one concern. Green roofs are especially workable with new construction. Morrison explains that he may call for as many as two feet of soil or other foundational material on a rooftop. Then come trees and shrubs, which may retain as much as 40 percent of rainwater—water that "never hits the 'ground,'" simply evaporating in warm weather. Morrison has even retrofitted Public School 6's rooftop to include a greenhouse and an urban garden. As much as 95 percent of a green roof's rain or snow evaporates there, never becoming runoff.

At Lawrence Hospital, not only did the green roof capture so much rainwater and snowmelt that only one of the runoff storage tanks that the original designers planned was installed, but "we took it one step further as we developed the green roof," Morrison says. "Most institutions have (closed circuit) camera systems. We said, 'Let's put cameras on the green roof so that if you're in your hospital bed and can't get out, and you're not lucky enough to have a decent view, why can't you go to Channel Four and see what's going on on the green roof? . . . For people who are really in tough shape you can cut flowers and bring them to them: 'They came from the roof.' They can see if there's birds or butterflies or bees going on." Hopper adds, "I think you see the same thing with productivity, with people who are less violent because they have access to green spaces." Connections with Landscape can heal any number of wounds.

Those green roofs are something of a Mark K. Morrison Landscape Architecture specialty. Turns out they do more than look pretty, cool buildings and cities, and uplift people's spirits. They also provide habitat. Morrison says, "The green roof of The Visionaire," located in southern

Manhattan, "is on the thirty-fifth floor of the building. There's crickets. Several kinds of bees. Wasps. Butterflies, birds, all kinds of good things up there thirty-five floors up. So you have this kind of patchwork mosaic that goes through the city" as green roofs multiply dozens of stories high. "If you're going to take it off the ground, we'd better put it back on the roof."

"Nearly 50% of impervious surface in highly urbanized areas is unused roof space," researchers Timothy Carter and Colleen Butler write. "Green roofs convert the impervious surface of a rooftop into multifunctional spaces in urban areas using vegetation, growing media, and specialized roofing materials. . . . As the land consumed by urbanization continues to outpace population growth, efforts must be made to create multifunctional land cover if some predevelopment ecological function is to be preserved."[12] Green roofs, then, may help recover some of what is lost when cities rise where trees once stood, making Hopper and Morrison's work less novelty than necessity.

How can other cities emulate New York's landscape architecture successes? Enlightened zoning, a key macro element, comes first. Smart growth—rules that promote building upward, resulting in lots of tall buildings with shops and offices on lower floors—is essential, as is making automobile drivers pay (literally or figuratively) while providing plenty of public transportation.

As for what the city could do better, Morrison and Hopper point to New York's stormwater retention and control regulations, in particular, as being behind the times. While they have played a key role in moving New York to the next level of sustainability, they don't go far enough. For instance, city guidelines treat impermeable pavements, which contribute to overloading the city's combined sewage system when combined runoff is at its worst, no differently than permeable alternatives that allow rain and snowmelt to move through the hard surface into slow-release catchment systems buried underneath sidewalks, streets, and parking lots. Permeable surfacing is mentioned in some of the city's green infrastructure documents, but it doesn't appear to have made it off the page and onto the pavement.

Deep Green Buildings

Usually, when one hears talk of a "green" building, it's in the context of the U.S. Green Building Council's LEED standards briefly mentioned earlier in this chapter. Those Leadership in Energy and Environmental

Design metrics establish a framework for builders and owners aiming to be environmentally responsible with their projects that is being adopted by cities, states, and foreign nations as part of their building codes.[13] But when Dickson Despommier talks about green buildings, he has in mind buildings that are literally green: green because crops are being grown there, making them deep green structures.

Despommier calls it "vertical farming," and it is potentially a way of growing food where increasing numbers of us live, in or near cities. The land area and energy needed to supply food to the ten billion humans alive at mid-century and to transport it to where we live will both be enormous. Starting with that problem, Despommier came up with vertical farming as a solution.

Despommier is a brash, unabashed proponent of an idea that has only begun to grow. If seen to fruition, vertical farming may fundamentally alter the Hudson region's Landscape and those far beyond. Skyscraper-based farms might make little difference to dirt farmers in the Hudson region, given that, as Todd Erling noted, New York State *must* import roughly half its food. But if the economics are powerful enough, vertical farming could spell doom for classical farming, raising questions (some of which Despommier is eager to answer) about the future of that acreage. Despommier's notions are cutting edge, and while it's not clear if they'll be blunted or will lay the scythe to traditional agriculture, they challenge the farming Landscape outlined in chapter 3 in fundamental ways.

Despommier's skyscraper farm fantasy bears few connections to the bulk of his research. A Columbia University public health professor, he's a worm expert, parasitic worms in particular; Despommier edited *the* book on the subject—his *Parasitic Diseases* is in its fifth edition, *The Vertical Farm* in its first.[14]

After a career devoted to ridding the world of such monsters, surely it was a leap to get to vertical farming? Not really. Despommier says, immodestly but honestly, "I'm a world expert in parasites. I recognize a parasite when I see one, and viewed from outer space, cities are the parasites and the land is the host. What's wrong with this picture? There are more cities now and more people now." Despommier is convinced we're living out an ongoing tragedy, one that could be avoided.

At root, then, vertical farms are his response to a population crisis that no one is paying much attention to and an environmental justice tragedy that too many are ignoring. "I want everybody to eat well and live well," Despommier says, "and then, by nature, we will have fewer children." Vertical farming as population control. Population control as essential to sustainability. It's not an unreasonable syllogism.

Or perhaps it is. "This is crazy: farming in a building," Despommier says, channeling his critics. "Who the hell ever heard of *that*? Well, you do everything else in a building, so why not? That's the point. We live in the built environment. We are totally accustomed to playing out our lives in a closed environment. We go outside to recreate, but we live in buildings from the time we go to work to the time we go to bed." We've brought nearly every other major human endeavor indoors because there is where they happen best. Why not farming?

One reason humans do so much indoors is because things can be controlled there like nowhere else. From temperature and lighting to cooking and relaxing to meetings and deadlines, interior spaces limit unknowns and cut down on uncertainty. Traditional farming, Despommier insists, is replete with both, making it a downright foolish endeavor. "Wherever you look," he says, "there's something that's going to short-circuit your farming project outdoors. Floods, droughts, bad weather—that includes hurricanes, tornadoes, hailstorms." He adds, "We can create a comfort zone for anything we want, so let's do it for our food as well." Viewed from any perspective other than romanticism, dirt farming is irrational.

Two logical points are central to Despommier's perspective on contemporary agriculture: dirt farming doesn't make much ecological or economic sense. "Farming is destined to failure because it is a nonecological activity in an ecological world," he says: an attempt to exert unecological control in the context of ecosystems, a practice doomed to failure and one that has spun off such bizarre practices as poisoning the land to encourage crop production. Removing farming from ecology hasn't worked; pesticides, GMOs, and the rest inevitably create ecologically damaging side effects, though Despommier is loath to come down too hard on genetic manipulation.[15] His solution is to "remove the ecology from farming so that we can control it just like we control our own temperature." Ecology writ large is one of those uncontrollable factors that confounds farmers. Why challenge it?

The corollary is also true. "We've only been farming for twelve thousand years, and it's wreaked havoc on the environment," Despommier says. Even in the face of Conrad Vispo's farm ecology evidence, Despommier doubtless would insist that little of ecological value can be found on the farm.

As for economics, Despommier decries the twisted logic of a global agricultural system where, for example, it pays even drought-stricken nations to sell what crops they harvest and purchase the same commodity on the market at a lower price from another nation. Despommier calls such an economic calculus crazy, and who other than a neoliberal economist could disagree?

The answer to the food insecurity that results from treating crops as no different from any other commodity is to eliminate the thing that makes commodities commodities: scarcity. Markets only arise when there is competition for goods. Why should there ever be any competition for something as essential as food? Chocolate or coffee, perhaps, but not carrots or cauliflower. Grown under certain, guaranteed conditions, there can be food aplenty for all, pulling the rug out from under speculators who care nothing for starvation or who embrace bizarre agricultural trade rituals.

Vertical farming holds the potential to reverse those nonsensical ecological and economic practices. Despommier insists we can grow food wherever we want. "All of these things that I'm suggesting doing in a multiple-story greenhouse have already been worked out carefully," he says. "So we have no technological breakthrough necessities."

Given the control over nearly every variable possible in greenhouses or vertical farms, "you can plan in advance how much crop you get," Despommier says. "The USDA says the maximum efficiency for planted crops outside in a field is fifty percent survival from seed to table. Fifty! Insect pests, plant diseases, a little drought, a little flood. That's the business model for a farm? Fifty percent? No one would invest in farming" without government subsidies. "If you put it in those terms, how could you choose any other than indoor farming," Despommier insists.

So why not do it? Some have, with small- to medium-scale vertical farms (up to ninety thousand square feet) opening in Chicago, Memphis, Michigan, and Brooklyn, although none appear to be very tall and some have no windows. Critics insist that the economics haven't been worked out yet but were addressed long ago for horizontal greenhouses, and Whole Foods seems comfortable enough with the financing to have given a $100,000 loan to the Chicago facility.[16]

Despommier, who advocates government-funded demonstration vertical farms to get the vision off the ground, bristles at the suggestion that because farming in tall buildings is untried, it's not worth doing. "Why do you insist that vertical farming be a viable business model [before the government or business supports it] when farming itself is not a viable business model?" he asks his critics. "Why are you being two-faced about this? I know why: because you don't want this, do you? Because this will make sustainable farming possible, whereas the other kind of farming is totally untenable."

There are other reservations as well: taste, unsuitability for certain crops, corporate control over the farms. Despommier calmly addresses most of those concerns but brusquely dismisses another: the fate of farming as we know it. "The poor dirt farmer has been extinct for centuries," he says. "We just haven't noticed."

Yet more concerns loom, from the expense of development to the emphasis on experts to energy use (for which Despommier advocates sustainable energy sources such as wind and solar power, as well as drawing energy from human waste; some of the early facilities are entirely indoors, and it is not clear what their energy sources are—prompting concerns about their sustainability). It's worth noting that in some form all of these objections may be leveled against our existing expensive, technocrat-controlled, energy-intensive agriculture and food system.

Despommier is careful to note that it's not farmers he objects to. He favors employing farmers who are committed to the land to re-create ecosystems on their former farms, with earth-cooling carbon capture a side benefit. "Let them farm the land the way they like to do it, and pay them for carbon credits and get them back caring for the earth, being stewards for the environment, and let the earth heal itself," he says.

Despommier would fundamentally alter many aspects of agricultural practice, a vital fixture in most advocates' view of a sustainable Landscape, and in so doing he adds another dimension to a preexisting tension among sustainability advocates. As peopled ecosystems, Landscapes must somehow include food production. Yet farming drastically affects a place's flora and fauna, posing problems for the ecology side of sustainability's triple bottom line.

Moving a substantial part of what's farmed—tree nuts and fruits, along with humanely treated livestock, do not easily fit Despommier's vision, so vertical farming will never completely replace dirt farming—into skyscrapers located within or near cities pulls food sustainability in a provocative direction. What mode of farming is best for ecology when everything—energy, efficiency, jobs, economic justice, food security, and the broader economy—is taken into account? Will farms be replaced by government-subsidized, carbon-trapping ecosystems, as Despommier imagines? And, given farming's historical ties to place, are Landscapes possible without traditional agriculture?

Ideal Human Habitat

Referring to former mayor Bloomberg's transportation commissioner, Janette Sadik-Kahn, Elliott Sclar says, "She's actually been taking streets back from cars and turning them over to bikes." That's exactly what

Transportation Alternatives has been advocating for years. "The future of cities is going to be more about walking and bicycling and mass transit," says Paul Steely White, the group's executive director. By those measures, New York City is rapidly approaching "the future."

"People see where this is going," White says. "It's not just environmental concerns. I think it's resource constraints, it's people seeing gas getting more expensive. It's the health issue. It's not about going to the gym to fight the obesity crisis; it's about building activity into our everyday lives." In a city where 149 walkers and eighteen bike riders were killed in accidents with vehicles in 2012, curbing automobile culture has the potential for improving drivers' emotional health as well as keeping pedestrians and cyclists alive.

With twenty-three employees, thousands of members, and tens of thousands on its e-mail list, Transportation Alternatives has become a force to be reckoned with in the city. Established in 1973, TA retained its early activistic status even as it developed to the point that former executive directors and employees now occupy important positions at City Hall.[17] It holds monthly meetings for borough activists, harangues unresponsive officials, and educates the public through an informative Web site, documentaries, even good old posters—including one that depicts fifty people in cars versus on a bus or on bicycles: the street looks more and more empty each step of the way, prompting viewers to reimagine a New York without motorized vehicles.[18]

TA's activism and sway in City Hall have resulted in a long string of successes. There are Sadik-Kahn's pedestrian plazas where street spaces have been rededicated to vehicle-free zones, more than four hundred miles of bike lanes painted onto the city's busy roads, off-street dedicated bike- and pedestrian-only paths first envisioned by Transportation Alternatives, and with its lobbying in 2014 the state changed the law to allow New York to establish a citywide maximum twenty-five miles per hour speed limit.

Perhaps its most notable recent achievement emerged in 2007, when Transportation Alternatives began pushing for a bike-sharing program along the lines of those found in Paris and other large cities. Primarily privately funded, Citi Bike finally got rolling in May 2013 to huge acclaim, with ninety-three thousand annual members paying $95 to join the bike share program in the first six months.[19]

(It's worth noting as well that Citi Bike is part of an emerging "sharing economy," a phenomenon that further enhances cities' sustainability. Zipcar is probably the most widely known example of the sharing economy, but it also includes Airbnb, a popular service for folks wanting to stay in others' homes for the night [with the owners present]. Citi Bike and Zipcar emphasize sharing things that are somewhat to very costly, large, and that city dwellers don't necessarily need all that often. Why buy when you can share?)

Neither success nor the hiring of numerous TA staff members to work in city government has curbed Transportation Alternatives' vision. It remains aggressive and high-minded, for example, when White speaks of the creation of vehicle-free lifestyles centering on public spaces. "The Greeks had this concept of the *agora,* which was fundamental to democracy," he notes. "People came to argue and give speeches and just talk politics. Once you tune into what's happening on Broadway or any number of streets that have been reclaimed here in New York in recent years, you do begin to see there's a lot more spontaneous interaction, a lot more lingering, and people talking to each other, not necessarily for the first time. You do run into people you know in New York City!" People hang out, chat, leaflet—they enact civil society: behavior not sanctioned by the government and not oriented toward the market but centered on the creation and maintenance of relationships, community, and democracy.

White adds, "I think when public space is habitable for people, they're not tuned into the television as much as they were before, and there's this vital public realm that I think is fundamental to democracy. It's not to say that the TV is evil or that even the suburbs are bad. It's just that without the public realm, without this common space, the commons, where people can mix and mingle and do, as Jane Jacobs described, this 'ballet of the street,'" something vital to ourselves and our democracy is lost.

In the reclaimed spaces that White extolls, the city's character changes. Consider, for example, the High Line, an unexpected park located on the abandoned route of an elevated freight train line that runs twenty-four blocks. Opened in 2009, it offers stunning views of the Hudson, Midtown Manhattan, even the Statue of Liberty two stories above the traffic. Or the section of Broadway that White mentioned: near Herald Square, blocks south of Times Square, which itself was put off limits to traffic a few years ago. Just down the way from the center of the tourist universe, no cars whiz past. No buses roar along. Customers duck into banks, restaurants, and shops. On warm summer evenings or sunny winter afternoons citizens and visitors linger huddled around tables or relaxed beneath umbrellas, enjoying a libation and city life moving at a remarkably—for its location near the heart of Manhattan—pedestrian, humane pace. Musicians strum, children giggle, and one cannot help but feel a sense of empowerment: here, for a time and in a small but precious space, the automobile has been banished from city culture.

Stumbling onto such "people-oriented streets" for the first time, "you could be an anthropologist discovering ideal human habitat," White quips. Championed by Danish urban designer Jan Gehl,[20] one finds that such spaces are where "you're happy, where you can actually meet your fellow citizens and talk and hear yourself think because there's no traffic noise," White says. People linger, and studies indicate that welcoming street spaces actually improve business for local merchants.

Isn't New York City the *last* place you would expect to see streets closed down to make way for a combination endless party/political discussion/meetup spot/family gathering place? Imagine the pressure to keep Broadway open to traffic: that wonderful strip of asphalt angling away from the Hudson toward the East River and downtown, a rushed motorist's delight.

Surely, if Broadway could be shut down, other core streets could be too—such as, for example, another Broadway, this one running through my professional hometown of Saratoga Springs. A miniature New York City—vibrant night life, public transit, cultural offerings from the nation's oldest folk club to Shakespeare in the Park and everything in between, a "smart growth" policy encouraging dense and diverse downtown development that is increasingly vertical, and a bustling local economy—Saratoga's heart is bisected by four lanes of hell with on-street parking to boot. Eighteen wheelers roar and rumble past. Unmuffled motorcycles tear along deafeningly as summer diners try to convince themselves that the people watching is worth the sounds and smells. One of the earliest cities to commit itself to reducing its carbon emissions, Saratoga Springs cannot seem to find the will to do to its main route what the big city two hundred miles south did: close parts of Broadway to traffic.

Transportation Alternatives sees direct links between the policies it advocates, such as making streets and street spaces more humane, and sustainability. "What's good for the planet is good for the people," White observes, quoting a TA board member. "There's not a dichotomy at all; in fact, there's a synergy between environmental development and design and what feeds us as people, what makes us happy." Getting around on foot or by bicycle cuts down on greenhouse gas emissions, promotes health, and reconnects us with our fellow citizens.

Looking at the changes going on around him on Manhattan and in his neighborhood in Brooklyn, where bike networks and quieter sidewalks take residents to farmers markets set up in plazas that used to be roadways, White muses, "I think what we're seeing is a compelling alternative lifestyle where all of a sudden it's easy to see how it all adds up." Walkable, bikeable residential areas mix with easy transit commutes and public spaces to produce cleaner air, richer, more meaningful social interactions, and lively local economies. "We're using fewer resources," White says, "and making cities more attractive."

Some dismiss Manhattan's evolving transportation model. David Owen writes, "New York City looks so little like most other parts of America that urban planners and environmentalists tend to treat it as an exception rather than a model, and to act as though Manhattan occupied an idiosyncratic universe of its own."[21] A bit defensively, Owen says the city's subway and bus lines often get overlooked in discussions about sustainable transportation, others' biases tending toward the hip, clean light rail systems created over the last couple of decades in St. Louis, Denver, Portland, Oregon, and elsewhere.

"But," Owen adds, "New York's public transit system is, far and away, the most successful in the United States, and the elements that have made it successful are the elements that are required to make transit successful anywhere," specifically, population density and strong disincentives to adopt alternatives (many of my students from the city don't know how to drive, since "no one," they remind me, owns a car where they come from).[22]

If people live close together, not flung far distances, and if driving is too costly or too big a pain (think time-consuming commutes and frustrating parking situations), they'll take transit or, increasingly, pick up a bike. In the process, the meaning of city life and living shifts, altering the city Landscape. The impersonal, destructive, dangerous city of the past emerges as welcoming, engaging, human-scale, and an alternative—*the* alternative?—to the unsustainable days of yore.

A There There

Where *do* cities fit within Landscapes? Are they so self-absorbed that they are cut off from everywhere else, as *The New Yorker* depicted on its cover decades ago: Manhattan as the largest part of the continent, separated from the rest by the broad Hudson River, with the Pacific Ocean a comparatively short distance away? Are they disconnected because they absorb—consume—so much from, and dump so harshly on, near and distant Landscapes that they become anti-Landscapes whose meaning has more to do with detracting from their world than infusing it with character? Or are there positive connections between cities and their environments?

Reflecting the sentiments of the best-selling *Last Child in the Woods*,[23] Mark Morrison makes a tragic observation: "There are still kids in Brooklyn, the Bronx that, if you take them to a park and they see a big tree, they get pretty upset. They cry because it's, like, what is that? What *is* that?" He added, "There's quite a difference between the natural environment and the urban environment, where the vast majority of people live. Thank god for the foresight of Central Park. Olmsted used the Catskill region as something to emulate in the overall landscape of Central Park."

Data in abundance support an anti-Landscape thesis regarding urban areas, the idea being that they create a "no there there," emotionless, anomic world for their residents. But to make such an argument stick, one needs to also consider suburban and rural life. Is the automobile essential to one's existence? Is it possible to get to work, pick up groceries, take the kids to a playdate, or go for a run on a nonmotorized path without first getting in a car? How seriously do local decision makers take planning for the future? Do they see climate change as something relevant to their community and something they have a responsibility to affect? How active is the citizenry in promoting and influencing local policies, and how vibrant is civil society generally?

My sense is that cities are, indeed, where we need to live if we take seriously the task of creating sustainable Landscapes. It *is* there that so much of the consuming takes place, but that's because so many of us are concentrated in urban areas, and that's a good thing. On a per capita basis there's a smaller "ecological footprint" to city life in a place like New York than anywhere else. And there is so much potential there. The school that Mark Morrison and Leonard Hopper retrofitted with a green roof and greenhouse? Students there are growing herbs that the kitchen staff incorporate into the children's meals. Citi Bike? Citizens are demanding bike rental kiosks in neighborhoods that don't have them. Historic buildings? New York's long-range plan (PlaNYC—see below) envisions the city working with preservation groups to improve their energy efficiency.

Urban areas are the indispensable bridge to sustainable Landscapes, offering more promise than problems for one simple reason: they are where we are. If we assume that large numbers of people are going to populate the planet, the options are for them to spread out or to live in concentrated numbers. Discussing the other end of the Hudson region,

Adirondack researcher Michale Glennon mentioned in chapter 2 that human disturbances as small as a hiking trail affect wild flora and fauna, so the choice seems ecologically obvious: we need to live in urban areas if we are going to be sensitive to the ecological side of Landscape's human-ecology equation.

There's another reason to encourage urban living: the "macro" argument. If "cities"—municipal governments, corporations, places of worship, advocacy groups, and the like—move toward sustainability, the effect is far greater than if atomized individuals or small enclaves, the "micro" side of life, make those shifts. Changes in public policy, corporate culture, and leadership by respected organizations in urban areas—those "macrolevel" developments mentioned earlier—have the potential to resonate throughout the region and beyond, bringing new meaning to humanity's interactions with the environments that support us.

Starting with the Michael Bloomberg mayoral administration, New York City began to treat sustainability as a holistic endeavor rather than a piecemeal undertaking and started to put to rest the notion that cities can only exist in tension with Landscapes. The city's marquee sustainability effort, PlaNYC ("Plan YC"),[24] has received international acclaim. Launched in 2007 with an eye toward shaping the city of 2030, PlaNYC's fourth-year update touted almost instantaneous accomplishments. For example, two hundred acres of new parkland brought an additional 250,000 New Yorkers within a ten-minute walk of a park, and the city saw a 13 percent cut in greenhouse gas emissions over 2005—a healthy start toward its goal of a 30 percent reduction (city government was on track to reduce its own emissions by 30 percent by 2017).

The plan's scores of initiatives and goals include emphases on planting one million trees (650,000 were in the ground by 2014), the creation of affordable housing, promoting residential growth near subway lines, and making roofs (almost 20 percent of the city's total area) more sustainable by turning them into energy producers or coating them to promote cooling. A Greenstreets program, around since 1996, now emphasizes green infrastructure, particularly using planters, plantings, and "blue roofs" to capture stormwater before it becomes runoff, and new policies aimed at the city's largest public and private buildings will cut energy use, save money, and create jobs.

Those from the eleven-by-two-mile island already tread lightly on the planet in numerous ways. David Owen notes, "Eighty-two percent of employed Manhattanites travel to work by public transit, by bike, or on foot,"[25] their smaller dwellings consume less energy to heat and cool than most, and because there's not much room there aren't a lot of electricity-sucking appliances to enlarge their ecological footprints. Indeed, Manhattanites generate about one-quarter as many greenhouse gases as the average American.[26]

Deepening Landscape Connections

Urban areas help us to see Landscape as an evolving concept. The essential human-environment connection is always there, as it inevitably is, but we can now understand it as a layered phenomenon. There is a macro stratum, how a locale interacts with far-flung Landscapes (for instance, the places to which New York City trash is transported each day) and with the biosphere, the one Landscape that unites all things. There's also the meso Landscape, which finds cities connected in intimate and, because of their size, profound ways to the nearby Landscape. For instance, in drawing water from the Catskills, commuters from nearby counties, and food from throughout the region, New York City enhances the sense that the Hudson region is more than the watershed's boundaries. Cities connect in complex ways with disparate places, and their reach is not always welcome; for example, many in the Catskills resent New York's ability to buy up huge parcels of land and, in the interest of protecting the watershed, place property off limits to the locals. Beauty and bitterness both may be components of a Landscape.

Then there's the micro layer, the city's immediate Landscape. It's one thing to say, as I did in chapter 3, that family farms are some of the clearest examples we have of a peopled Landscape. Farms are one (big) step from unadulterated wilderness, though Conrad Vispo reminds us that most include valuable ecological components. In contrast, the local Landscape in a city of eight million would appear to be as thoroughly domesticated as one could imagine. For a Landscape to exist, there must be an environment that people physically manipulate and to which people give meaning. Other than a few city block–sized parks, and an 843-acre one in the middle of Manhattan Island, where do we find "environment" in Gotham? Looking out past the Statue of Liberty toward the ocean, perhaps? Up the Hudson or East rivers? Is it broken up into the million trees that PlaNYC envisions shading scorched streets?

Paul White—like WeACT's Peggy Shepard—would say environment is in every breath New Yorkers draw and every sip of water they take. Their city is embedded in the Hudson Landscape as surely as Adirondack Park or Poughkeepsie. It is undeniable that large cities alter a region's

Landscape. Their gravity is immense and multidimensional. But they needn't be black holes. Far from it, they can be leaders, as we see in PlaNYC's numerous objectives.

In truth, of course, we all live with these macro, meso, and micro Landscape layers. Our suburban yards or urban streets embody some of the most important meanings in our lives. Signifying anything from family to danger, our micro worlds also are rich, if not always positive, sources of human-environment interactions ranging from the injustices of polluted neighborhoods and poorly constructed apartment buildings to the bucolic setting of semi-rural suburbia, where foxes scamper across backyards and hawks cruise overhead. In any event, those micro-Landscapes are inescapable. So, too, are the macro and the meso, though our connections to them often are not as immediate. There is, in the end, a multilayered Landscape in our cities. And by virtue of that fact, there is a there there as well.

Chapter 7

A Complete Disruption

Gavin McIntyre harbors some lofty ambitions. "Our mantra as a business is to be the sustainable material science company of the twenty-first century, the analogue to Dow or DuPont from the twentieth century," he says with an engineer's matter-of-fact confidence. And the ingredient that will put his company on the map and challenge synthetics, the equivalent of Dow's Styrofoam or DuPont's nylon?

Mushrooms.

McIntyre's company, Ecovative (think "innovative" with a hard-e "eco" prefix), got its start when he and business partner Eben Bayer were undergraduates at Rensselaer Polytechnic Institute in Troy, New York, a couple of miles down the Hudson from the company's present-day facilities on Green Island.[1] Their Product Design and Innovation dual major with Mechanical Engineering challenged them to address serious human concerns, and in their senior thesis they wrote about the potential of mushrooms—fungi—as an insulator, having found that the fungi-infused structural insulated panel that they created (grew, actually) scored a high R-value and was fire-resistant. Nonflammable, no volatile organic compounds, no carcinogens, no synthetic chemicals: a dream product for the building industry and homeowners alike, one would think, the opposite of the stuff made by those "material science" behemoths found at big box retailers.

Harkening back to E. F. Schumacher's *Small is Beautiful*, McIntyre matter-of-factly says that Ecovative's perspective "is trying to approach a steady-state economy. We're here on Spaceship Earth and we have a finite resource allotment. The inputs that we have are solar exposure. So to truly sustain as a people, we need to be within the steady state of the ecosystem, meaning that we're not taking out more than we're putting back. I think that's precisely what we do here at Ecovative. We draw upon evolution as an engineer." He calls his creations "self-propagating, self-replicating biopolymers," and they reflect capitalism's future as it must someday appear if our economic system is to survive.

That's because, as community sustainability advocate Scott Kellogg puts it, "We've reached the limits as to how large the economy can expand. We don't see the economy as being a subsphere of the global ecosystem; we see the global ecosystem as being an externality to the economic sphere." But if McIntyre and others are correct, the processes that will remake our economy, and, therefore, that will play central roles in the remaking of our Landscapes, are already underway.

In their influential book *Naural Capitalism*, Paul Hawken, Amory Lovins, and Hunter Lovins note that "the economics of resource productivity are already encouraging industry to reinvent itself to be more in accord with biological systems."[2] Products such as Ecovative's, which, when tossed into a garden bed or a compost pile after use, break down into mulch in a couple of weeks, stand at the cutting edge of both capitalism and Landscape reconstruction. Without them, sustainable capitalism will continue to be an oxymoron.

We saw in chapter 1 that almost from the moment of its arrival in the Hudson River region, capitalism transformed the Landscape. It was an economic system that drew beaver, fresh water, clean air, trees, Native Americans, indentured servants, soil, tenant farmers, minerals, factory workers, energy, slaves, and today's service sector employees into it and that produced necessities, luxuries, waste, misery, a way of life, and widespread destruction. This chapter presents green business as a break from the past: full of potential, focused on the triple bottom line, and less riven with contradictions. Following a discussion of Ecovative, we explore the saga of the Hudson region's first legal distillery since Prohibition. Next, localism's connections not just to economy but to community emerge from the efforts of ReThink Local, and then there's the story of how Jiminy Peak Mountain Resort coaxed profit from a zephyr. Creativity, insight, and more than a little necessity all play a role in the invention or reinvention of these firms, as they must in the reinvention of the Hudson region's Landscape.

Starting with a Problem

As Ecovative got going after Bayer and McIntyre's May 2007 graduation, the plan was straightforward: use some sort of crop waste as the anchor and food source for mycelia, the filaments that provide mushrooms and other fungi with nutrients. Let them grow for a few days between a couple of pieces of oriented strandboard, then sterilize it all and voila! structural insulated panels, SIPs, with fewer human and ecological pitfalls than any others, the kind of simple, effective design you'd expect to find in a science fiction novel as the basis for an entire civilization—or at least that civilization's buildings.

Bayer and McIntyre "bootstrapped" the company by winning a couple of business plan competitions, parlaying that early capital into more by landing state and federal grants, then attracting outside investors, amassing a total of roughly $30 million in capital through 2013, Ecovative's fourth year of production. In that time the company grew from two founders and a bit of office space to sixty employees and forty thousand square feet, and it has taken home national and international prizes for innovation and environmental responsibility.

While that initial plan to build a better SIP didn't pan out, the simplicity of the vision is instructive. Classic SIPs sandwich an insulating layer of polystyrene between two pieces of oriented strandboard (OSB). They're not as popular with builders as stick frame construction, and they cost slightly more, but they are said to produce quieter homes, possess better insulating qualities, and even the standard ones may improve indoor air.

Ecovative's chief mycologist Sue Van Hook explains that to make the typical SIP "you *glue* the polystyrene to the board, which is really toxic and the most expensive part. With our material, you *grow* it to that OSB—no glue—and it's *way* stronger in attachment." Van Hook handed over a mushroom-based piece of SIP as she was talking, and I couldn't resist trying to separate the two strandboard pieces from the off-white fungi-crop residue mixture, reminiscent of the chalky exterior of brie cheese, in the middle. Nothing doing.

Unfortunately for Ecovative, there wasn't much doing in the SIP world, either. "We wanted to start down that pathway," Van Hook says, "but getting into the building market is tough to do with an unproven product, a lot of [building code] standards to meet, and the recession hit." Plus, the profit margin was small, as it tends to be for building products, and Ecovative would have been under pressure to produce huge quantities—something its limited manufacturing facilities would not allow. "We had to make a choice," Van Hook says. "Can we do this in this market or do we need to pivot? The choice was to pivot."

For Ecovative, pivoting was not much of a challenge. The basis of their core product in hand, the issue was the best use to put it to. Regardless of how the fungi are employed, the fundamental approach is the same.

Van Hook explains, "You put the slurry mixture" of live fungi and crop residue "in a form for a few days and it grows beautifully to the form. You just pop it out," sterilize it, and it's ready for use.

In short order the Ecovative team realized that "the obvious thing was protective packaging," Van Hook says, referring to the ubiquitous "Styrofoam" (usually a misnomer—it's molded polystyrene) inserts that separate a product from its box. "Where we found our price breakpoint was with things that weighed more than fifteen pounds," says Van Hook. Heavier items—for instance, stereo receivers or computer monitors—need denser, slightly heavier protection against breakage, and Ecovative's product fit the bill.

Smaller companies contracted with Ecovative for their packaging needs, then moved on. Other, larger ones replaced them, and things were looking good. "The big break came when Steelcase, the largest office furniture manufacturer in the country, Dell Computers, Puma, Crate and Barrel: we started getting big names," Van Hook says. Ecovative began to take off.

Van Hook is an old friend—we taught together at Skidmore College until she left in 2010, as excited to be working with McIntyre and Bayer as she was disappointed in the cancellation of her mycology course. She found the young entrepreneurs when a colleague shared a local newspaper article about what they were up to, and from their first conversation she knew she wanted to be involved with Ecovative. Supported by Skidmore's biology labs and Rensselaer's business incubator, Ecovative's first two years were largely spent experimenting.

Van Hook did the testing, exploring the characteristics of different mycelia, and she continues to craft solutions to problems. In fact, problems are at the root of Ecovative's approach. "The reason why we were successful," McIntyre says, "is that when you look at our technology, it didn't start with an idea. You know, 'I have a really cool widget that I think people will buy.' It started with a problem. It was, 'Hey, there's this toxic foam stuff out there that we consume fairly regularly and is non-compostable.' I think the technologies and products that tend to survive are those that start with problems rather than with ideas. Where we are today as a society, there are plenty of problems out there that could use some new ideas and strategies."

"The idea is so disruptive," Van Hook says of Ecovative's humble yet paradigm-shifting innovation, using a word that is growing in popularity to describe industry-altering inventions. "It's completely new technology. It's not a slight adjustment. So many of the sustainable businesses we're seeing, it's like making one slight little improvement using a little less energy or a little less plastic. This is complete disruption of an existing industry."

In capitalism's incessant rush for the new and the better, and for all its vaunted creativity, at times it races right past answers. Fungi, after all, are the yeasts that raise bread and bubble beer. They impart taste to cheese and nutrition to tempeh. In cooking they provide texture and unique character; in medicine they are responsible for life-saving antibiotics, most notably penicillin.

But those in the packaging business have never given biocomposites like the fungi–crop residue marriage created by Ecovative a chance, stumbling headlong toward plastics that are chemically so complicated, and ecologically so dead and foreign, that it may take hundreds of thousands of years for them to break down into nontoxic constituents. By contrast, "What is unique about Ecovative is our entire process is earth-friendly," says Van Hook. "It's earth-aligned, it's cradle-to-cradle. We take plants and fungi from the earth. We borrow them for a little time. And then we put them back in the earth.

"You go home at the end of the day every day, even though you work hard, but you feel really good about what you're doing. And you know it's the new economy."

Only in his late twenties, McIntyre talks business like a grizzled veteran. Potential investors, for example, are shunned unless they are "individuals, firms, or companies   strategic partners—that bring some value to the business." Without connections or expertise, "what's the point?" he asks rhetorically. Known, big-volume customers get most of the attention, while the odd order for a surfboard core—a sample board sits invitingly just inside Ecovative's front door—may not be filled for some time. "Those customers likely aren't going to come back," McIntyre says. "You buy a board and you're done."

By making those smart business decisions, in roughly two years of production Ecovative was profitable—or would have been had McIntyre and Bayer not reinvested the profits into the company. Whether the question is who's allowed to invest, who sits on the board, or when the company makes a profit, it all boils down to strategy: what can Ecovative get out of it? What makes the best business sense?

But this isn't the usual business sense. A major part of the company's disruptive character is its adherence to the triple bottom line. Van Hook recalls a conversation at a company retreat where a designer spoke up in front of the entire company on behalf of the line workers, courageously complaining about lesser pay; McIntyre and Bayer responded, revealing that for the first three years everyone at the company was paid the same, except them. The founders weren't taking home a dime.

There's even more about Ecovative that's innovative from a sustainability perspective, most notably its organizational behavior, which involves evaluating everything from just how sustainable Ecovative really is to who has a say in the company's direction. "Internally, we assess ourselves using lifecycle assessment tools," McIntyre explains. "That allows us to identify where our largest burdens are on the planet. So, for example, when we got started in Two Thousand Nine producing product, the big energy burden was transportation. The reason was we were shipping cotton gin waste from Texas to New York to process. Since then, we've transitioned to corn stover that we source from within two hundred fifty miles of this facility."

Ecovative still has plenty to do to fulfill the ecological bottom line. Thing is, it knows it. Today, for example, 60 percent of their energy use is through the natural gas dryers integral in their processing; they hope to replace the dryers with microwave technology powered by the hydroelectric dams less than two miles upriver. Doing so will cut their energy requirements by 70 percent. It's all just a matter of saving the money to purchase the microwave dryers.

What's next for Ecovative? McIntyre has not given up on his original dream of growing those SIPs. Already confident that they have a winner there, he is now looking to do the engineered wood industry one better. He explains that yesterday's synthetics are not only outdated by sustainability measures, they don't even make sense according to classic business's metrics. "The first engineered wood plant in the United States was actually here in New York," McIntyre says. "It was founded in Nineteen Sixty-Three, and the cost for resin was three percent of the total cost of goods sold. Today, if you look at the cost breakdown for, say, medium-density fiberboard, that resin cost ranges anywhere from thirty-five to forty percent of the total cost. So it's a substantial increase in price." The difference has to do with the higher price of oil, from which the synthetics are derived, and from regulations founded in human health concerns. Fungi may be the answer to lowering those costs.

Ecovative is also looking at using plant phenols, powerful chemicals that may be used to disinfect the fungal spawn, much of which is imported from Africa and India. "What it presents us with," says McIntyre, "is a plant-based solution to disinfecting our raw material that kills off all the bad stuff that we don't want but still allows our fungus to grow." It seems that Ecovative is bent on disrupting an already disruptive system.

That sort of behavior is fundamental to the creation of revived Landscapes. Sustainability entails infusing old ideas such as product packaging or SIPs with new meaning through new behaviors and reconceptualizations of the old. As a result, entrepreneurs don't look at what was the same way anymore. Imagine unpacking a new computer monitor and, instead of tossing the crumbly, oversized polystyrene blocks into the trash, you break up the Ecovative packing material for mulch in your garden (the mycelia aren't alive, so you won't get mushrooms instead of mums) or toss it into the compost heap? In such a future, everything takes on new meaning, as does your connection to Landscape.

Proof of Concept

Ralph Erenzo uses fungi and promotes sustainability by doing so, too, but otherwise his product has little in common with what Ecovative creates.

It's whiskey.

Whiskey and more, actually, but the essential ingredient is alcohol derived from the work of fungi. In 2003 Erenzo and Brian Lee established Tuthilltown Distillery, the first legal whiskey and spirits maker in the Hudson River region since Prohibition. "Before Prohibition, there were over a thousand distilleries in New York," says Erenzo, trim and relaxed sitting in front of a huge stainless steel distilling kettle. "Every farm community had a mill and a distillery. They worked together. When the price of corn dropped or the market fell out and it was too expensive to ship it, they brought it to the distillery, made liquor out of it, and there's *always* a market for alcohol." If Ecovative represents sustainable business's creative future vision, Tuthilltown is, in many ways, a return to a time gone past, with a twist.

In founding the distillery, Erenzo says, "our goal was, first, to make money—make a living. But, second, we wanted to affect agriculture. We wanted to prove a point: that there were better things to do, and we could do them, with the materials at hand to help farmers want to stay in business rather than every time some developer knocks on their door with a multimillion dollar check in their hand: we didn't want the farmers to be thinking of that check. We wanted them to farm." Without a hint that the pun is intended, Erenzo adds, "It was very much a proof of concept project as well, and now it's been proven out."

Tuthilltown has become a catalyst for farmers near their New Paltz–area location. "A lot of them are changing over their growing habits to meet our needs," Erenzo says. He tells a story about sourcing corn for whiskey reminiscent of Ecovative's experience with cotton gin waste, though the distances aren't as great. "We were buying our corn from Cochecton Mills, on the other side of the Catskills"—so far away you can see Pennsylvania from the parking lot. "One day I was over at Bev Tantillo's farm and we got to talking. I was looking for a farmer who had a combine," the huge harvesting machines that strip the kernels from the cob in one operation—the kernels are all Erenzo is interested in. The Tantillos had sold their combine to Cochecton Mills, "which meant," Erenzo says, "Cochecton Mills was sending a five-ton truck across the Catskills, picking up all the corn bulk, bringing it back to Cochecton Mills, putting it in bags, and then driving it over here" to the distillery. In other words, Erenzo was buying corn from fields practically visible from his distillery . . . only the corn first traveled a hundred and twenty miles.

It didn't take long for Erenzo and the Tantillos, fourth-generation farmers, to come to terms. "Now," says Erenzo, "Lenny Tantillo puts the one-ton totes on his flatbed, drives them over here—three miles—and we pay them. They get a better price. We get a better price. The money stays in town," perhaps being spent as many as seven times before it leaves Ulster County. "That's really wonderful for rural economies, especially rural farm economies," he says.

> And we know who we're dealing with. We give them the seed. We are financially responsible for the crop. That takes the financial burden off the farmer for buying the seed. He knows he's going to sell every bit of it. And we know what we're getting. We're trying to avoid using GMO corn. We have varietal corn that we've sourced that we've had grown for us as seed corn, and now we use that. That's what we give to the farmers. So it works very well all around and it closes off that loop locally.

The local connections don't stop there. Tuthilltown's indigenous apple brandy, planned for the near future, will begin at nearby Jenkins-Lueken Orchards, where the distillery has already leased 150 trees and grafted on old Hudson Valley cider apple stock—bitter to the taste when fresh off the tree but complex in character, perfect for transforming into unique nectar in the still. Erenzo says, "It makes good business sense and good neighborly sense to know the people you're doing business with, to be close to their needs as well as your own, and it's good financial sense to source locally."

In their local partnerships, Tuthilltown, Tantillo, and Jenkins-Luek-en are helping to transform the Hudson region's Landscape into one that is ecologically and economically sound, and they are doing so through positive steps that smack of resistance to the dominant, Landscape-destroying paradigm. Tremendous amounts of carbon-producing fuel once wasted on hauling the same corn over a mountain range and back are no longer being used, neighbors are working together toward the same end, sustainable corn seed has displaced GMO corn, and local businesses' proceeds are churning through a small town's economy.

Erenzo makes no bones about it: making money came first for him and supporting local farmers second. But he recognizes and embraces the sustainability that developed as an offshoot of his attempts to fulfill those goals. Along with sustainable sourcing have come other green initiatives. Tuthilltown constructed two reed beds to filter their liquid waste rather than paying by the gallon to have it carted away by a septic company, and when I spoke with Erenzo they were planning to purchase a furnace that would burn their solid (plant) wastes to provide all of their heating needs, "so grain comes in or apples come in," he says, "and nothing but alcohol goes out. . . . These things, sure, they're good for society and they're great for the farmers and for the environment, but they're also extremely cost effective." As sustainability advocates have argued for decades, there's money to be made in eliminating waste.

The grandson of Italian and Irish immigrants, Erenzo was born in Manhattan. His family moved to northern Westchester County in time for Ralph to witness a housing boom overrun the area's farms between fifth and twelfth grade. A Navy veteran without a college degree, he returned to Manhattan and lived there for twenty years, much of it doing television production or running a business constructing and managing climbing gyms.

His dream was to move to the 'Gunks—the famed Shawangunk Ridge, the East's foremost climbing venue—and open a business catering to his Manhattan clientele eager to climb the real thing. The land purchased, Erenzo ran up against well-heeled, anxious neighbors who delayed the project until he threw in the towel. Having run up bills, Erenzo and his partners sold off chunks of the property until it shrunk to 7.8 acres—the land where the old barn that is Tuthilltown's home stands. There is a silver lining, though: "It's a lot easier to make money, and you can make a lot more money, making whiskey than making beds for climbers," Erenzo says with a laugh.

Getting the distillery up and running took two years. Business partner Brian Lee was an engineer with a newly minted MBA who was looking for a hands-on opportunity, and he found it after speaking with Erenzo. The two didn't know each other well, but the match—Erenzo's property and Lee's capital—worked. New York had just passed a law allowing operations such as the one they planned, but numerous regulatory hurdles lay ahead. The following two years were spent snipping that red tape and preparing the granary building that now houses the distillery; it needed everything from Sheetrock to supporting columns to a water well, and Erenzo and Lee did almost all of the work themselves.

Erenzo's stove and an old teakettle were their first stills, though Erenzo and Lee visited other distilleries, attended technical seminars by the makers of their stills, and relied on Internet sites to help them grasp the process of turning apples into vodka and corn into whiskey. Ultimately, the big challenge was with the fungi—getting the fermentation process down—but Lee took the lead in figuring it out.

"There's no manual for this," says Erenzo. "We had to make it up as we went along." Lee and Erenzo, whose title is Master Distiller, eschewed the standard practice of hiring someone else to make their hooch for them. Erenzo explains, "Our mentality was, there are guys back in the woods with no teeth and a kindergarten education and they're making money making alcohol. We should be able to figure this out! Plus, we knew if someone came and did that, they'd be showing us how to make *their* alcohol, not ours, and we wanted to make it our way. We were absolutely convinced we could do it."

Tuthilltown began with apple vodka "because we're in the middle of apple country and we could see that the apple growers were struggling against way-underpriced juice products coming from China, table apples coming from Chile and Peru." Partnering with the region's apple growers would be good for both sides. Next came whiskey. Six months after receiving their license to distill, they finally got the formulas down, and 375 milliliter bottles labeled

HUDSON
New York Corn
WHISKEY

started lining the shelves. It and numerous other libations produced by Tuthilltown have been hits with critics and have won dozens of awards in juried competitions. The drinking public seems to like the stuff, too; the distillery store contributed $250,000 to Gardiner's economy in just its first six months—with no advertising.

In the early days Erenzo loaded up the bottles in his car and carted them to liquor stores, bars, and restaurants, serving as his own salesperson. It was Tuthilltown's story, he says, that got him to the front of the line to give his pitch no matter where he went. His rap? "I'm not a liquor salesman. I made this. It's the first whiskey made in New York since Prohibition. . . . They couldn't believe that we'd pulled it off and that it was good! We surprised everybody, including ourselves."

In the shadow of the steep cliffs of the Shawangunks, a stunning landscape feature, Erenzo is modeling how to reshape a Landscape using good business sense and a concern for community and connection. Those things were misplaced in classical capitalism, the old model in which profit was measured only one way and everyone from suppliers to consumers were means to that end. Tuthilltown Spirits shows a company can pull down profits aplenty—so much so that William Grant & Sons, owner of Glenfiddich, bought the whiskey line and distributes it globally—and still make a difference locally.

People, Planet, Business

That spirit of localism reflects a back to the future movement that will be central to the sustainable economy of tomorrow. Like Erenzo, Ajax Greene was drawn to the corner of Ulster County near the Shawangunk Ridge by the superb rock climbing. Greene was one of the world's top climbers in the 1970s—he made the first single-day ascent of Half Dome in Yosemite Valley—and when it came time to settle down after a peripatetic young adulthood that saw him pioneering routes across the globe, the 'Gunks were where he chose to call home.

By then an experienced—and, by his admission, not always successful—"serial entrepreneur," in 2012 Greene hatched the idea of an organization that would promote local businesses in the Hudson Valley. Involved in BALLE, the Business Alliance for Local Living Economies,[3] from its early days, Greene also envisioned supporting those businesses as they shifted toward sustainability.

With startup funds provided by the Local Economies project, part of the New World Foundation, that kernel of an idea became ReThink

Local, a "nonprofit collaborative of businesses, farmers, artists, and independent workers working to co-create a better Hudson Valley," says the group's board chair, Scott Tillitt. It promotes "a Hudson Valley that is locally rooted, human-scale, vibrant, sustainable," and committed to the triple bottom line, Tillit notes. "It's grounded in sustainability in a very broad sense: not just environmental sustainability, but social sustainability, economic sustainability, spiritual sustainability."

And, following BALLE's lead, a key theme for ReThink is "place matters," Greene says. "Every place you go is unique, so why not have that uniqueness come out?" Why leave home if, on your travels, you eat at the same chain restaurants that you frequent at home? "That's where I think the localism is so beautiful. You come here, and if you're not from here you experience what it's like to be here."

A big part of that here-ness localists embrace is a sense of community. Ironically, though, many of the business owners who might join ReThink, particularly those who embrace its emphasis on sustainability and other shared values, don't know it exists. Mentioning the story of Agnes Devereux, the owner of the Village Tea Room Restaurant in New Paltz where we met, Greene says that "she was doing all these great things, but she had no idea that there was a name for it or a community around it. People are hungry to connect with like-minded folks. . . . There may be lots of people doing cool things, but they don't know there are other people doing cool things, and we're starting to connect them."

Greene's commitment to sustainability began almost organically as a result of his rock climbing. His formative years were heady days for environmentalism, which saw all of its major policy successes coming in the decade following the first Earth Day in 1970. In the summer of 1980 Greene had an epiphany, realizing that "the world was going to hell and I had to do something about it." In time he melded environmental and business sensibilities, the latter particularly important because, Greene says, "I viewed economy as probably one of the most unifying things that human beings have on the planet, so that became my passion: How we can reinvent the economy so it's sustainable on the level of people and planet?"

He first gave it a try with a company called Ecotrek. It manufactured high-quality outdoor apparel and backpacks that were made almost entirely from recycled materials and were themselves recyclable. The *Christian Science Monitor* reported that Ecotrek helped "displaced Berkshire-area factory workers set up worker-owned cooperatives" and that it planned to hire as many as twenty to sew for them.[4]

The company didn't make it, but Greene says he learned a lot about creating a business while free climbing out ahead of the sustainability curve. "That was a challenging time," says Greene, "where now, I would say, everyone is hungering to learn what we were learning back then." Since the mid-1990s he has found himself combining his people-planet outlook with a sense of individuals' need for community and the ethics of sustainable capitalism to the point that his business advising work is exclusively with companies and organizations that emphasize "corporate social responsibility."

That includes supporting the 120 members of ReThink. They and others are on individual and communal trajectories through three sorts of transformation, Greene says. The first is personal, "waking up and saying, 'I want my life to be different,' " including business owners who want their companies to reflect their values. "That sort of authenticity around your values is a key part of business going forward. . . . Independent businesses: they should be talking about who they are and what their values are, because that's how they're going to drive their margins."

The second transformation is rooted in public policy. Greene is working with others to create a New York chapter of the American Sustainable Business Council, a three hundred thousand–member "progressive Chamber of Commerce" that will lobby for socially responsive legislation.

Finally, businesses large and small are assuming leadership roles in sustainability, something Greene knows of from his Ecotrek days and that he continues to encourage. Greene insists companies have no choice but to become socially responsible, comparing our times to those shortly after the fall of the Iron Curtain. He says, "In Nineteen Eighty-Nine when the Wall collapsed, we saw the failure of communism. In my opinion, in Two Thousand Eight with the collapse of Lehman [Brothers, the huge financial services company], we saw the collapse and utter failure of unfettered capitalism. It hasn't died, yet, but it's in its death throes." Unlike the old, the new capitalism will attend to the triple bottom line, will be firmly rooted in community, and will be responsive to consumers' values.

Greene says, "I'm a complete, utter believer: the future of the economy is based in independent, locally owned businesses," adding, "They're going to be what becomes and drives the economy, particularly here in the mid-Hudson Valley." Convinced that we are nearing a "tipping point," Greene says, "I think if we look back ten to thirty years from now, we'll see a massive change having happened over this next period."

In 2013, ReThink commissioned a study to explore just how big that change might be for the mid-Hudson economy. Greene says it indicated that 77 percent of local restaurant dollars and 55 percent of retail dollars recirculate within the mid-Hudson economy, significantly higher rates than nonlocal, nonindependent businesses that send profits straight to the home office. More startling, Greene says, "We estimate that if the mid-Hudson community shifted ten percent of their shopping from nonlocal to local and independent organizations, that would create four hundred seventy-five million new dollars in economic activity" in the area each year.

That kind of money can bring about tremendous change in subregions such as the mid-Hudson. In an era when wealth concentration is greater than ever in America's history, and when there is tremendous political resistance to taxing the wealthy to redistribute income, buying local may become a primary means of promoting equity—and may, as a result, play a vital role in the emergence of new Landscapes.

Spinning the Meter Backward

On its way to cutting costs, Jiminy Peak Mountain Resort found sustainability—and a whole lot of attention. Spreading down a Massachusetts mountain overlooking the headwaters of Kinderhook Creek, a Hudson River tributary that meets the big river fifty-one miles and one state away, Jiminy has become a draw for skiers in the winter and environmentally conscious conference goers much of the rest of the year, not least because of Zephyr, its 1.5 megawatt wind turbine visible from the slopes and from miles around.

There's no escaping the fact that ski resorts and sustainability don't go hand in hand. To begin with, steep mountainsides must be clearcut to create the ski runs and spaces for restaurants, shops, and lodging, wiping out large swaths of habitat in the process. Driving to and from the slopes, skiers pour tons of carbon and other pollutants into the atmosphere. And while there they often rely on energy-intensive snow making and indoor (even outdoor) heating, as well as resource-intensive restaurants, restrooms, lit slopes for nighttime skiing, and more. But as ski resorts go, Jiminy has become a model for moving toward sustainable recreation.

Jim Van Dyke is vice president of environmental sustainability at Jiminy. Fit and in his fifties, Van Dyke's family settled in the Berkshires in 1970 after his father retired following a long career in the Air Force.

Jim began working at Jiminy to pay for his ski habit and his community college education in nearby Pittsfield, and he's been there ever since. Known for taking the lead on the resort's new projects, Van Dyke was at the center of things as the Jiminy ownership began realizing it needed to do something about its energy usage. "Before we started any of these initiatives," Van Dyke says, "Jiminy Peak would use about nine million kilowatt hours a year. That's *a lot* of power. In the wintertime, we would peak at three megawatts of demand between lifts, lights, snowmaking, and buildings. It's mind boggling." Indeed, it is. Calculations differ, but it's safe to say that one megawatt is enough to power the needs of four hundred to nine hundred homes; Jiminy's annual electricity needs were easily the equivalent of five thousand to 7,500.

In the late 1990s, Jiminy's management began looking for ways to trim that demand. The Environmental Team, headed by Van Dyke and including line employees from all over the resort, was already in place, and in short order it identified changes that cut 2.3 megawatts, almost one-third, simply through conservation:

- compact fluorescent lights and fixtures were installed in buildings;
- energy-efficient lighting began to be used on the slopes;
- heat from the snowmaking air compressors was captured, warming four buildings 1,000 hours of the year;
- and improvements were made to the snowmaking process— the largest single user of power at the resort—including better motors on the snow guns and water pumps, allowing them to reduce the time it took to produce a given amount of snow.

Thanks to financial incentives from the local utility, each of the major retrofits paid for itself within two years. It all happened "without a lot of fanfare," Van Dyke says.

Jiminy opened in 1948. With a loyal clientele established over fifty-five years, what was the value in trumpeting all that environmental responsibility? In hindsight, Van Dyke says Jiminy should have turned its conservation efforts into good PR, "but that wasn't the reason to do it. The reason to do it was it made sense. To put that in perspective, we're a business. Our business . . . is not to save the environment. That wasn't one of our mission items at that point." It made sense because it improved the financial bottom line.

Jiminy *exists* to use the environment—not in the abusive way of, say, a strip mine, but few recreational activities manipulate nature like ski resorts. The clearing of trees to create the runs and the rest is only the start. Even in the wet East, snow often has to be made before anyone can play in it, and Jiminy uses 120 million gallons of water a year for snowmaking, plus another 1.6 million for domestic water usage. Wells drilled around the property supply guests' and the food services' water needs, and like the more obvious energy-saving efforts, water conservation helped reduce the resort's electricity bill.

Van Dyke explains, "Whether it's low-flow toilets, which are plumbing standards, or a no-flow waterless urinal that saves forty or fifty thousand gallons of water a year, that's water we don't have to draw"—pump, a considerable energy expenditure—"out of the ground. It's good for the environment. It's good business for us, and it's another line item on the list of environmental things that we do." An on-site secondary treatment facility purifies wastewater and discharges it into the ground.

But at seventy-five times the domestic usage, snowmaking is Jiminy's water—and energy—hog. Before being sent to water guns to make snow, water is pumped from local streams when flows are above a set level and stored in either of two reservoirs. One near the base of the mountain holds six million gallons and feeds the snowmaking equipment along the upper part of the 1,150 feet of vertical rise on the mountain. The other holds twice that and is located near the summit of Potter Mountain, allowing the water that is pumped up to it at night, when electricity rates are lowest, to power the snow guns on the lower third of the slopes on its own—gravity and the resultant pressure are all that's needed to make snow.

In another bid to conserve electricity, both reservoirs are chilled: warmer water from lower in the reservoirs is sprayed over the surface. It cools as it falls back into the reservoir, taking the temperature from the lower forties to about thirty-five degrees. When the near-freezing water is shot from the snow guns, it needs less compressed air to do the job, since the droplets freeze more quickly. Less air pressure equals less energy use.

From waterless urinals to reducing air compressor workloads, by the early 2000s Jiminy had done all it could to conserve short of shutting down. So when electricity rates increased by nearly 50 percent, management knew it needed to find some other way to trim the bill from its remaining seven megawatts of usage. "When you're using that kind of power, that's a lot of money," Van Dyke says. "As with any business, what are you going to do with that? You're going to absorb as much of it as you can, and beyond that you have to pass it on to your customer in one form or another. Is it an increase in lift ticket price? Is it an increase in your room rate? Is it your hamburger that costs fifty cents more?"

Looking at ski industry trends, the folks at Jiminy knew they could not raise prices forever. Skiing is a discretionary activity, and they worried that skiers would go elsewhere or simply quit the sport altogether. National statistics bear out the problem: for decades visits to the slopes have been almost flat, even with the booming popularity of snowboarding. Jiminy's president, Brian Fairbank, charged Van Dyke's Environmental Team with finding a way to save even more.

The team was stuck, in no small part because of Jiminy's commitment to quality. Many of the ideas the group came up with, such as co-generation of electricity, were well outside of the resort's core competencies and would require new employees, thereby adding costs, not lowering them, and compelling the business to extend itself in directions away from what it was committed to doing well: providing a great guest experience.

Then a former employee who was back for a day of fun on the slopes suggested that Van Dyke look into placing a windmill on the breezy back side of the mountain to produce electricity. Van Dyke's response was immediate and unequivocal: "No. Never thought about a wind turbine and probably never will think about a wind turbine." A year later, the ex-employee, by then working for a renewable energy firm in nearby Albany, New York, was back. He convinced Jiminy to pony up $1,000 for a feasibility study. It and another indicated there was enough wind to power two large electricity-producing windmills near the summit.

Jiminy's management began to realize that only a big leap, such as one represented by the purchase of a wind turbine, would save it more money. It would have to invest to save. Invest a lot: $3.9 million when the final tab was in for just one windmill, including various studies, and permitting; the state supported the purchase to the tune of almost $600,000. Over the course of a couple of years, Van Dyke explored the alternatives, initially recommending a one-megawatt turbine but for financial reasons settling on a 1.5-megawatt General Electric model. Plans to bring the windmill on-line in 2006 were delayed, but "Zephyr" began generating electricity on August 1, 2007.

In ways planned and unplanned, the 253-feet-tall giant on the mountain, with its 123-feet-long propellers, changed Jiminy forever. It proved its value the instant it began generating electricity. Because Zephyr is behind the meter, the commercial side of the resort actually uses the windmill's power directly; if you're riding a chairlift and Zephyr is spinning, chances are the electrons powering the lift come from the turbine, not from the grid. (At the time, state regulations dictated that residential needs on the mountain, like those of condominium owners, must be supplied by a utility company.) That arrangement is also crucial because, when demand at Jiminy is low, Zephyr produces excess power that is sent out to the grid. Initially, the resort was paid the wholesale price—about half of the retail value of that electricity. So the primary advantage of Jiminy's investment in Zephyr during the early years was its ability to produce electricity on-site, not selling power on the open market. In other words, once Zephyr was up and running it did "spin the meter backward," as residential solar and windmill installers like to say, but in its first couple of years it only spun half as fast backward as it did going forward.

At sixteen cents per kilowatt hour, Jiminy's price for power when Zephyr was installed, and 6.7 megawatts of annual demand, the turbine had the potential to save the resort a lot of money. Zephyr generates about 4.6 megawatts of power annually. Given the resort's uneven power demands—huge for perhaps four months a year but very little for the other eight—Jiminy only uses half of those 4.6 megawatts (ironically, 2.3 megawatts: the same figure as was saved through conservation), with the rest going out to the grid.

Skeptics dogged the Zephyr project. Early on, it was local residents who were concerned about horror stories associated with wind turbines: ruined views, odd sounds, and diced-up birds were the major ones. Anxious about adverse publicity, Jiminy contracted for studies examining potential habitat loss, animal kills, and damage to Native American archaeological sites in the one-acre area that was disturbed by the wind turbine construction. All came back negative.

The matter of the view, though, was and is a tough one. The huge windmill is visible from Stephentown, New York, clearly out of place among the greenery that paints the mountainside. But as environmentalist Bill McKibben has argued, if we want to enjoy the benefits of electric power, shouldn't we be reminded where it comes from?[5] One or two residents have complained about a low hum, and under the right conditions Van Dyke says the turbine is audible but—to him—not troubling. There were a couple of dead sparrows found in the vicinity of the windmill, literally only two in the first years of operation, likely a regrettable result of Zephyr's spinning blades (the tip speed can approach two hundred mph).

But one critic stands out in Van Dyke's mind. The president of the National Ski Areas Association brought the folks at Jiminy back down to earth, giddy as they were over the tons of free publicity Zephyr attracted from *Time* to CNBC. The NSAA president pointed out that Jiminy had wandered from its own commitment to emphasize their core competency. Van Dyke recalls him asking Fairbank, " 'You're a ski area operator. You're a resort operator. Is this going to drive people to come to your resort?' The phrase he used was, 'Is this going to make the cash register ring?' We didn't know the answer to that." It sounds like a narrow view of things, particularly from a sustainability perspective: If it doesn't contribute *directly* to your business's single bottom line, what good is it? Saving money is all well and good, but would Zephyr *make* Jiminy any?

Turns out, it did. Not a chairlift, not a lodge, not a new mogul run, at first marketing a *wind turbine* just didn't sound sexy to the folks at Jiminy. Soon enough, they realized that Zephyr could be the entrée to Jiminy's rich conservation story: in roughly ten years, it cut half of its dependence on outside electricity, equal parts from conservation and from the three-armed spinning thing that quietly (at least from the slopes) goes about its business while customers cavort in its shadow.

It was a story Jiminy had never told: a two-decades'-old green team, all those retrofits in the lodges and on the slopes, and now Zephyr. Van Dyke finally realized, "The wind turbine: that may be why people come to the resort or why news agencies come to the resort, but we've got a lot of stuff to talk about besides that. Every single one of those [conservation efforts] was successful, some more than others, and they made sense from both a business standpoint, which was the first reason we did it, and then from a green standpoint, which is a benefit of doing the first one."

The four years following the 2007 startup of Zephyr were each record breakers for Jiminy. "That doesn't happen," says Van Dyke. "In the ski business you get one good year out of seven: that is the average." Factors including good skiing weather played a role in Jiminy's great run post-Zephyr, but the wind turbine "is a very large part of it. It's a very large part of it," Van Dyke insists.

In the winter, guests can get as close as one thousand feet from the turbine, and in the summer Jiminy hosts tours that include a gondola ride up the mountain, an alpine slide ride down, and a visit to Zephyr in between—all for nine dollars. They've yet to offer one of the no-reservations-required tours where no one showed up. "Who would've thought?" Van Dyke asks incredulously.

But from a business standpoint, as that NSAA president insisted, what really matters is that the world is beating a path to Jiminy, and it is. Corporate retreats and small conferences select the resort because they want to talk about "green things," seeing the great spinning trillium up the mountain as inspiration. "People started coming because of this," says Van Dyke. Nearly a quarter of the skiers and other guests say they visit Jiminy at least in part because of its green initiatives. Standing out in a group not known for its environmental virtues, Jiminy demonstrates the potential of medium-sized businesses (it was sold for $27 million in 2009, then leased back to a group including Fairbank) to discover their importance in Landscape creation.

There were disappointments after Jiminy made its big investment in wind energy. For one, Zephyr has yet to achieve the full expected annual output of 4.6 megawatts. Making things worse, in the first years after it went on line in 2007 the wholesale price of electricity tumbled from eight cents per kilowatt hour to two cents, threatening to lengthen the payback period from the 7.5 years Jiminy's management had planned on. However, in 2008 Massachusetts enacted a Green Communities law to promote clean energy. It allows the resort to receive credit from its utility for the full *retail* value of the power produced by the turbine that is sent out to the grid, not the half-price wholesale rate of its first couple of years. The effect is that today Jiminy only pays an electric bill three months out of the year. As a result, it recouped its investment in Zephyr months ahead of schedule.

The lessons Jiminy has learned from its hike along the sustainability path are substantial, Van Dyke says. Most importantly, there is no reason for just any business to drop nearly $4 million on a wind turbine to make a dent in its energy usage. "Looking at the conservation work we did [before installing Zephyr]," which conserved half as much energy as the wind turbine produces, "we didn't spend four million dollars on that work. Whether it's your home, your school, your business, your city hall, whatever: put solar panels on the roof. Use your compact fluorescents. Yeah, they're expensive, but they *really do work*. You will be amazed at how much energy you will save if you do that." It's a lesson in picking the low-hanging fruit first.

Many assume that, because of conservation's potential to add to the financial bottom line over time, businesses already must be doing all they can to conserve. The fact is, many do not. A 2009 U.S. Department of Energy review of federal and state studies indicated that merely switching to more energy-efficient lighting—one of the first things Jiminy did— could reduce energy use between 3 and 12 percent in existing commercial buildings; implementing a full slate of changes, such as replacing old heating and air conditioning units with more efficient ones, could save 10 to 20 percent, and adding lighting and other sensors could double those savings.[6] The potential is even greater in small commercial buildings, where a group headed by the National Trust for Historic Preservation estimates that "[c]ost effective energy savings of more than 45% are possible," with a range of between 27 and 59 percent depending on variables like climate zone location and type of commercial activity.[7] Even Jiminy, with its unusual energy demands, approached those figures.

As news of Zephyr's wind-driven energy savings spread, other ski resort operators, and small business people having nothing to do with the industry, began phoning Van Dyke to ask for advice. Sustainability opened up new business possibilities outside of Jiminy's core competencies, and EOS Ventures was born. A renewable energy company specializing in comparatively small-scale projects—such as the ten-turbine windmill array on the ridgeline across the road from Jiminy—in its first three years EOS installed five megawatts of solar electricity-generating photovoltaic panels and six megawatts of wind (Zephyr included). EOS has now designed and built renewable energy projects from Maine to Pennsylvania.

Like none of the other businesses profiled in this chapter, Jiminy came to sustainability through the back door. As Van Dyke freely admits, economic profit drove all that Jiminy did. Yet it became a poster child for energy and water conservation, and it proved to be a good community citizen as well, taking pains to consult with two towns about its wind turbine plans and literally answering every question that residents asked of it. The key lesson is that Landscape change does not have to be guided solely by those deeply committed to sustainability at the outset. Many paths lead to sustainability.

Stumbling to Sustainability

While several observations about the future of the Hudson region's Landscape stand out from these stories, perhaps none is more noteworthy than that last one—one drawn from the experiences of both Tuthilltown Spirits and Jiminy that gains prominence thanks to its contrast with Ecovative: sustainability does not have to come first for a business to accomplish it. Green businesses like Ecovative that put triple-bottom-line sustainability front and center from the start are less important than *greening* business: taking seriously the hard work of reorienting a business toward sustainability, even if that greening is foremost about profit. Most businesses aren't green; the quicker they can get to sustainability, the better for all of us.

Neither Tuthilltown nor Jiminy set out to embrace sustainability. Ralph Erenzo and Jim Van Dyke each said more than once that their respective companies were there to make a buck first. Yet they each found that incorporating local ingredients, conservation, or huge investments in renewable energy could *immediately* benefit the company. Each profited enormously from sustainability. As René VanSchaack puts it, "With rare exceptions, the economics are positive on most anything you can think of environmental." Relating a conversation with a developer who griped that conservation set-asides undermined the affordability of his townhomes, VanSchaack recalls saying,

> Wait a minute, here. So what are you saying to these people? Are you marketing to them, "Come up here and buy my weekend townhouse in the middle of blacktop jungle?" No. If you've got smart salespeople, they're taking that back road in, and those people are looking around seeing farm fields. They're coming up over that ridge and dropping back down again and they're going, "Wow, this is where my little townhouse is going to be. Cool!" You're selling this [place]. This has got value to you.

Green begets green, but many business owners don't grasp that point.

Environmental activist Manna Jo Greene sees the same sort of lack of vision in many entrepreneurs. Speaking of her interactions with economic development and tourism advocates, she says,

> A development project is proposed, and you just support it because it's going to create jobs and more cash flow. Okay. But what if you make it the greenest project it can be? Think about the multiplier effect! People come to see this amazing project in, say, Kingston: ninety percent of the energy is generated on-site and the buildings are super-insulated and they use nontoxic materials that are locally sourced and so forth. They're going to go, "Wow, did you see that?" The next time they come, they're going to bring their friends or their family.

Word spreads and Landscapes change. In a sense VanSchaack and Greene are noting old news, but it bears repeating because so many businesses have yet to get the message: in their haste to land the quick sale, too often growth advocates sacrifice what's good for the local economy over the long term (to say nothing of what's good for people and the planet).

The assumption is that firms have to wait for sustainability initiatives to repay themselves: those lightbulbs/new air conditioning units/solar panels take *years* to pay off, the story goes. Thing is, sustainability pays immediately *and* in the long term. The instant Zephyr came on line, Jiminy Peak stopped paying its utility for a large part of its electricity; the full payback period might have been the hoped-for ninety months (it proved to be less), but the resort began profiting from its investment on August 1, 2007. Ralph Erenzo and his nearly-within-sight neighbors down the road at Tantillo's Farm each profited the moment the first ton of corn came off of that flatbed truck at the distillery.

Landscapes won't change if we wait for every business to be replaced by one founded on sustainability principles. Ecovative was created as a triple-bottom-line corporation, but that ideal type remains rare. Ajax Greene understands as much as he recruits skeptical small business owners, and he takes it upon himself to point out the benefits of going green.

This chapter also helps us to understand that sustainable companies benefit Landscapes in a host of ways—not "the Landscape" but *Landscapes*. Those businesses that are intimately tied to a place (an apt example is Pleasant Valley Farm from chapter 3) do help re-create the relationship between people and a given place first and foremost. But Paul and Sandy Arnold's commitment to sustainable agriculture is such that they host annual gatherings where dozens of others in their family-farming network come together to learn from them, master farmers and businesspeople that they are. Few of their guests share their Landscape, but many of them share their vision. What benefits one Landscape in a spatially immediate sense benefits others elsewhere.

Likewise, when Jiminy Peak produces its own electricity, the ramifications are almost certainly greater outside of the Hudson River region than in it. Somewhere, one of its utility provider's power plants is burning a lot less coal or fracked natural gas, or perhaps it is able to send more hydropower to others thanks to Jiminy. As a result, an asthmatic child breathes more easily, a rural water well is a bit less likely to be polluted.

Looking back on my conversations with sustainability advocates, one of the things that most impressed me was how certain they were that the economy must change. Both production and consumerism are at fault. Production occurs at the level of the firm and is deeply embedded in the growth-oriented logic of capitalism. Most consumption is done by individuals and families (not other firms or governmental entities) and responds to the allure of the commodities produced by corporations: the new smart phone, automobile, swimming pool, granite countertop, treadmill, skirt, or shirt. So long as we tolerate production without higher principle and consumption without conscience, Landscape re-creation is not possible.

Jeff Golden, co-founder of the Common Fire communes, observes,

> One of the places that I feel like our society, and perhaps our species, has gotten most off-track is, it's easier sometimes to focus on quantifiables like dollars, so we've lost track of money being a means to an end, something that is to achieve something else. But it has become an end in itself, and so we start feeding ourselves on the concept of more, more, more and lose sight of the quality. In the loss of the quality . . . you lose track of the metric of what does sustainability even mean.

Such an environmentally and economically unjust society, argues Golden with considerable understatement, "is not exactly what we want to be sustaining." Similarly, David Kooris, who, as vice president of Regional Plan, regularly worked with local and state officials in the greater New York metro area, says,

> As long as we point to those same indicators, whether it's GDP or the stock market, the common indicators of success—those indicators that don't incorporate long-term environmental impacts or social health into the equation—we're constantly going to be steered down the wrong path. That's what's really fundamental: coming to consensus as a society that those metrics that we use to measure our progress towards something better. If they don't include long-term impacts, we're constantly going to be running circles around this conversation.

"Off track" or "down the wrong path:" either way, Landscapes profoundly influenced by profit-maximizing corporations do not operate as they must if planet-people-profits are to work together toward the same ends. Is Landscape re-creation a subject that the wealthiest individuals, the corporations they oversee, and the politicians who possess the power to steer localities, regions, states, and the nation in more sustainable directions want to discuss?

Melissa Everett thinks it is. Everett's Sustainable Hudson Valley is a nonprofit that serves as a catalyst for for-profit innovation in the Valley. It's her view that best business practices are increasingly environmentally responsible. "Environmental protection has been a game of stop development, and land development has been a game of outwit the environmentalists," she observes. "The notion of the working landscape and natural resource–based industries and serious attention to zero waste production, zero environmental impact production are just being understood. There needs to be a way that dynamic development and vigorous environmental restoration can go hand in hand."

Similarly, Auden Schendler writes that "business is both the cause and the victim of environmental decline. . . . Climate change threatens every business on the planet, and business is the primary cause of it. . . . [I]f business is in large part the cause of the planet's problems, then it can also be the solution."[8] Some insist that such "second wave" outlooks are establishing themselves in the Hudson region. Amidst the epic 2011 debt ceiling fight in Congress, Rep. Paul Tonko, whose district includes Albany and environs, wrote, "The federal government would do well to use the Capital Region as a template to putting our country back to work, especially in the ever-growing green technology and clean energy sectors."[9]

Tonko noted a Brookings Institution report that found the Albany-Schenectady-Troy metropolitan area was home to "a higher concentration of clean jobs than any other major metro area in the country," making it "a surprise leader in the clean economy" with one in every fifteen jobs falling under the clean economy rubric, not least because of General Electric—Jiminy Peak's Zephyr was designed by GE, and some of its components manufactured in the Capital Region.[10] The report defined *clean economy* as "economic activity . . . that produces goods and services with an environmental benefit or adds value to such products using skills or technologies that are uniquely applied to those products."[11] In 2010 those goods and services were valued at more than $1.2 billion in the Capital Region, largely thanks to those GE jobs.

Yet looming in the background of Tonko's enthusiasm and Brookings's cheerleading is the problem of greenwashing: putting an environmentally friendly face on business as usual. GE was a founding corporation on the Dow Industrial Average in 1896, and no corporation has been listed on the Dow longer. It stands as a paragon of growth. As Gus Speth puts it, "In the recent past, and in the present, the economic growth actually experienced has been and remains the principle source of our environmental problems."[12] GE is doing good things for the planet, but to what end? If it made less profit—focused less on growth—how much more would it do? How might it become a leader in promoting equity?

One measure of that new sustainability sensibility is that the classic measure of economic growth at the national level, Gross Domestic Product, is under assault from economists. Writing in *Nature*, one of the foremost scholarly publications in any discipline, Robert Costanza and colleagues observed, "The emphasis on GDP in developed countries now fuels social and environmental instability. It also blinds developing countries to possibilities for more-sustainable models of development."[13] They note that cleanup costs following environmental disasters such as oil spills and those linked to climate change, such as megastorms, actually *increase* GDP. Despoiled Landscapes are good things.

In old capitalism's perverse calculus, such twisted thinking makes perfect sense. But it doesn't if one takes seriously the planet's future or humanity's . . . or even capitalism's. Costanza's group notes numerous alternatives to GDP, including the Genuine Progress Indicator, which has been adopted by the State of Vermont. Such metrics typically include dozens of variables but are all aimed at measuring how effectively a jurisdiction tends to the triple bottom line, not old capitalism's anachronistic single one.

The most widely read work advocating a different tack is *Natural Capitalism*. There, entrepreneur Paul Hawken and long-time sustainable energy advocates Amory and Hunter Lovins argue, "Capitalism, as practiced, is a financially profitable, nonsustainable aberration in human development."[14] As Ajax Greene puts it, "I haven't had anyone explain to me how you have endless growth in a closed-loop system like planet earth. . . . We're talking about running out of *everything*." Holding up a cell phone, he asks, "How can I make that if I can't get the rare earth elements that go in it because we ran out? There is going to be a complete reinvention of the economy." And as economies go, so go Landscapes.

Chapter 8

A Landscape to Fight For

"There's probably no part of the country that's more organized than the Hudson River Valley," says long time environmental advocate John Mylod, adding, "There are more organizations—local, state, federal, non-profit—that all operate in the valley here, trying to move their messages and their missions to make for a better community. Once you decide you want to put a power plant or some gigantic factory in the backyard, it triggers all kind of responses that are remarkable."

It does indeed. It was here that the environmental movement—not environmentalism, an ideology, but an actual grassroots movement—was reborn in the 1960s. Fifty years later, veterans of that fight such as Mylod and two generations of younger activists stand on guard for the places they love, from the Hudson's headwaters all the way to The Battery on the southern tip of Manhattan.

In a word association game, "environmentalism" is frequently the first response to the "sustainability" prompt. The connection is apt, of course. What, after all, in casual parlance is to be sustained if not the environment? Who will do the sustaining or be advocates for it? Environmentalists.

Yet just as business often has ignored people and the planet in pursuit of profit, so, too, have environmental organizations paid little attention to reforming economy and promoting equity. But not in the Hudson region. Here, as elsewhere, environmentalists have been the foes of business, but in the region they also have created strong connections with the for-profit world and are leading advocates for equity, particularly through environmental justice, as the stories below demonstrate.

In this chapter, we encounter groups and organizations conscientiously striving to create a new Hudson region Landscape, each using some combination of grassroots involvement, traditional organization, and science. There are small bands of activists pursuing citizen science—sometimes to the dismay of government agencies—as well as quiet land trusts that preserve key ecosystems by creating preserves out of them. There is also a paradoxical environmental group that exists with one foot in boardrooms and another on the deck of its activist-minded Dutch sloop, another that is the region's granddaddy of them all, and yet another that fights pollution with vigilance, data, and the threat of determined courtroom action.

Battling for the Battenkill

Doug Reed projects what most of us would expect from a solitary woodworker plying his trade. A bit quiet, straightforward without being rude, driven to see a task through: that's Reed, a founding member of the Battenkill Conservancy.[1]

"Kill" is Dutch for stream or creek, and kills dot the Hudson region: Fishkill, Wallkill, Moordener Kill, Roeliff Jansen Kill, and more. The Battenkill, rising in Vermont and nearly sixty miles long, is a bit more than a creek, large enough to boat in well upstream from its outlet at the Hudson. The Battenkill is also beloved of fly fishers, canoeists, and others who want nothing more than lively sport or a quiet day on the water.

Another group wants more than anything to know that the Battenkill is there for its own sake, a nurturing, thriving ecosystem. That's where Reed comes in. He was working in his furniture making shop on Route 29 in East Greenwich one day when someone walked in and said, "You should come to a meeting. We're starting a Battenkill Conservancy." The wry Reed "immediately thought, 'I don't want any part of this. They're going to ask me to do something!' I had no idea what a 'conservancy' does, but it probably means volunteering a lot of time." Yet, there in the Greenwich Library no one asked anyone to do anything. One speaker described a water watch group he had founded in North Carolina, and it prompted Reed to stroll down to the Battenkill behind his shop one day not long after. He looked closely at the water, noticing all the life there that he'd never seen before. "I discovered, sure enough, there's a lot of things going on," Reed recalls. "All I used the river for was swimming every now and then."

He was hooked. That was 1990, and ever since his niche with the Conservancy has been stream monitoring. By examining the aquatic insects in the streambed repeatedly over weeks, months, and years, "you can tell an awful lot about water quality," says Reed. "I thought, 'That's really interesting! Look at these insects!' They were fascinating under a microscope. You've never seen anything like them. They exist all around the world. Many are the same species, though there's *seven hundred* varieties of caddis flies and May flies and stone flies. They exist right here."

It wasn't long before he realized he couldn't do the work on his own. One person passed him to another, and soon Reed was in touch with a biology teacher from up the 'kill in Arlington, Vermont, who encouraged him to contact River Watch Network in Montpelier. Reed arranged for a River Watch workshop, and forty people from across the Albany region attended, eager to investigate and advocate for the streams out their back doors. Over the next several years, River Watch worked with Reed not only to develop stream monitoring on the Battenkill but to create "a much larger, whole Hudson River watershed volunteer stream monitoring program," he says. From recruiting and retaining volunteers to the actual monitoring to writing grants and creating networks, River Watch showed Reed the ropes, then he took it from there.[2]

In the early years, high schools along the length of the Battenkill from its Vermont headwaters to its confluence with the Hudson undertook the monitoring. Plied with cider doughnuts, biology classes aided by Reed or another River Watch expert would all venture out on the same day to take the same measurements and samples at designated locations along the kill. More recently the model has spread throughout the region, supported along the 150-mile tidal section of the Hudson (well south of the Battenkill) by the state Department of Environmental Conservation's (DEC) Estuary Program. Each October on "Snapshot Day" more than three thousand students obtain data on sixty or more sites, sending their results to a central repository where it is compiled for use by those students and by college and agency researchers.[3]

The Conservancy's stream monitoring program falls under the general label of "citizen science," and not everyone thinks it's a good idea. The DEC, for example, long pooh-poohed citizen scientists. Reed and others responded by asking Cornell University to vet their methods. The key to producing legitimate science, Cornell said, was documenting the group's methods, and that's how Reed trains his monitors. The benefits, he insists, are clear: "It's useful to have many more eyes on the water than just what the state can do because right now they can't do anything" due to years of budget cuts. "And their record is pretty poor of protecting rivers *before* they get polluted. God knows, it's much harder to clean them up after they are polluted"—witness the Hudson PCB cleanup.

River Watch groups don't need much money to get started or to keep going. Reed recalls receiving a state grant for $5,000 early on that he thought was an immense windfall; their largest grant ever was $92,000. Reed oversees coordinators from the Hudson headwaters south all the way to Westchester and Rockland counties, the New York City suburbs. With no staff other than Reed, 80 to 85 percent of the funding, the majority of which comes from state grants, goes to equipment and consultants, although he also often manages to rope in established natural scientists to aid the groups' work at no cost.

Reed and others collaborated with two experienced River Watch staff members to produce a "Guidance Document,"[4] a 138-page how-to manual for stream monitoring that is so user-friendly yet detailed that it "has really brought in a lot of people without having to have a tremendous amount of training sessions," says Reed. He conducts workshops a couple of times each year, estimating that since he started Hudson Basin River Watch in 1990 hundreds of teachers and thousands of their students have attended the sessions, where they learn about essential stream-related biology and geology topics, how to test water chemistry, and more.

Behind citizen science is the imperative to nurture Landscapes, infusing them with meaning through caring enough about them to give them regular checkups. Reed says, "We've got to start somewhere, teaching kids—citizens—to care and understand why water quality is so important. So we started with the schools. We gathered them all together one year at the State Museum (in Albany) before a panel of experts—EPA and New York State agency people. They were totally impressed" by every aspect of the program, Reed says: the rigor, the care, the scope, even the quality of the data.

Fickle state agencies eventually shifted their emphasis from school-based research to adult citizens groups, and most in the network of local stream monitoring organizations had to follow the money or end their efforts altogether. The Conservancy managed to keep its school program alive through its own funding, and school districts up into the Adirondacks still fund students' stream research. One high school teacher in the nearby Mohawk River watershed actually begins work with students when they are in middle school, and eventually they become "expert taxonomists," Reed says, not to mention polished public speakers. "They find pollution. They're taught how to present these findings at town meetings not as shrill whistleblowers but just as concerned citizens. Because they're kids and they speak, with practice, very articulately about these issues, the town boards and planning commissions are just blown away. They'll sit up and listen to a kid." Along the way those children learn advanced science and how to handle themselves when they're put on the spot in challenging public settings.

Stream monitoring is environmental direct action: science-based citizen advocacy, protest by knowledge creation—a form of bearing witness. The results are shared publicly, including with reluctant regulators whose notion of science does not include volunteers, however carefully trained, and whose agencies do not have the funds or the bodies to undertake precisely that science. So the work can be thankless.

"You're not paid well," says Reed a bit glumly. "There's not instant gratification. It takes decades to see a change. If you find someone who's positive and isn't just running down the agency or running down the system or just constantly negative, it's just like a breath of fresh air. So I kind of feel like a cheerleader. I don't feel positive and optimistic all the time." Then, brightening, he adds, "But just having people be positive to me about what I'm doing, I realize that's the way it works. That's the way you really get things done." Whether it's getting the work done, presenting the results, or lifting one another's spirits, tomorrow's Landscapes will emerge from today's relationships.

An effort to cement the relationships between stream-focused groups is seen in the Hudson River Watershed Alliance, on whose board I sat with Doug for several years. The Watershed Alliance is a clearinghouse for information, a conduit for science-oriented and more traditional advocacy groups alike to communicate about issues vital to the region's rivers and streams.

One of the supposed hallmarks of science is that it is open to evaluation by all. In practice, that dictum usually means that science's ostensible democracy is available to those who know the methods, theories, software programs, literature, and so on; to the rest of us it's a black box, a closed world.[5] Yet Reed and his volunteers crack open the shell that college professors, industry scientists, and government regulators have created for *their* science, forcing transparency where it ostensibly is found as a matter of course and empowering people young and old to speak with confidence about the waters around them. Whether it is school groups or adults conducting research and acting on behalf of local waterways, Landscape advocates are carving out a place for civil society and democracy through sampling and analysis.

A Million Little Things

On January 27, 2014, the Hudson region lost its most visionary sustainability advocate, Pete Seeger. A folk musician who stood up to the House Un-American Activities Committee in the 1950s, marched arm in arm with Dr. Martin Luther King in the 1960s, penned songs such as "If I Had a Hammer" and "Where Have All the Flowers Gone?" and who stirred the region's environmental soul in the 1970s by bringing the people to the Hudson River, Seeger was known to all as "Pete." He literally launched one of the most vibrant regional environmental organizations anywhere in the country, setting sail aboard a replica Dutch sloop to encourage citizens from the Hudson headwaters to Manhattan to clean up their river, preserve their land, and embrace their neighbors.

The group that fundraised for the sloop called itself Hudson River Sloop Restoration, Inc., and named the sloop *Clearwater*. The *Clearwater* was christened using Hudson River water on May 18, 1969, in South Bristol, Maine, where it was constructed thanks to $181,933 in donations, many of which, Manna Jo Greene says, came from schoolchildren pitching in nickels, dimes, and quarters when Pete's banjo was passed during fundraising concerts.[6] On August 1, the "sleek ship," impressive at 76 feet long with a 106-foot mast and more than 4,300 square feet of sail, arrived in its home waters after stopping for twenty-five fundraising concerts on its way from South Bristol, "her green hull cleanly slicing through the fetid waters of New York harbor," reported the *New York Times*.[7] The paper quoted New York mayor John Lindsay as vapidly pronouncing, "We need this kind of thing. . . . We're very much in favor of clear water."[8] (Lindsay was actually serious about sustainability, creating the research group that is today's GrowNYC, profiled in chapter 3.)

While the harbor has yet to be restored to pre–European contact quality, in no small part thanks to Pete's work it and thousands of other American waterways have been protected over the last forty years. The organization created to build *Clearwater* today goes by Hudson River Sloop Clearwater, Inc., but most know it by the same name as the sloop. Important as the boat is to Clearwater's efforts, the sloop is only one side of what it is all about.

Manna Jo Greene knew Pete well, having served since 2003 as Clearwater's Environmental Director. Over the intervening years she has played a role in nearly all of the region's major environmental struggles, most notably over the Hudson River PCB issue and the relicensing of Indian Point Nuclear Power Plant, which looms just down river from Clearwater's headquarters in Beacon.

Greene says Pete's vision has set Clearwater's course. "Forty years ago we were living in an environment that was foully polluted," she observes, "our social structure was contentious and dysfunctional. Pete had a vision of a clean Hudson River and a world that works for everyone, where people lived in harmony with each other and with the environment. . . . He had the creativity and the genius to think, 'If I build a boat and it's a beautiful boat and it captures people's attention, we sail up and down the river, that's going to draw people to the river. And once he got them there, he used the power of song to inspire them."

Grassroots social movements had always employed song. Labor, feminist, civil rights: in each movement music played a central role in educating, encouraging, and emboldening activists to become activists. But environmentalists were lyrically mute. The behemoths, including today's major environmental organizations such as the Sierra Club and National Wildlife Federation, don't sing. Similarly, the AFL-CIO doesn't sing, nor does the National Organization for Women or the NAACP. In fact, large *organizations* rarely resemble grassroots *groups* along many important dimensions, including culture, yet it is at the grass roots where the impetus for change so vital to a social movement occurs: at the level of real people and their real problems.[9] That is where Pete and the other musicians who sailed with him up and down the Hudson felt Clearwater needed to be found. If they could get the people singing and down to the water, the river might "once again run clear," as Pete sang.[10]

Over time, Clearwater created a niche for itself between the extremes of grassroots-only and interest group–only activity, with the majority of its time and effort spent on the former. Greene, whose activism goes back to the civil rights movement and who was elected to the Ulster County Legislature in 2013 (late in the campaign, Pete performed at a benefit concert), says, "Outreach, grassroots organizing: that's Clearwater's forté—community organizing—and we do it at the grassroots level. We also, of course, work with elected officials, municipalities, and other organizations. But going into a community, listening to people's concerns, and helping them address what impacts them is really central.

"You know, Pete said that making the world a better place is not going to come from a few big things. It's going to come from a million little things. I think that underlies everything that we do."

An example of Clearwater's grassroots-level efforts is its Green Cities initiative, found in five river towns. Key to Green Cities and most other Clearwater projects is that they are "community-led," Greene insists. "We're there to facilitate and provide support. We're not there to tell the community what their most important priorities are." The results span the gamut. In the struggling city of Newburgh, for example, a fitness trail designed by community members and lined with trees planted as part of the state's "Trees for Tribs" program will run along Quassaick Creek to a small, largely ignored lake, encouraging residents to experience a place many overlooked and to appreciate it as "a jewel in the middle of their community to be protected," Green says.

Clearwater promotes grassroots involvement in a host of other ways. In Peekskill, Beacon, Poughkeepsie, and Kingston a climate justice project first aided residents in identifying pollution sources and populations that were experiencing environmental injustices, then in uncovering points vulnerable to rising sea levels. The cities are subject not only to higher Hudson River tides created by climate change but are likely to be affected by tidal surges caused by more frequent hurricanes as well.

In December 2011, Clearwater hosted a meeting of representatives from the towns' respective Climate Justice Councils, which were instrumental in the localities' climate justice investigations. The result is likely to be a strengthened, more resilient grassroots that is less apt to become the path of least resistance when faced with external challenges, because each community now understands it is not alone.

Additional benefits from Clearwater-supported projects spread in multiple directions. For instance, the Green Jobs initiative—part of its Green Cities work—not only helps train young people from river cities for employment in fields related to energy efficiency and "green infrastructure," it has the added benefit of cooling communities. Echoing themes that ecologist Gary Kleppel mentioned in chapter 2, Greene says that the tree planting undertaken by Green Jobs participants affects "micro climates. You allow these plants that weren't previously there to serve an ecosystem function and to generate more oxygen and improve the air that people are breathing."

Many of the participants are high school dropouts; the government grant–funded projects that they are working on pay for classes to prepare them for their GED exam, and the skills they acquire on the job get them ready for sustainability-oriented careers. Greene says, "In every one of those projects we are actively involving inner-city youth and making sure there are stipends to pay them, so they not only are thinking of it as an educational opportunity but as a job with a job's responsibilities—we're focusing on career opportunities for them."

With their grassroots emphases, Green Cities and Green Jobs make Clearwater sound much like Sustainable South Bronx, profiled in chapter 5. In some of its other core issues, however, at first blush Clearwater seems little different than its bulky environmental interest group cousins. For example, for decades it has fought to close Indian Point Nuclear Power Plant and advocated dredging the Hudson to remedy the worst of the river's PCB contamination. Plenty of other environmental organizations did the same.

But even here we see what distinguishes Clearwater. It practiced consciousness raising in Indian Point's backyard when it worked with the Peekskill community to develop an environmental justice inventory. And although the question of whether or not to dredge the Hudson was a contentious one, Clearwater did its best to nurture community ties rather than enter the fray as the all-knowing environmental organization from downriver. "During that campaign," says Greene, "there was a very adversarial relationship between the people in the mid-Hudson area, where a lot of the environmental groups were located, and the local people in Fort Edward, Hudson Falls, and the upper Hudson where the dredging would take place."

The upper-Hudson folks argued to let sleeping sediment lie; dredging, they said, would only stir up the contaminants, in the short term sending the toxic PCBs into the water column and potentially contaminating drinking water supplies, while over time dredging's benefits would be no greater than allowing the worst of the poisons to continue to be covered by fresh layers of silt flushed down the river. Environmental organizations, Clearwater and Scenic Hudson included, insisted that if not dredged the PCBs would be dispersed more widely and would continue to make their way into the food chain as currents, propeller-driven boats, and animals that scavenge on the river bottom stir up or consume the contaminants. Hudson River fish, long off-limits for human consumption, might never again be edible, which was not only a sad commentary on the ecological side of Landscape, it had important ramifications for the emerging Hudson Landscape's equity emphasis, disproportionately affecting poor families dependent on the inexpensive food and recreation sources that the Hudson once provided.

Reflecting on years of tense public hearings, Greene says, "We were careful to listen to the concerns of the upriver community and to support them as much as possible. Over a period of about five years, from Two Thousand Two, when the (final decision to dredge) was issued, we gained the trust of the people in the upriver communities, and that relationship shifted one hundred eighty degrees. It became a relationship of collaboration instead of confrontation. That, to me, is a huge success for the river, for the communities, and for the relationships.

"I think now there is a much more unified Hudson River consciousness."

Such a notion must be heartening to John Mylod, the former Clearwater executive director and a licensed commercial fisher since the 1970s. As he considers the world today's Clearwater faces, Mylod notes, "It's all very different. It's all still very important, however. No matter how much we think things have improved—well, you can sit back for a minute—you really can't because the issues may be slightly different but they are still constant, and you really have to try to do the right thing, whatever that is."

Another environmental activist once told me, "Out of the confrontation comes the illumination." Perhaps the struggles over contentious issues such as dredging will lead to a new, unified Landscape understanding, which Greene insists is emergent. Many of the ingredients are there. An influential, grass roots–focused environmental group like Clearwater understands its opponents and sees them as human beings, not as an opposition to vilify. It listens and looks for ways to build bridges and mend fences. And it recognizes that so many in the region, like those upper-Hudson residents who dearly love the river, see in this place something special. "I've traveled the country," says Greene, "and when I come home to the Hudson Valley, I take a sigh of relief because I see great potential here for a transformation—a transformation that can be replicated in other places." The transformation in this region is underway, and compelling it will be a new, transformed meaning emerging from conflicts such as those over the PCBs.

"You Guys Gonna Do Something about This?"

As a first-year student at Vassar College in the mid-1970s, Karin Limburg landed a summer job working for Clearwater. She was hired as a researcher for People's Pipewatch, a Clearwater creation funded by proceeds from one of Pete's concerts. Limburg cruised the Hudson with an out-of-work roofer named John Cronin, checking the discharge pipes from factories and other polluting sites to ensure that the provisions of the new Clean Water Act, passed by Congress in 1972, were being adhered to.

Quite often, Limburg and Cronin found, the filth polluters were dumping into the river was not reflected in their permits. "A few of them were grossly polluting," Limburg recalls. "It was a fantastic experience for a college kid to go through, especially in those days when pollution was so, so visible." She and Cronin were particularly careful to follow prescribed methods for collecting the samples, since attorney Tom Whyatt, whose official title was The Riverkeeper, wanted to build court cases against those who were dumping.

In time, Limburg and Cronin took newspaper reporters and officials from the newly created Environmental Protection Agency out on the water to share their shocking findings, prompting the *New York Times* to report that Limburg and Cronin identified fifty-seven illegal discharges during their summer of research.[11] "When we started to document it," Limburg says, "we started to realize that some of these companies were really, really seriously violating their permits."

They arrived at those conclusions with the assistance of high school teacher Richard Knable, who established an aptly acronymed, state-certified laboratory, SEWER—Student Educational Workshop in Environmental Research—run, as the name implies, with the help of his students. Their work resulted in New York's first successful prosecution under the Clean Water Act.[12]

Three decades later, a group known as Riverkeeper is still doing that work, pursuing a mixture of activism, science, and litigation that place it in a unique position among the region's environmental organizations.[13] It began in 1965 as the Hudson River Fishermen's Association (HRFA), when *Sports Illustrated* writer and avid angler Robert Boyle organized a group of river lovers who recognized that "the river was so badly polluted that the fisheries were in jeopardy," says Alex Matthiessen, who was Riverkeeper (executive director) when I spoke with him but has since moved on.

Like Limburg and Cronin, Boyle and others witnessed what was happening to the river *from the river*. Trolling about, they saw and smelled the pollution and grew enraged at its effects: ducks that drowned when their feathers became soaked in oil, inedible fish and crabs, and long stretches of the Hudson incapable of supporting life. Matthiessen says, "This was before the modern environmental movement. There wasn't a Clean Water Act. There wasn't a National Environmental Policy Act. They didn't know what to do."

They toyed with a few ideas, the first reminiscent of the most extreme of the radical environmentalists who followed two decades later. Wondering "how could they physically stop the polluters from despoiling their beloved Hudson River," says Matthiessen, HRFA members considered dynamiting a cooling water intake at the Indian Point Nuclear Power

Plant or similarly destroying the Penn Central Railroad's discharge pipe, which poured waste oil directly into the river. "These guys were very angry, and there really weren't a lot of options for them at that time," Matthiessen says.

Ultimately, they choose a less destructive, more creative path. After repeated attempts to prod the U.S. Army Corps of Engineers, which then had jurisdiction over water quality in New York harbor, into action and refusing to be put off by statements such as, "'We're dealing with top officials in industry, and you just don't go around treating these people like that,'"[14] the HRFA proceeded to treat them just like that. They sued. Wielding two pre-turn-of-the-twentieth-century laws that no one paid much attention to as legal cudgels, HRFA argued that Penn Central's pollution illegally defiled the Hudson. They won, pocketing half of the $4,000 bounty, as the law allowed.

More lawsuits under the New York Harbor Act and the Federal Refuse Act followed—these against industrial giants such as Ciba Geigy and American Cyanamid—resulting in more bounty money, in time amounting to enough to hire someone to do what Boyle and his cohorts had been doing for years: keep watch over the river, documenting polluters and compelling them to follow the law or pay for flaunting it.[15] The person they hired was Karin Limburg's fellow People's Pipewatch observer, John Cronin.

In 1986 HRFA changed its name to Riverkeeper, but its approach has always been the same: enforcing the laws already on the books by gathering evidence on the river. Riverkeeper is the Hudson's Department of Justice, and the FBI's investigative role is played by a boat captain, John Lipscomb. On a trip with him from Troy south to the city of Hudson, he seemed to know every outlet pipe and its history. The latest concern was a restaurant whose sewage backup problems prompted it to reroute waste from a toilet directly to the river. Bad enough, but in this case the raw sewage first splashed onto a city-owned dock. A disgusted boat launch manager first called Riverkeeper, *then* the state DEC.

This Department of Justice's prosecution arm is populated by attorneys working for Riverkeeper, the best known of whom is Robert F. Kennedy Jr., son of the former U.S. attorney general. Unlike many government-brought enforcement actions, all Riverkeeper usually has to do is threaten legal action and corporate or governmental miscreants clean up their act. That's because when they do head to court, Riverkeeper almost always wins—as it repeatedly did in its earliest cases. It has brought suit or threatened suits large and small, including those against:

- the DEC for deregulating some intensive dairy operations, waste from which could foul Hudson tributaries;

- Atlantic Richfield Company for extensive PCB pollution in Hastings, New York;

- the New York Thruway Authority and the construction companies building the new Tappan Zee Bridge for both improper dredging methods and poor monitoring of dredging operations' effects on endangered sturgeon;[16]

- the City of Poughkeepsie for essentially closing a public dock when it rented sixty feet of a sixty-eight-foot dock to a commercial sightseeing vessel;

- Exxon, which, in the 1980s, anchored tankers near Franklin D. Roosevelt's family home in Hyde Park (a National Park), where they flushed their tanks of any jet fuel that remained after offloading their cargo in Albany, then took on fresh water for use at a refinery in Aruba;

- and they have twice sued the U.S. EPA, alleging it was not implementing part of the Clean Water Act that requires power plants to use the best available technology to prevent fish and other organisms from being drawn into cooling systems.

On any given day, Riverkeeper has twenty to twenty-five active legal cases ongoing, with more than one hundred investigations underway. Often, they are the only cops on the beat. Matthiessen says, "There's been so many examples where we've talked to some of our friends on the DEC staff who, when we've been looking at a particular case of pollution, have said, 'So, you guys gonna do something about this? We really need some help'. . . . They're actually looking to Riverkeeper to do the work that they're supposed to do."

Matthiessen says Riverkeeper has not only won in the courts and in its major campaigns, but also through

the impact we've had on the culture. I think there's renewed pride in the river. Riverkeeper has been the leading group in restoring water quality over these last couple of decades. It's just a matter of stopping polluters from polluting. Once you stop discharging pollutants into the river, it largely cleans itself. It's the cleanup of the river that has restored pride in the river among people, among municipalities, and there's been a renewed investment into the river: protecting it, gaining access to it.

He adds, "The Hudson is much, much cleaner than it has been in decades, and each day it gets cleaner. . . . The river has come a long way. We are *most* of the way to a fully restored Hudson River, but we still do have some major obstacles to overcome."

Some are a bit ironic. For example, as Riverkeeper and other regional environmental organizations succeeded in protecting the river, allowing it to do that self-cleansing, developers came to realize the Hudson is a "huge resource for them" and have flocked back to the river's edge, building on the abandoned brownfields, Matthiessen says. Now, new construction threatens to block local residents from the river. As I mentioned in chapter 5, such access is a matter of equity, the argument being that the river's edge is the people's space, not solely the province of those who can afford the most expensive view.

That such properties are once again in high demand is testament to the river's shifting meanings. Where once its surface was an oil slick, its depths a sewer, and its shores a garbage dump, today living along the Hudson is a marker of status. With status often comes exclusion, the very opposite of equity, making access a new and unanticipated front in struggles over sustainability.

Really Wonderful Places

Across the United States, local land trusts have been created to conserve places that otherwise might have been given up for development. The largest of them all, the Nature Conservancy, made a name for itself by purchasing property or development rights, and it plays a major role in wildlife preservation both nationally and internationally.

But local land trusts don't enjoy the Nature Conservancy's economic power and must operate using resources such as public policy and persuasion, along with whatever funds they can muster. In the Hudson region they go by names like Saratoga Preserving Land and Nature (Saratoga PLAN), Mohonk Preserve, and Orange County Land Trust. One of the most dynamic is the Columbia Land Conservancy (CLC), which has emerged as an essential element in sustainability efforts in its home county.

CLC's mission is simple yet sweeping, even daunting: to conserve the farmland, forests, wildlife habitat, and rural character of Columbia County. "Traditionally," notes executive director Peter Paden, "the bread and butter work of land trusts—and there are many, many land trusts in the country, different sizes, different scope, different breadth of program—but the one thing that almost every land trust does is conservation easements."

The nation's 1,700 land trusts rely on such easements more than any other tool in their kit. Paden explains, "Essentially, a landowner voluntarily agrees to give up a substantial amount of development potential on land." The landowner still owns the land under a conservation easement, and it can be sold or leased, but the portion covered by the easement is permanently off-limits to housing construction, road building, or any other kind of development. Land trusts hold easements, counting the acres represented in them among their conservation accomplishments. CLC's two hundred easements total 23,500 acres, more than 5 percent of the total land area in Columbia County, most representing farmland or former farmland.

Helpful as they are for conservation purposes, easements are also burdensome. "Easements come with great costs," notes Paden. "We have to steward them and monitor them and deal with landowners. It's all part of what we do, but there's a big external cost associated with an easement."

Paden became executive director of CLC after almost thirty years as a government and private attorney in New York City, the last stint with a multinational law firm of more than eight hundred attorneys. He purchased a home in Columbia County in 1979 and sat on CLC's board for more than twenty years before taking over daily supervision of the operation, so the move was not a leap into the unknown.

He notes that another approach to conserving land while keeping it in owners' hands is New York's Farmland Protection Program, begun in 1996. Although it suffered with little or no funding during the worst years of the Great Recession, state appropriations for the FPP have begun to improve. Paden explains that, working through local government and groups such as CLC, the FPP funds development rights purchases. "We can just buy it from somebody and essentially give them the cash value of their development rights," says Paden. "It ends up with a very similar-looking easement, but the farmer—instead of donating it—has actually taken the cash value out of his land and put it in his business or his estate or wherever." As with easements, the purchase of development rights does not affect things like farming activities; cropping, grazing, and the like go on just as they did before.

Given the costs to CLC of overseeing easements and the poorly funded FPP, Paden says his organization has embarked on several alternative land conservation strategies. One is an innovative farmer-landowner match program. He explains, "There are a lot of people who own farmland who aren't farmers who are thinking—instead of paying someone just to brush hog the field and keep it clear—maybe they'd like to put it back into production." Livestock owners graze their animals on hundreds of acres owned by others, while matches involving vegetable farmers have resulted in formerly fallow five-acre parcels once more growing produce. CLC offers workshops that cover the legalities and practicalities of the matching program, which has gotten off to a fast start and serves as an antidote to the farmerless farmland phenomenon mentioned in chapter 3.

As a complement to its four core emphases of farmland protection, forest preservation, wildlife conservation, and safeguarding the county's rural character, Paden says support for good land use planning is central to CLC's work. Christine Vanderlan, a CLC staff member, is an experienced planner, and she works with localities throughout the county, almost always at no cost for her consultancy, including conducting popular training programs for planning and zoning board members that run the gamut of sustainability-oriented themes from managing storm water runoff to creating and using conservation advisory commissions.

Such planning-oriented work led to the creation of the Harlem Valley Rail Trail, a beautiful paved recreational path running twenty-three miles in Columbia and Dutchess counties through forests and past farm fields, linking small communities with one another and with a popular state park. The type of project typically undertaken by local government, CLC stepped in and "wrote the grant that got the money for the state to buy it," Paden notes. "There are people all over the county interested in creating trails," so much so that CLC is supporting locals planning on developing a countywide trail system that will do what the Harlem Valley Rail trail does but throughout the 636-square-miles county.

Reflecting on CLC's location and its range of activities, Paden says, "One of the ironies of Columbia County is there's all this big open space, but there are relatively few public open spaces. We don't have that many state parks or forests, almost no county parks. There's very few places for people to go and get outdoors into all this wonderful stuff that you see when you're driving around." In the early 1990s, CLC set about changing that incongruity, purchasing 225 acres that became the Greenport Conservation Area north of the river town of Hudson. It has grown to 715 acres, and CLC now manages nine such parks across the county, outright owning seven of them.

"They're really wonderful places," Paden says. "They're quite varied. They're pretty heavily used. You can bird watch and hike and fish and snowshoe. They're a real asset for the county." They also help connect people to place. Paden notes, "In addition to doing conservation, we talk about building and maintaining a constituency for conservation. . . . Even in Columbia County, a lot of kids don't know where their food comes from, don't know anything about wildlife. So providing occasions for people to get out and make connections with the world seemed important to us." A full-time environmental educator works with thousands of school children, families, and seniors to help them appreciate and learn from the places CLC has managed to preserve.

What limits CLC's work? Money. "What we do is expensive," Paden says, adding,

> What we could do if we had a project acquisition fund: we know twelve farm families in this county right now who would like to do (an easement) to save their farm, keep it in farming. We know lots of incredible rich and wonderful land that's for sale that could be bought that would make wonderful parkland or very limited development land. We just don't even begin to have the assets—we don't have the beginnings of a project acquisition fund. If we had three more staff people, if we had two more educators, if we had one more person working on some of our projects, we would be busy from day one and we'd be able to get more done.

The lack of funding for CLC means missed opportunities not only to purchase land or easements but to educate even more policymakers and schoolchildren, to support community gardening, and more. And that unfulfilled potential means that Landscape creation and preservation will be considerably greater challenges in years to come.

A Force for Sustainability

Scenic Hudson is the region's "Big Daddy," the environmental organization with the most clout and the richest history. There are other key players in the region as well. The Open Space Institute uses its hundreds of millions of dollars in assets to purchase land for conservation and recreation, with a reach that extends throughout the region. The Appalachian Mountain Club, the nation's oldest environmental organization, has a strong presence in Massachusetts and Vermont. In the Adirondacks, the Adirondack Council, Protect the Adirondacks, the Adirondack Mountain Club, Adirondack Wild, and others are active defenders of the Hudson headwaters. And scattered throughout are local advocacy groups such as the Rensselaer Plateau Alliance and Catskill Mountainkeeper.

But Scenic Hudson, historically focused on the estuarial Hudson Valley but recently beginning to branch out, is the one that stirs the green imagination. It grew out of one of the formative moments in contemporary American environmentalism, the struggle to save Storm King, a majestic mountain rising 1,380 feet straight out of the Hudson River, from becoming a generating plant for New York City's power provider, Consolidated Edison. Without Scenic Hudson's leadership, American environmentalism would not exist as it does now, nor would the sustainability impetus. It is highly likely that the nation would be more industrialized, the land more ravaged had that fight not gone the way it did. Something like the *Storm King* court decision would have happened somewhere in the United States by now, but at what cost to the land? And most importantly, the acknowledgment that plants and animals have rights might never have come about.

Standing as a sentry at the north end of a small but impressive range of mountains known as the Hudson Highlands, Storm King got its name because dark clouds often encircle its summit. For fifteen years, starting in the mid-1960s, a metaphorical hurricane whipped that part of the Hudson. When it was over, activists had put Storm King on the map, forever altered American environmentalism, and had given the Hudson region's foremost environmental organization its start.

On its face the fight was over development, namely Consolidated Edison's plan to pump water up one side of the mountain at night to an eight-billion-gallon reservoir it would construct near the summit, then release the water during the day to spin power-generating turbines at the base of Storm King Mountain when demand was highest. In terms of physics, the plan was foolish—it would use more electricity than it would produce. But Con Ed cared only about the economics, and from a business perspective the scheme was genius. Because of the differential value of electricity at night versus during daytime hours, it was a sure moneymaker.

The real fight, though, was over views and more. The Storm King facilities would scar the mountain and mar the landscape. Already despised—Robert Boyle noted at the time, "For years, Con Ed has been a notorious dispenser of high-priced electricity (the highest of any major utility in the nation)"[17]—Con Ed soon became reviled.

Boyle and other activists arranged creative protests to demonstrate to Con Ed the public's opposition to its Storm King plans, including one night when the citizens of Croton-on-Hudson, at the foot of the mountain, turned out their lights en masse. Boaters staged a "sail-in," and "Dig They Won't—Save Storm King" bumper stickers abounded, the latter a response to Con Ed's motto—its actual motto!—"Dig We Must."[18]

For years Boyle and the Scenic Hudson Preservation Conference, formed in 1963 to fight Storm King, duked it out with Con Ed and with the Federal Power Commission. Frances Dunwell wrote, "The Storm King battle . . . was deeply rooted in activism of the 1960s and a sense, widely shared, that America's post–World War II passion for growth needed to be tempered with an equal passion for conserving our unique heritage. Ultimately, it was the story of people rallying to maintain our nation's cultural and spiritual connection with nature."[19]

Con Ed's plan not only would destroy views, it would wipe out habitat and kill fish and other marine organisms in huge numbers, as Scenic Hudson argued in FPC hearings and then in the courts. Today, we take the legal importance of positions such as those for granted, but we can only do so because of the Storm King struggle. At that time it was novel to suggest that environmental harm itself was unjust apart from direct human interests.

The turning point in the fight came when the Second U.S. Court of Appeals sent the FPC's decision in favor of Con Ed back to the commission for review. It was also a turning point in American environmentalism. A band of citizens had halted what went on under the banner of "progress," stopping in its tracks a regional Goliath. As Tom Lewis wrote in *The Hudson*, "For the first time in U.S. history a group of citizens had used the power of the courts to thwart the will of two bureaucracies [Con Ed and the FPC] that had always had their way."[20]

Ultimately, Scenic Hudson rewrote U.S. environmental law. As Christopher D. Stone noted in an influential article, a new meaning for the concept of "standing" emerged; in an instant, trees and rocks could sue for their rights.[21] Water, forests, fish, views: those things and more emerged from Storm King with new meaning. Here, in this place, humans would not be the sole measure of all things.

It was a remarkable moment. A centuries-old legal tradition treating "nature" as merely utilitarian, exclusively as property, was fundamentally altered. Storm King advanced the truth, ignored since Henry Hudson's arrival, that our well-being is inextricably tied to that of the nonhuman—and even nonliving—world around us. Biogeophysical landscapes themselves could be harmed, this new, modern legal construction goes. They, too, enjoy rights through their aggrieved human advocates.

As is inevitable with Landscapes, the new people-place nexus reflected a new image back on the society doing the meaning making as well. The simple, noble, essential notion of citizenship mattered once more. In the stances that HRFA, Clearwater, and Scenic Hudson took against corporations such as Con Ed and Penn Central, the people spoke, resisting unalloyed corporate greed masquerading as public good and exposing the collusion of government and industry. In their successful struggle to create a Landscape that once more intimately linked humans and place, the people found one another and the power of the commonweal.

After Storm King, that understanding of the potential for a shared, sustainable destiny has never gone lacking in this region, and today more people and organizations than ever are committing themselves to that end.

Scenic Hudson executive director Ned Sullivan notes his organization "continues to be a force for sustainability today," opposing power projects and advocating for smart growth. Scenic Hudson's influence in the Hudson Valley difficult to overestimate. It has created or improved sixty parks and owns thousands of acres, has helped preserve dozens of farms, and is a forceful environmental advocate in Albany.

Among its key current initiatives, Sullivan emphasizes two that have much to do with energy: advocating that new electric transmission lines follow preexisting corridors, rather than destroy farms and forests, and fighting the transportation by rail along the Hudson of bituminous oil, which has the potential to sink to the bottom of the river in the event of a derailment, making it almost impossible to clean up. (Residents in Albany are fighting a plan at the port to create facilities to liquefy that heavy oil, which tends to thicken in the winter, so that it can be transferred from rail cars to barges and tankers. From anxieties about derailments to concerns about heat, noise, light, and fumes, the proposed facilities raise a host of environmental justice issues.) Scenic Hudson is also lobbying the de Blasio administration in New York City to safeguard the city's regional foodshed—its farms—with the same sort of investment that it has put into its watershed, which could mean hundreds of millions for farm easements and development rights.

Emerging from its grassroots beginnings, Scenic Hudson demonstrates the potential scope of a large environmental organization. Though today it relies more on experts than citizens to get the work done, its vigilance and advocacy remind us that the region's environment is both constantly under threat and full of potential as a sustainability leader, something Scenic Hudson's founders recognized more than fifty years ago.

New Understandings of the Mud Puddle

What are the looming struggles facing Hudson region environmental advocates? According to Manna Jo Greene, twin issues must be acted upon immediately: addressing climate change and developing alternative energy sources. She says, "It's clear that we're in a climate crisis, and we need to take *drastic* measures. We mainly need to invest in installing the infrastructure for renewable energy"—solar panels, windmills, tide-driven turbines, and the like. "Once we invest in the infrastructure, the fuel is free! You don't have to pay the sun or the wind or the water or the power of the moon to pull on the tides. Energy efficiency and renewables: this is the decade. We either do it or we kiss it all goodbye." However, she insists it won't come to that—at least not near her home. "I believe that the Hudson Valley is poised to become a region that models the transition to a green energy economy because the environmental ethic is now very strong and deeply ingrained."

Ned Sullivan sounded a similar theme. He noted that instead of adding those new transmission lines to carry energy from upstate New York to the New York City metropolitan area, policymakers should promote "a more sustainable system of electric generation and transportation that would be based more on locally generated, sustainable, green power that would rely on conservation of energy, that would have microgrids, and that would be a spur to photovoltaics and geothermal energy." Such efforts, shifting investment away from transporting electricity from large centralized generators to local sites that would draw power from renewable sources, could make the region a model of sustainability.

How can it fulfill that vision? Coming to common understanding—shared meaning—is essential. The last thing we need today is the tone that seems to prevail. From Congress to the local town hall, we appear loath to agree about something as fundamental as survival. Better to stop a functioning government or to ignore vexing issues staring us in the face than to pull together to address the worst crisis humanity has ever witnessed. At the grass roots, the world of real people where Manna Jo Greene lives and works (including as an elected official in her home town), Washington's spiteful, stuck-in-the-mud attitudes don't seem to hold sway. "I'm talking about listening for a different perspective so you can learn," she says.

> I'll give you an example. I once took a biodiversity training because I wanted to do a biological assessment of my back yard—a portion of the Town of Rosendale. I wanted to learn about my most immediate environment. In the process of this training, they took us out to see what wetlands were and the different habitats and what lived there. We saw what looked like a giant mud puddle. It was an intermittent woodland pool, a vernal pool. Prior to this experience, I just thought of that as a big muddy spot that, if I wanted to get from here to there in the woods, I had to go around it. And when they had us look at what was living there and the value of the fact that it was intermittent, so that salamanders and frogs could reproduce there without worrying about fish eating their eggs, it shifted my consciousness. Instead of a big, muddy area that I wanted to avoid so that I didn't have to get my boots dirty, it became a living part of the landscape.

> The whole landscape went from something that was two-dimensional and there for my enjoyment—oh, look how beautiful this picture is!—to what it supported in terms of life. . . . Had I not taken this course and listened for the learning, it would still be a big mud puddle that I needed to avoid.

Listening and learning: the power of empathy, of standing in an ecologist's shoes—or a neighbor's—to change meaning is what Greene has in mind. In those cases, what we learn is not simply information; it is another's standpoint: their way of viewing the world, the meanings that they infuse it with, and the factors that influence those others people's viewpoints.

Peter Paden suggests that sharing a place can be the starting point for finding common ground. The challenge, he says, is "making people see common connections and common points of interest across lines that typically divide people. There's a lot of them-and-us in every world, including this one, and land use issues can be very divisive very easily. I know because I used to litigate them. But I think there's also a tremendous basis for people to find common interest. . . . It's a question of finding ways of having those conversations in a positive context rather than not."

That Greene and Paden would advocate the same need—to empathize and to acknowledge the connections to place we share in common—is remarkable because each of them is battle-scarred: Greene the tenacious environmental advocate, Paden the hard-nosed litigator. They know what it is like to refuse to bend, yet both are wise enough to admit that we walk together into our future. Our lives are bound up one with another's, and the Landscapes we need to create must be the products of listening, learning, and processes that lead to finding common ground. They do not have to emerge through confrontation, but they do need to be conscious if they are to serve as guideposts along the way to a better future. That is the place that the *Clearwater*, whose home port resides in the shadow of Storm King, is taking us to.

Conclusion

A Practical Revolution

One crisp November afternoon, I heard a cacophony of squeaks and squawks coming from high overhead. Looking up, I saw hundreds of starlings flying toward the setting sun . . . and far higher a jet happened to be heading in roughly the opposite direction, white contrail streaming and bright light gleaming off its silver skin. For an instant I reveled in the contrast: nature versus artifice, pure opposed to profane, simplicity set against the complex. And then I recalled that starlings are invasives, having been released into Central Park a century ago by a Shakespeare aficionado.

The way to sustainability has not been made easy. Invasive species such as those starlings, combined with institutional racism, bizarre farm and land use policies at multiple levels of government, and endless challenges to creating localism in a global economy, create roadblocks to lasting communities, economies, and ecologies. No one knows those barriers better than the Hudson region's sustainability advocates, yet they persist. They moan, groan, and gripe. But they also smile, laugh, and joke, coming across as far more upbeat than downcast. Realists to a person, they also are optimists. We can get to sustainability, they insist, and this book is the story of how they and their organizations are charting that path.

In the Introduction, I discussed the two foci I planned to thread through each chapter. First, there was inspiration, the stories of sustainability entrepreneurs in the Hudson region and their remarkable achievements. My hope is that their creativity, passion, and commitment to bringing about a sustainable planet will spark the same sort of action in others. Second, I wanted to bring insight to their work by identifying what a sustainable social construction of the human-nature relationship, under the label of a new Hudson region Landscape, might look like. That meaning-filled Landscape needs to be a conscious choice to serve as both guidepost and metric, giving direction while also providing activists and policymakers with a set of goals—and perhaps even standards to be used to judge our progress as we strive toward sustainability.

In the pages that follow I first combine inspiration and insight, pulling together some of the key aspects of that new Hudson region Landscape to paint an integrated picture of what may come about. Next, I consider what some argue is an emergent counter-notion to sustainability, "resilience." I conclude by sharing a couple of lessons I take from spending time with the remarkable people in this book.

Insight from Inspiration

While my previous treatment of Landscape-related insights has not integrated observations from across the chapters, here I do so. As a book about one region's uncoordinated yet inspiring efforts to work with place and people to bring about a new and lasting tomorrow, it is important both to appreciate how those efforts can be conceptually linked yet stay grounded in the realities that gave rise to those insights.

Core Sustainable Landscape Characteristics

My conversations with sixty-two scientists, farmers, planning experts, business owners, environmental activists, and others point to several core characteristics of sustainable landscapes. These themes each emerged across multiple chapters.

One cluster of characteristics includes the observations that farming families, cities, and communities all will be essential components of lasting Landscapes. For example, the closer our food is grown to the customers who purchase it, the more sustainable the resulting food system is. The surest way to keep food local is to create policies and social climates that encourage and reward family farmers such as the Arnolds and McEnroes from chapter 3 by making it easy for them to stay on the farm and seamless for them to get farm products to market (Dickson Despommier's reservations regarding "dirt farmers" notwithstanding). Silly fights like whether Ray McEnroe's farm stand is too large to qualify as such (which occurred at the town level) or whether Ralph Erenzo's distillery counted as a farm (necessary to qualify Tuthilltown Spirits as a particular distillery type, a struggle he waged with the state) exemplify the myriad barriers encountered by sustainability entrepreneurs. Provisions should be made to fast-track sustainability organizations through bureaucracy at all levels.

As we saw in chapter 3, ties such as those GrowNYC has forged not only benefit city residents, they resonate throughout their Landscape. Such is true in general with cities' sustainability potential. Occasionally, ironies emerge; New York's infrastructure sprawl, represented by a municipal water system that stretches more than one hundred miles, promotes forest preservation in the Catskills as an integral part of New York's effort to avoid installing a costly water filtration plant.[1] But for the most part the links are less ambiguous, like the regionwide economic benefits that accrue from local producers (farmers and otherwise) selling their goods nearby in the city. What we find is that cities are a bridge to sustainable Landscapes, enabling the sorts of energy savings, transportation systems, and economic connections without which we will never attain lasting societies.

Cities far smaller than New York can play positive roles in regional sustainability, acting as incubators for creative community sustainability solutions—witness Radix's work in Albany. Another example: cities that practice "smart development" and provide transportation alternatives to the automobile benefit their Landscapes and others by curbing global greenhouse gas emissions.

On a similar theme, cities and towns alike—wherever populations are concentrated, with all of the attendant potential human and environmental benefits—tend to prompt more local commerce of the sort that ReThink Local promotes. Localism encourages the recirculation of monetary capital rather than its exportation, and other kinds of capital are likely to grow as a result. I'm thinking here of "social capital": rich networks of friends and contacts that encourage stronger communities. Those communities may be built in a host of ways, from creating community-based businesses to shopping at those establishments to using the kind of local path system to get around mentioned in chapter 4. In addition, the literal building of communities—as policy, through sustainable land use planning of the sort that Marirose Blum Bump encouraged, or through particular structures, such as those that Françoise Bollack, Mark Morrison, and Leonard Hopper are known for—is essential.

Intentional Landscape Creation

A theme that runs through all of the foregoing points is that Landscape creation needs to come about through sets of intentional, well-considered actions. By choosing to focus development in a village, town, or city, and thereby spare precious farmland, as Red Hook and Greene County have done, we conscientously construct sustainable Landscapes through policy and action. Similarly, in chapters 3 and 8, we heard that shared experiences of the land also are important in creating sustainability. That land does not have to be located on a rural farm; it may be an inner-city community garden, the Walkway over the Hudson (the world's longest pedestrian bridge, preserved and rehabilitated thanks in part to Scenic Hudson), or a hiking trail to Mt. Marcy or Mt. Greylock—respectively the highest peaks in New York and Massachusetts and both in the Hudson watershed. What's important is that we appreciate and share the beauty and value of a place's soil, rock, ice, flowing water, flora, and fauna.

For that to happen, those places need to be accessible to us. The work of Columbia Land Conservancy and other regional land trusts is vital in this regard, as are Riverkeeper's and River Watch's efforts to ensure that the public has easy access to rivers and streams and, once there, that they can enjoy them without anxiety. In urban areas, initiatives such as those in New York City to ensure that everyone can walk to a park in ten minutes or less are key to furthering those people-place connections that advocates say are vital to creating and maintaining sustainability.

We will need to create Landscape through other means, too. Politically and interpersonally, compromises will likely need to be made. Manna Jo Green articulately voiced the imperative to listen to others, and Jeff Golden encouraged us to meet our fellow community members on their ground. Such empathetic approaches to difficult questions sound Pollyannaish in an era where our highest elected officials regularly yell at one another from entrenched ideological positions. Of course, few of them are much vested in sustainability; perhaps rather than looking to them for answers, we should act on our own and demand that they follow.

Finally, the natural and social sciences are likely to play key roles in nurturing Landscapes. Both can provide some of those guideposts I mentioned earlier; for example, how well are we doing at slowing the spread of invasive species? How is ecosystem health faring? Human health? What do our alternative GDP indicators tell us about how happy and fulfilled our communities are (and have those alternatives been adopted; in the Hudson region, only Vermont has done so)? And, of course, are today's Landscapes the Landscapes we want? How can we improve upon them?

Stepping Up and Acting Up

Revising and reviving Landscapes takes effort. Pete Seeger would remind us that we cannot create a sustainable Hudson region, or any other, standing alone. It may take a million little acts to bring about change to a regional Landscape, but the action will need to be taken in concert with one another: a million letters written, customers frequenting local stores, bicycle commuters, citizen scientists. Whether coordinated or not, an awareness of all that activism is vital; communication and connection, through the groups we act with and the larger organizations we join and support, will be key.

As I asked in chapter 2, who will act for ecology? Who will act for Landscape broadly? Activism, we heard, is vital for farming, for environmental justice, even for creating the disruptions that are at the core of a sustainable economy, something Sue Van Hook of Ecovative suggested. Resisting the tug of the quick buck and the big box store is part of that picture as well for those wishing to support local businesses. Activism and resistance, as I found repeatedly in my conversations, are integral to Landscape creation. Both carve out places for civil society, too, and in so doing they draw us together. Perhaps a bit surprisingly, one dimension to sustainability activism and resistance is it becomes democracy in action.

Missing Links

Those broad themes run through these pages: the intimate connections between cities, farming, and community; the value of localism; intentionality; respect and empathy; awareness, communication, shared experience, action, and resistance. All are essential to realizing sustainable Landscapes. These general concepts are rooted in dozens of things the people I spoke with have done. They design green roofs for skyscrapers and dream of green skyscrapers for growing food. They investigate environmental insults as scholars and activists. They promote small, local businesses and, on a wave of mycelia, imagine displacing Dow Jones Industrial–listed corporations as economic elites. They promote environmental justice and advance environmental agendas by hobnobbing with elected officials.

The list of sustainability-related accomplishments across the region is impressive, but in three key ways it falls well short of the ideal. Advocates rightfully speak of the crucial place that transportation and energy must play in the creation of sustainable futures, two areas the region has struggled with, and the third missing piece is regionwide planning. It is important to acknowledge that those things do not appear often enough on these pages. My purpose was to highlight what is being done, here, and transportation and energy, in particular, are not being attended to as they must for the Hudson region to attain sustainability.

New York City is a model regarding transportation, of course, and some other cities and towns in the region are working toward solutions for moving people around better. Bus lines crisscross Albany and Saratoga Springs, New York, for example, and many in Williamstown, Massachusetts, and Bennington, Vermont, are able to walk just about everywhere they need to go. But Saratoga constructed a huge new parking garage in an homage to its vehicle-centered culture rather than provide incentives for riding the bus (or disincentives for parking). Commuters in the Albany area face a daily nightmare on its roads and highways, which do not include a single high-occupancy vehicle lane to promote something as basic as carpooling.

Far worse, outside of the New York metropolitan area, rail lines—what Scenic Hudson's Ned Sullivan terms the "spine" of the region's sustainable transportation infrastructure—go completely unused for commuting. Most in the upstate, New Jersey, and New England portions of the Hudson region are as wedded to their automobiles as anyone in Los Angeles or Atlanta. No serious transportation proposals exist at the subregional level to comprehensively slow sprawl and promote in-city residence. (Plenty of communities are doing what they can on their own to create local [as opposed to regional] sustainability. The Town of Malta, New York, is a fine example of a traditional bedroom community that saw an opportunity to do things differently through land use planning).[2] In short, for most of the region, transportation policies to promote sustainability do not exist.

If anything, the energy situation is even worse. Sustainable energy's importance is twofold: replacing greenhouse gas–emitting, or habitat-destroying, sources of energy while providing adequate amounts for residents, businesses, and services. On occasion, we saw mention of energy success stories: Ecovative's efforts to shift from its dependence on natural gas, talk of locally based microgrids that draw from solar and wind power as an alternative to centralized high-voltage lines, and, of course, the remarkable story of Zephyr at Jiminy Peak. But those things are hardly a beginning. Making things worse, the region is also a corridor for the transportation of dangerous Bakken crude and Alberta tar sands oils that are unsustainable, ecologically destructive, and raise serious environmental justice concerns. The relevant rail and river travel is beyond the control of state officials, though that is not the case for the proposed liquefaction project in Albany.

One bright spot regarding energy is the Regional Greenhouse Gas Initiative (RGGI), a compact among eight northeastern states—including all five in the Hudson region except New Jersey, which pulled out in 2011 after Gov. Chris Christie claimed it would never work—to curb carbon dioxide emissions from power plants. Begun in 2008, it became the first market-based effort in the United States to cut greenhouse gas emissions. RGGI ("Reggie") has been wildly successful and will trim more than $2 billion from the lifetime energy bills of three million affected households and twelve thousand businesses while pumping $700 million in energy investments into the states.

New Jersey's intransigence notwithstanding, RGGI played a major role in establishing the Northeast as the nation's leader in reducing carbon dioxide pollution over its first five years of operation.[3] The market-driven "cap and trade" system is periodically revised to reduce carbon emissions; in 2014, the new cap for the eight states was slashed 45 percent because the program already had accomplished its goals. It lowered the emissions benchmark from 165 million tons annually to 91 million. Beginning in 2015, the cap will be reduced each of the next five years by 2.5 percent. The effect on consumers? An increase of less than 1 percent on their monthly bills in the short run, with those billions in savings coming in the future as the initiative's various conservation and efficiency programs bear fruit.[4]

The region's increasing commitment to renewable energy sources is also worth noting, not least because many of the CO_2 reductions under RGGI have come from shifts from carbon-intensive, unsustainable coal and fuel oil to less carbon-intensive, unsustainable natural gas. Permanent energy sustainability is possible only through renewables. To its credit, New Jersey is second only to Arizona in providing incentives for photovoltaic installations. In 2014, New York continued its efforts to catch up, with a nearly $1 billion boost to the 2012 NY-Sun Initiative. In the initiative's first two years, state-funded projects avoided 116,000 tons of greenhouse gas emissions. That program was largely intended to boost efforts to wean solar from government incentives, even as libertarians such as the infamous Koch brothers pour millions into ad campaigns intended to "unplug solar power by killing governmental preferences for the solar power industry" in favor of coal.[5] (New York also has created a "Green Bank," a public-private partnership to spur "clean" [not necessarily all sustainable] energy development in the state with upward of $1 billion in total investment.)[6]

Thanks to those state initiatives, solar panels began appearing on Hudson region buildings in increasing numbers in the early 2000s, and there are hundreds of small photovoltaic and wind turbine installation companies in the region in addition to the big one, GE, the manufacturer of Jiminy Peak's Zephyr. Yet there are no broad-scale energy policies in the region to promote Ecovative-style disruptions to spur sustainable energy projects. Microgrids of the sort that Ned Sullivan mentioned are well and good, but, as he implied, state governments need to use their regulatory power over utility providers to make such innovations a reality rather than relying on piecemeal (albeit large) funding commitments such as the NY-Sun Initiative.

Of these three shortcomings—transportation, energy, and planning—the latter is the closest to being rectified, at least in New York. There, Gov. Andrew Cuomo announced a "Cleaner, Greener Communities Program" in 2011. State-funded, locally produced regional sustainability plans were developed in less than eighteen months for all areas of the state. Those efforts took place on the heels of the creation of a regional economic development planning process. The state contemplates integrating the two and is making $90 million available to implement the plans.

The prospect of sustainability planning being meaningfully woven into economic development is exciting, but what will actually happen is unclear. In addition, regional planning is not the same as regionwide planning: planning for the Hudson River watershed as a whole, including areas of states outside of New York (which has the strongest planning program in place). Watershed-based planning's virtues are easy to see for water quality purposes, but they are broadly relevant, too. Economies and commuters often are linked within watersheds. Plenty make the drive from southwestern Vermont or northwestern Massachusetts to Albany's Capital Region for work every day, for example, and many do their shopping there; the flip side is lots of us living in that area recreate in the Green Mountains or the Berkshires. The Hudson's watershed is about more than where water flows. Money, culture, play, and shared destiny flow there, too.

Enter Resilience

Late in the writing of this book I realized that several people I interviewed had used the word *resilience,* and I became intrigued by the word. One who mentioned it was farm ecologist Conrad Vispo. He said that while we may have lost the basis for sustainability along the way to today, we can get it back. We need look no farther than the Hudson region for evidence that the ecological component of sustainability, at least, is recoverable. "There is resilience," he said, pondering the stunning reality that 150 years ago 80 percent of Columbia County, like virtually all the others in the region, had been cleared of trees; now the county is 80 percent forested.

Vispo continued, "We had this place open. Things can come back. To throw up your hands and say, 'We've screwed everything up, that's it.' No. Things can come back. This landscape has changed dramatically. We've had turkeys come back, beaver come back. On the other hand, even a hundred and fifty years ago we were able to essentially clear the whole thing. So we can have major effects . . . on the landscape."

Another person who mentioned resilience was local business advocate Ajax Greene. Speaking about which businesses will be in the best position to withstand the vicissitudes of the climatological and economic changes that are coming down the pike, Greene said, "Local and independent will do really well. They will be far more resilient and able to change than large, entrenched organizations, who I think are going to be crushed, in large part, by the changes." Short supply chains and close community support are likely to position nonfranchised small stores and restaurants in ways that will see them survive the challenges that likely lie ahead.

Finally, I used the word myself. As I reflected on Clearwater's efforts to unite disparate communities in chapter 8, I observed that resilient grassroots environmental groups, those that are networked with others and therefore understand that they and their communities are not alone, are less likely to be victimized by governments and business interests seeking to locate development where resistance is weak.

No doubt some who mentioned resilience had read Andrew Zolli and Ann Marie Healy's *Resilience: Why Things Bounce Back*, published in 2012.[7] Zolli and Healy insist that sustainability is passé. In a *New York Times* op-ed piece, Zolli argued that "the sustainability regime is being quietly challenged" and that "a new dialogue is emerging around a new idea, resilience: how to help vulnerable people, organizations, and systems persist, perhaps even thrive, amid unforeseeable disruptions. Where sustainability aims to put the world back into balance, resilience looks for ways to manage in an imbalanced world."[8]

There is a lot to like about resilience. It implies that we can almost endlessly adapt built environments, economies, perhaps even whole communities and societies, to successfully confront a future of endless uncertainty. That's a reassuring message. Given the correct technologies, and enough money, we can bring stability to a world gone haywire. Cities, buildings, economies, and more can be made more resilient, so the concept is refreshingly flexible and relevant to an era where instability has become a given rather than a rarity.

Resilience is a virtue of considerable power. I'm reminded of the Taoist notion of bending without breaking. When a powerful force is about to overwhelm you, do you stand stiff, stubbornly resisting and risking almost certain harm? Or do you shift, lean, and perhaps avoid until you can stand straight once the danger has passed? Resilience has been around a long time, and there is much wisdom to it. Why construct rigid structures, inflexible infrastructure, and unyielding social systems in an era full of unknowns?

But the truth is, sustainability is revolutionary. Is resilience? "Balance" is not what the sustainability advocates with whom I spoke embrace. Ecology recognizes that ecosystems are in a constant state of flux, Ecovative's disruptive path is all about rejecting the economic balance of power, Paul Arnold must remain flexible on his farm because of imbalances beyond his control, and environmental justice firmly rejects the status quo. It is resilience that sounds safe, as if it holds the potential for keeping climate change's effects at arm's length while life goes on as usual. Meanwhile, sustainability aims to upset the applecart that gave us climate change.

The word *revolution* was not raised once in my five dozen interviews, but it is what many obliquely referred to, as when they suggested that development decisions be directed by environmental concerns and when farmers shared success strategies with one another and created community with their customers. Overthrowing local growth coalitions and converting cold capitalism to community: that's revolutionary. Revolutions bring about sharp breaks with the past, and in its quiet way sustainability is heading just there. Resilience seems a necessary tool for coping—it is often used as a synonym for "adaptation," an essential component in confronting climate change—but will we get to a new social, economic, and ecological place merely through resilience?

We find creeping but nevertheless revolutionary changes when city streets are reclaimed by pedestrians and when local storekeepers band together to challenge the primacy of multinational corporations. I see sustainability in those things, not resilience. Moreover, when developers are compelled to set aside much larger pieces of land for conservation than the law requires, and when environmental justice organizations play central roles in reinvigorating their neighborhoods, something radically new is taking place. Something more active and less reactionary than resilience is going on.

The sustainability revolution is a practical one. It's not simply rooted in a moral imperative that some social movement or religious cult created out of whole cloth or in accordance with holy writ. Sure, there is a moral side to it. But it is practical in multiple senses. Foremost, of course, the evidence that we must act to curb environmental abuses from pollution to climate change to species extinction is a scientific certainty. Those phenomena are not opinion, nor is acting on them optional. There are other practicalities, too. People are committed enough to the triple bottom line, for example, that they are staking their businesses, careers, and reputations on it.

How revolutionary is resilience? It is being taken seriously as a topic of study in numerous disciplines. For those areas where resiliency overlaps with—and, in Zolli's view, stands to replace—sustainability, we need to ask of it some serious questions. For instance, is there space in resilience for equity? Is there concern for ecology? Resiliency may imply revolutionary design, but will those designs end up being the next wave of urban renewal, displacing the poor and persons of color as powerful interests build ill-conceived, wasteful megaprojects? Will we, in our rush to construct resilient places, exacerbate the very climate change they are meant to address? Does resiliency mean a loss of the moral and political will to reverse the horrors of climate change? To the extent that resiliency implies large expenditures of public funds, how realistic is it? Will resiliency be adopted by entrepreneurs and entrepreneurial organizations in the ways that sustainability has been?

Some resilience advocates frame it as a component of sustainability, and doing so makes lots of sense.[8] However, pitting the concepts against one another because resilience seems to be the next new thing risks reducing both to fads. Sustainability advocates should build and plan with resiliency in mind without losing sight of triple-bottom-line goals.

Lessons Learned

My favorite moment working on this project came during my three hour conversation with René VanSchaack, literally on the banks of the Hudson River. It's when, as I relate in chapter 4, he said,

Time in and time out again, all up and down this Hudson Valley, these communities have said, 'Oh, wait a minute. We need to think about saving some of this.' Well, you know what? They're about two hundred subdivisions too late. They're about five shopping centers too late. They're about two industrial parks too late. . . . We've been satisfied with 'we got the little green medians and we're gonna do some trees in them. And you know what, beyond the loading dock we'll leave a half acre. And when you add it all up.' Add it all up? There's no value when you add it all up!

It's an odd quote for an optimist to glom onto. There are tough lessons in those few sentences, lessons reflected elsewhere on these pages. Sustainability cannot be undertaken piecemeal, for instance. We cannot expect to add up small accomplishments and find we have attained more than the sum of their parts, particularly when so much has already been sacrificed at the altar of economy. Yet we are doing precisely that. The inspiring work to effect sustainability occurs here and there in cities and towns, through the efforts of nonprofit organizations, and by intrepid corporations. Disturbingly little coordination exists among those sustainability-oriented organizations. Moreover, in this perilous time too many governments at all levels stand frozen, following rather than leading just when we need open discussion about our collective future and careful guidance to arrive there the most.

In VanSchaacks's observations there's also the sobering possibility that everything we do may be for naught. If we are two hundred subdivisions too late all throughout the region, what's left to save? Where are the wild places? Where is the wildlife? Where, in endless suburbia, are the connections to neighbors and the lasting relationships that Jeff Golden would say characterize community? Is all gone? One thing we're certainly too late for is climate change; Doug Burns and Tim Howard make clear that it is a fact of our lives. One study even suggests that if we stop emitting carbon into the atmosphere today, the climate will not return to what our great-grandparents knew as normal for a thousand years.[10]

There's also the lack of political will implied in VanSchaack's comment. Where are the Marirose Blum Bumps saying that community and collective character are what really matter, not economic development or flying through town on Interstate-wide "streets"? Where are the Michael Bloombergs, conservatives who embrace sustainability and climate science, risking beratement from the head-in-the-sanders in their political party? A couple or ten or twenty of them is not enough. Where are the Gavin McIntyres, putting sustainability front and center in their business models, and the Jiminy Peaks, which found sustainability to be a gift that not only made the continued existence of their business possible, but helped it thrive?

VanSchaack's quote stays with me so because of why he said it: *this* is the mentality that sustainability advocates are up against. Ignore the big picture. Ignore everything but our wallets or getting reelected. Ignore all the science and much of the public sentiment. Ignore the future, even what's in our own children's best interests to attend to. Short-term greed, happiness, pleasure, and expediency are all that matter, ignorance be damned.

But, of course, what compels VanSchaack and the dozens of others with whom I spoke is the opposite of those things. Each in their own way, they work to bring about a new, sustainable Hudson region Landscape. In them, insight has triumphed over ignorance, courage over cowardice, concern over moral blindness, and responsiveness to social need over the narrow-mindedness of personal greed. Their efforts are too fractured to be called a social movement, yet they build communities when they can: Paul and Sandy Arnold with other farmers, Peggy Shepard in West Harlem, and GrowNYC in schools, gardens, and greenmarkets. Ajax Greene's work with small businesses leaves him convinced that a new economy is just over the horizon, and Ecovative, like many businesses in the region, is already there. Doug Reed and Clearwater are empowering citizen scientists and inner-city youths with knowledge, jobs, and hope.

They are each driven to create a better place, rejecting the laissez-faire defeatism inherent in today's pet phrase: Eh, what are you gonna do? And together these revolutionaries, like thousands of others, give the lie to the truth VanSchaack identified. Perhaps at the end of the day, when they add it all up, this region—already a leader in sustainability—will be sustainable once and for all.

Methodological Note

As an ethnographic endeavor, this project included one unique component. Qualitative researchers commonly record their interviews, but because I intended to produce a parallel documentary film, I videotaped nearly all of my conversations. Using Apple's Final Cut Pro editing software, I captured the footage, labeling each clip using key words in a process that loosely mimicked the coding regime used in grounded theory methodology.[1] Then I ordered those clips in Final Cut's "timeline," the portion of the software's window that allows one to shift around pieces of a film until the flow seems correct. In this case, the timeline allowed me to line up the clips so that I could easily transcribe the relevant quotes into each chapter. As I wrote, I interpreted the materials to identify the relevant insights that emerged out of my research participants' comments.

True grounded theory methods are substantially more rigorous than the approach I took: sensibly so, since in its purest form the inductive grounded theory approach's object is to identify theoretical propositions that may be tested using deductive methods. My purpose was not so lofty. The insights I hoped to glean from my conversations with sustainability advocates were not intended as theoretical conclusions but as characteristics of a sustainable Hudson River region's Landscape. To the extent that I succeeded in that end, all credit goes to the flexibility of grounded theory methods.

Creating Sustainable Communities: The Film Version

Rik Scarce has produced a parallel documentary film that features many of the people, places, and issues explored here. For more information, visit sustainingthisplace.net.

Notes

Introduction

1. Auden Schendler, *Getting Green Done: Hard Truths from the Front Lines of the Sustainability Revolution* (New York: Public Affairs, 2009), 70.

2. Simon Schama, *Landscape and Memory* (New York: Alfred A. Knopf, 1995), 6–7.

3. J. Sanford Rikoon, "Wild Horses and the Political Ecology of Nature Restoration in the Missouri Ozarks," *Geoforum* 37 (2006): 200–11.

4. Stella Čapek, "Of Time, Space, and Birds: Cattle Egrets and the Place of the Wild," in *Mad about Wildlife: Looking at Social Conflict over Wildlife,* ed. Theresa Goedeke and Ann Herda-Rapp (Boston: Brill, 2005), 195–222.

5. Jan E. Dizard, *Going Wild: Hunting, Animal Rights, and the Contested Meaning of Nature* (Amherst: University of Massachusetts Press, 1999).

6. Rik Scarce, "What Do Wolves Mean? Social Constructions of *Canis lupus* by 'Bordertown' Residents," *Human Dimensions of Wildlife* 3, no. 3 (1998): 26–45; Rik Scarce, "More than Mere Wolves at the Door: Reconstructing Community Amidst a Wildlife Controversy," in *Mad about Wildlife: Looking at Social Conflict over Wildlife,* ed. Theresa Goedeke and Ann Herda-Rapp (Boston: Brill, 2005), 123–46.

7. Simon Dresner, *The Principles of Sustainability* (Washington, DC: Earthscan, 2008), 1.

8. World Commission on Environment and Development, *Our Common Future* (New York: Oxford University Press, 1987).

9. Ibid., 9.

10. Joan Fitzgerald, *Emerald Cities: Urban Sustainability and Economic Development* (New York: Oxford University Press, 2010), 18.

11. Andres R. Edwards, *The Sustainability Revolution* (Gabriola Island, BC: New Society, 2005).

12. John Elkington, "'Towards the Sustainable Corporation: Win-Win-Win Business Strategies for Sustainable Development," *California Management Review* 36, no. 2 (1994): 90–100.

13. C. P. Snow, *Studies in Words* (New York: Cambridge University Press, 1960), 37.

Chapter 1. How We Lost Sustainability

1. Information about "Cooper's Cave" may be found at: http://sgfny.com/Coopers-Cave.htm.

2. Pete Seeger, "Sailing up My Dirty Stream," Fall River Music, 1961.

3. Oliver A. Rink, "Seafarers and Businessmen: The Growth of Dutch Commerce in the Lower Hudson River Valley," in *Dutch New York: The Roots of Hudson Valley Culture*, ed. Roger Panetta (New York: Fordham University Press, 2009), 7–34.

4. Robert Boyle, *The Hudson: A Natural and Unnatural History* (New York: W. W. Norton, 1969), 86.

5. David Stradling, *The Nature of New York: An Environmental History of the Empire State* (Ithaca: Cornell University Press, 2010), 16.

6. Ibid.

7. Adriaen van der Donck, *A Description of the New Netherlands* (Syracuse: Syracuse University Press, 1968), 5.

8. Stradling, *The Nature of New York.*

9. Ibid., 20.

10. Max Weber, *The Protestant Ethic and the Spirit of Capitalism* (New York: Penguin Classics, 2002).

11. Vernon Benjamin, "The Algonquins in Context: The End of the Spirituality of the Natural World," in *America's First River: The History and Culture of the Hudson River Valley*, colls. Thomas S. Wermuth, James M. Johnson, and Chistopher Pryslopski (Albany: State University of New York Press, 2009), 33.

12. Dennis J. Maika, "Encounters: Slavery and the Philipse Family, 1680–1751," in *Dutch New York: The Roots of Hudson Valley Culture*, ed. Roger Panetta (New York: Fordham University Press, 2009), 35–72.

13. Stradling, *The Nature of New York*, 53–54.

14. From the 1820s on, steam power was increasingly commonplace in the city, and coal was used for home heating and cooking as well. See: Edwin G. Burrows and Mike Wallace, *Gotham* (New York: Oxford University Press, 1999), 442.

15. Hugh O. Canham, "Hemlock and Hide: The Tanbark Industry in Old New York," *Northern Woodlands* 69 (Summer 2011): 36–41.

16. Ibid., 40.

17. David Stradling, *Making Mountains: New York City and the Catskills* (Seattle: University of Washington Press, 2007), 117.

18. N.Y. Const., art. XIV.

19. Boyle, *The Hudson*, 93–94.

20. Mark Kurlansky, *The Big Oyster: History on the Half Shell* (New York: Ballantine, 2006), 259.

21. Stradling, *The Nature of New York*, 182.

22. Environmental Protection Agency, "Niagara Mohawk Power Corp. (Saratoga Springs Plant)," http://www.epa.gov/Region2/superfund/npl/0202182c.pdf.

23. Blake Jones, "Report: Finch Paper a Top Polluter," *Post-Star* (Glens Falls, NY), March 29, 2012, http://poststar.com/business/local/report-finch-paper-a-top-polluter/article_7147efb6-7930-11e1-b847-0019bb2963f4.html.

24. Matthew L. Wald, "Nuclear Plant's Use of River Water Prompts $1.1 Billion Debate with State," *New York Times*, August 23, 2010.

25. Sanford Gifford, *Storm King on the Hudson*, National Academy of Arts, c. 1865.

26. James O'Connor, *Natural Causes: Essays in Ecological Marxism* (New York: Guilford Press, 1998), 332.

27. Ibid., 235.

28. John Bellamy Foster, *The Vulnerable Planet* (New York: Monthly Review Press, 1994), 124.

29. Allen Schnaiberg and Kenneth Alan Gould, *Environment and Society: The Enduring Conflict* (Caldwell, NJ: Blackburn Press, 2000).

30. K. William Kapp quoted in John Bellamy Foster, *Ecology against Capitalism* (New York: Monthly Review Press, 2002), 37.

31. Gert Spaargaren and Arthur J. Mol, "Carbon Flows, Carbon Markets, and Low-carbon Lifestyles: Reflecting on the Role of Markets in Climate Governance," *Environmental Politics* 22, no. 1 (2013): 176.

32. Ibid., 176–77.

33. Gert Spaargaren, "Ecological Modernization Theory and the Changing Discourse on Environment and Modernity," in *Environment and Global Modernity*, ed. Gert Spaargaren, Arthur J. Mol, and Frederick H. Buttel (Thousand Oaks, CA: Sage, 2000), 53.

34. John Hoffmann, "Social and Environmental Influences on Endangered Species: A Cross-National Study," *Sociological Perspectives* 4, no. 1 (2004): 82.

35. Arthur Mol, Gert Spaargaren, and David Sonnenfeld, "Ecological Modernisation: Three Decades of Policy, Practice and Theoretical Reflection," in *The Ecological Modernisation Reader*, ed. Arthur Mol, Geert Spaargaren, and David Sonnenfeld (New York: Routledge, 2009), 4.

36. Information is available online at http://www.bire.org and at https://www.ibm.com/smarterplanet/ca/en/water_management/examples/index.html.

37. I have consciously avoided wading into the esoteric details of the scholarly debate between critical ecologists/eco-Marxists and eco-modernists (not to mention other theoretical and activistic perspectives). My object is not to pick sides in those debates but, rather, to offer the two perspectives as useful

filters—each in its own way—for understanding the Hudson region's socioecological history.

38. James Gustave Speth, *The Bridge at the End of the World* (New Haven: Yale University Press, 2008), 100.

Chapter 2. A Place under Siege

1. Aldo Leopold, *Round River* (New York: Oxford University Press, 1993), 165.

2. William R. Catton, *Overshoot: The Ecological Basis for Revolutionary Change* (Urbana-Champaign: University of Illinois Press, 1980).

3. John Muir, *My First Summer in the Sierra* (Boston: Houghton Mifflin, 1911), 211.

4. Working with undergraduate students, my Skidmore College colleague Kyle Nichols has conducted some pathbreaking research on logging's effects on "stream morphology"—the shape of streambeds—in the Adirondacks. See: Caroline Loehr, Jonathan Reeves, and Kyle K. Nichols, "How Large Were Floods Caused by 19th and 20th Century Splash Dams in the Upper Hudson Watershed, New York?" 2010 Geological Society of American Annual Meeting. Abstract available at: http://gsa.confex.com/gsa/2010AM/finalprogram/abstract_179186.htm.

5. Boyle, *The Hudson*, 231.

6. Lawrence C. Skinner, "Distributions of Polyhalogenated Compounds in Hudson River (New York, USA) Fish in Relation to Human Uses along the River," *Environmental Pollution* 159, no. 10 (1987): 2565–74. However, ecological studies are mixed. One team of researchers has found that *populations* of certain fish—as opposed to individual fish—do not appear to have been harmed by PCBs. See these studies, which were funded by General Electric, the corporation responsible for the release of the PCBs into the Hudson; also note that these studies are of the "lower" Hudson, not the section of the river most heavily contaminated by PCBs. See: Lawrence W. Barnthouse, David Glaser, and John Young, "Effects of historic PCB exposures on the reproductive success of the Hudson River striped bass population," *Environmental Science and Technology* 37 (2003): 223–28; and: Lawrence W. Barnthouse, David Glaser, and Liane DeSantis, "Polychlorinated Biphenyls and Hudson River White Perch: Implications for Population-Level Ecological Risk Assessment and Risk Management," *Integrated Environmental Assessment and Management* 5, no. 3 (2009): 435–44.

7. Because they feed on insects, tree swallows are often used to test for contamination in sediment. Recent Hudson River research on the birds includes: C. M. Custer, B. R. Gray, and T. W. Custer, "Effects of Egg Order on Organic and Inorganic Element Concentrations and Egg Characteristics in Tree Swallows, *Tachycineta bicolor*," *Environmental Toxicology and Chemistry* 29, no. 4 (2010): 909–21.

8. Hudson River Natural Resource Trustees, *Work Summary and Data Report: Collection of Bats from the Hudson River, New York, 2001 and 2002 Samples* (Silver Spring, MD: U.S. Department of Commerce, 2007).

9. There are many sources of information on PCBs generally and in the Hudson River particularly. Among those most useful to me have been a report issued in 2001 by the U.S. Department of the Interior, the National Oceanic and Atmospheric Administration, and the New York DEC that is available at: http://www.dec.ny.gov/docs/wildlife_pdf/fishinjury.pdf; the EPA's Web sites for the Hudson PCB issue generally, available at: http://www.epa.gov/hudson/; and the EPA's Hudson River dredging Web site at: http://www.hudsondredgingdata.com/.

10. See: http://www.dredgingtoday.com/2010/05/02/usa-general-electric-estimates-first-phase-of-hudson-river-dredging-at-561-million/.

11. Gerald B. Silverman, "GE Expects to Complete Dredging of PCBs in Hudson River in 2016," *Bloomberg BNA* (January 2, 2014), http://www.bna.com/ge-expects-complete-n17179881070/.

12. Kenneth A. Gould, Allan Schnaiberg, and Adam S. Weinberg, *Local Environmental Struggles: Citizen Activism in the Treadmill of Production* (New York: Cambridge University Press, 1996), 167.

13. Robert Costanza et al., "The Value of the World's Ecosystem Services and Natural Capital," *Nature* 387 (15 May 1997): 253–60.

14. Karin Limburg, *The Hudson River Ecosystem* (New York: Springer, 1986).

15. One volume that gives a sense of the approach that Limburg, Swaney, and other historical ecologists take to their research is: John Waldman, Karin Limburg, and David Strayer, eds., *Hudson River Fishes and Their Environment* (Bethesda, MD: American Fisheries Society, 2006).

16. Interested readers may enjoy two exceptional histories by Tom Lewis and Russell Shorto: Tom Lewis, *The Hudson* (New Haven: Yale University Press, 2007); Russell Shorto, *The Island at the Center of the World: The Epic Story of Manhatttan and the Forgotten Colony That Shaped America* (New York: Vintage, 2005).

17. Robert Costanza, Bryan G. Norton, and Benjamin D. Haskell, eds., *Ecosystem Health: New Goals for Environmental Management* (Washington, DC: Island Press, 1992), 4.

18. One summary of the peer-reviewed literature on hiking trails may be found at: http://science.natureconservancy.ca/centralinterior/docs/ERAtoolbox/9/Trails.pdf.

19. Michale J. Glennon and William F. Porter, "Effects of Land Use Management on Biotic Integrity: An Investigation of Bird Communities," *Biological Conservation* 126 (2005): 499–511.

20. Ted Gup, "100 Years of the Starling," *New York Times*, September 1 1990.

21. J. Madeleine Nash, "Invasion of the Zebra Mussels," *Time*, January 21 1991, 63. An important review of zebra mussels' effects on the Hudson River's

ecology is: David L. Strayer, Kathryn A. Hattala, and Andrew W. Kahnle, "Effects of an Invasive Bivalve (*Dreissena polymorpha*) on Fish in the Hudson River Estuary," *Canadian Journal of Fisheries and Aquatic Sciences* 61 (2004): 924–41.

22. For a helpful summary of the complex phragmites history and the challenging literature, see the Web page created by Cornell professor Bernd Blossey: http://www.invasiveplants.net/phragmites/natint.htm.

23. For more information, see: http://www.nps.gov/plants/alien/fact/aial1.htm.

24. New York State's invasive species list may be found at: http://www.dec.ny.gov/animals/265.html. There do not appear to be any published ecological studies of mitten crab in the Hudson River. However, a study from Delaware Bay indicates that the crab is likely to become well established in the Hudson's waters: Charles E. Tilburg et al., "Transport and Retention of the Mitten Crab (*Eriocheir sinensis*) in a Mid-Atlantic Estuary: Predictions from a Larval Transport Model," *Journal of Marine Research* 69, no. 1 (2011): 137–65.

25. Carol Demare, "Once a Beauty, Beastly Plant Can Burn," *Albany Times Union*, July 6, 2011.

26. The U.S. Environmental Protection Agency has a useful Web site on ballast water, found at: http://water.epa.gov/polwaste/vwd/ballastwater/invasive_species_bal_links.cfm.

27. Stephanie R. Hanson, David T. Osgood, and David J. Yozzo, "Nekton Use of a *Phragmites Australis* Marsh on the Hudson River, New York, USA," *Wetlands* 22, no. 2 (2002): 326.

28. D. L. Strayer, "Alien Species in Fresh Waters: Ecological Effects, Interactions with Other Stressors, and Prospects for the Future," *Freshwater Biology* 55 (Supplement 1): 152–74.

29. Mike Lynch, "The Alpine Zone: A Rare Glimpse of the Past," *Adirondack Daily Enterprise,* August 30, 2008, http://www.adirondackdailyenterprise.com/page/content.detail/id/502185.html?nav=5046.

30. Intergovernmental Panel on Climate Change, *Climate Change 2014: Impacts, Adaptation, and Vulnerablility* (Geneva: United Nations, 2014), http://ipcc-wg2.gov/AR5/report/final-drafts/.

31. Jerry M. Melillo, Terese (T. C.) Richmond, and Gary W. Yohe, eds., *Climate Change Impacts in the United States: The Third National Climate Assessment.* (Washington, DC: U.S. Government Printing Office, 2014), http://nca2014.globalchange.gov.

32. Ibid., 7.

33. Douglas A. Burns, Julian Klaus, and Michael R. McHale, "Recent Climate Trends and Implications for Water Resources in the Catskill Mountain Region, New York, USA," *Journal of Hydrology* 336 (2007): 155–70.

34. Nathan P. Gillett et al., "Ongoing Climate Change Following a Complete Cessation of Carbon Dioxide Emissions," *Nature Geoscience* 4 (2011): 83–87.

35. A comprehensive and oft-cited review of the research on global ecological responses to climate change is: Camille Parmesan, "Ecological and Evolutionary Responses to Recent Climate Change," *Annual Review of Ecology, Evolution, and Systematics* 37 (2006): 637–69.

36. Manfred Metzler, "Foreword," *Endocrine Disruptors Part I* (New York: Springer, 2001), xii.

37. Brian Nearing, "Tiny Beads Water Peril," *Albany Times Union*, May 15, 2014.

Chapter 3. A Constant Bounty

1. Michael Pollan, *The Omnivore's Dilemma: A Natural History of Four Meals* (New York: Penguin, 2006), 240.

2. Jaspar Dankers and Peter Sluyter, *Journal of a Voyage to New York* (Brooklyn: Long Island Historical Society, 1867), 120–21.

3. Stradling, *The Nature of New York*, 58.

4. USDA Economic Research Service, "State Fact Sheet: New York." Online. Available at: http://www.ers.usda.gov/data-products/state-fact-sheets.

5. Charles L. Redman, "Introduction," in *Agrarian Landscapes in Transition: Comparisons of Long-term Ecological and Cultural Change*, ed., Charles L. Redman and David R. Foster (New York: Oxford University Press, 2008), 4.

6. Pleasant Valley Farm's online presence is through Facebook at: https://www.facebook.com/pages/Pleasant-Valley-Farm/242214617771.

7. Stephanie Strom, "Has 'Organic' Been Oversized?" *New York Times*, July 8, 2012.

8. Figure refers to national farming income; see: U.S. Census Bureau, *Statistical Abstract of the United States: 2012* (Washington, DC: U.S. Government Printing Office, 2013), 544.

9. McEnroe Farm's Web page is at: http://www.mcenroeorganicfarm.com.

10. Wendell Berry, "Whose Head Is the Farmer Using? Whose Head Is Using the Farmer?" in *Meeting the Expectations of the Land: Essays in Sustainable Agriculture and Stewardship*, ed. Wes Jackson, Wendell Berry, and Bruce Colman (San Francisco: North Point Press), 23.

11. Mireya Navarro, "Bloomberg Plan Aims to Require Food Composting," *New York Times*, June 16, 2013.

12. GrowNYC may be found online at: http://www.grownyc.org.

13. Brian Nearing, "Food Grown by Friends, Neighbors," *Albany Times Union*, May 15, 2014.

14. Capital District Community Gardens' Web site is: http://cdcg.org.

15. Sara J. Scherr and Jeffrey A. McNeeley, eds., *Farming with Nature: The Science and Practice of Ecoagriculture* (Washington, DC: Island Press, 2007).

16. Judith D. Soule and Jon K. Piper, *Farming in Nature's Image: An Ecological Approach to Agriculture* (Washington, DC: Island Press, 1992), 113, 121.

17. Randal S. Beeman and James A. Pritchard, *A Green and Permanent Land: Ecology and Agriculture in the Twentieth Century* (Lawrence: University Press of Kansas), 153.

18. Field Goods' Web address is: http://www.field-goods.com.

19. USDA Economic Research Service, "Organic Production." Online. Available at: http://www.ers.usda.gov/data-products/organic-production.aspx#. UyBtDFxVMdc.

20. Leonard Charles et al., "Where You At? A Bioregional Quiz," *Coevolution Quarterly* 32 (Winter 1981): 1. Several updated versions of the quiz may be found online.

21. Railex press release available at: http://www.railexusa.com/site/press1. php?id=184, May 7, 2012.

22. Data from: Census of Agriculture, *Geographic Area Series 1987 Census of Agriculture* Part 32, New York (Washington, DC: U.S. Government Printing Agency, 1987) and from the online Census of Agriculture at: http://www.agcensus. usda.gov/Publications/2007/Full_Report/Volume_1,_Chapter_2_County_Level/ New_York/st36_2_008_008.pdf.

23. For information, visit: http://www.wwoof.net.

24. CRAFT's Web site is at: http://www.craftfarmapprentice.com/farms. php.

25. The Farm Hub initiative is supported by a grant from the Local Economics Project of the New World Foundation. The Web site is: http://www. localeconomies-hv.org/initiatives/farm-hub/.

26. Alan Beardsworth and Teresa Keil, *Sociology on the Menu: An Invitation to the Study of Food and Society* (New York: Routledge, 1997), 257.

27. Just Food's Web page is at: http://www.justfood.org.

28. Michael Pollan, "How Change Is Going to Come in the Food System," *The Nation*, October 3, 2011, 24.

29. Paul K. Conkin, *A Revolution down on the Farm: The Transformation of American Agriculture Since 1929* (Lexington: University Press of Kentucky, 2008), 205.

30. Jennifer Cockrall-King, *Food and the City: Urban Agriculture and the New Food Revolution* (Amherst, NY: Prometheus Books, 2012), 312.

31. Syane Roy, "The Promise of Alternative Retailers" in *Food Access in Low-Income New York,* ed. Ben Bakelaar et al. (report, New York City Coalition against Hunger, 2006), 29.

Chapter 4. Two Hundred Subdivisions Too Late?

1. Virginia H. Dale, Rebecca A. Efroymson, and Keith L. Kline, "The Land Use-Climate Change-Energy Nexus," *Landscape Ecology* 26 (2011): 756.

2. For information about the Centers and Greenspaces plan, see: http://www.redhook.org/PDFs/TaskForce/Report2.pdf.

3. Pace University's Law School in White Plains, New York, provided training to representatives from the Town of Red Hook and the villages of Red Hook and Tivoli. See: http://www.pace.edu/school-of-law/red-hook-tivoli-intermunicipal-task-force-lula-case-study.

4. See: http://smartgrowthny.org/history.shtml.

5. Matthias Ruth, "Introduction," *Smart Growth and Climate Change: Regional Development, Infrastructure and Adaptation*, ed. Matthias Ruth (Northampton, MA: Edward Elgar, 2006), 3.

6. See: http://www.smartgrowth.org/why.php.

7. See: http://www.smartgrowth.org/engine/index.php/principles/.

8. For more information about Regional Plan Association, see: http://www.rpa.org/; and for information about New York-Connecticut Sustainable Communities, go to: http://www.sustainablenyct.org/.

9. James Gustave Speth, *The Bridge at the End of the World* (New Haven: Yale University Press, 2008), 76.

10. Andreas R. Edwards, *Thriving Beyond Sustainability: Pathways to a Resilient Society* (Gabriola Island, BC: New Society, 2010), 76.

11. Edwards, *The Sustainability Revolution*, 109.

12. See the executive summary of the "Rising Waters" final report: http://www.nature.org/media/newyork/rw_070509_exec.pdf.

13. The list of adaptation strategies may be found in the appendix to the "Rising Waters" report and is available at: http://www.nature.org/media/newyork/rw_062409_app.pdf.

14. Rockland County is close enough to the mouth of the Hudson River that the water is brackish, necessitating removing salt from the water. For information about the proposed facility, see: http://sustainablerockland.org/?page_id=2.

15. Political sociologists have written extensively about "local growth coalitions." The most notable among them is William Domhoff; see his *Who Rules America? Challenges to Corporate and Class Dominance* (New York: McGraw-Hill, 2009).

16. For an example of the Partnership's work, see: http://www.clearwater.org/biodiversity/vanschaaken.pdf. The Coxsackie Creek Grassland Preserve was also created out of a deal that VanSchaak brokered: http://www.greenelandtrust.org/index.php?option=com_content&view=article&id=16&Itemid=25.

17. Boyle, *The Hudson*, 82–83.

18. One brief, helpful overview of clustered development was written by the University of Minnesota Extension. See: http://www.extension.umn.edu/distribution/naturalresources/components/7059-01.html.

19. Information about the APA's policies—which, in some ways, reflect a smart growth approach—may be found in their *Citizen's Guide to Adirondack Park Agency Land Use Regulations*, http://www.apa.state.ny.us/Documents/Guidelines/CitizensGuide.pdf.

20. Mark Roseland, *Toward Sustainable Communities: Resources for Citizens and Their Governments*, rev. ed. (Gabriola Island, BC: New Society, 2005), 19.

21. Tom Daniels, *When City and Country Collide: Managing Growth in the Metropolitan Fringe* (Washington, DC: Island Press, 1998).

22. Simon Dresner, *The Principles of Sustainability* (Washington: Earthscan, 2008), 174.

23. For information, see: http://www.hudsongreenway.state.ny.us/home.aspx.

24. For information, see: http://www.hudsonwatershed.org/.

Chapter 5. Remaking Communities

1. Scarce, "What Do Wolves Mean?"

2. Chris Maser and Christine Kirk, "Sustainable Development," in Maser, *Resolving Environmental Conflict: Towards Sustainable Community Development* (Delray Beach, FL: St. Lucie Press, 1996), 166.

3. Stradling, *The Nature of New York*, 176.

4. Lisa W. Foderaro, "Rake the Leaves? Some Towns Say Mow Them," *New York Times*, November 25, 2013.

5. Peter Freund and George Martin, "Driving South: The Globalization of Auto Consumption and Its Social Organization of Space," *Capitalism, Nature, Socialism* 11, no. 4 (2000): 51–71.

6. Robert Bullard and Beverly Wright, *The Wrong Complexion for Protection: How the Government Response to Disaster Endangers African American Communities* (New York: New York University Press, 2012), 15.

7. Robert Bullard, *Dumping in Dixie: Race, Class, and Environmental Quality*, 3d ed. (Boulder: Westview, 2000), 3.

8. Valerie Gunter and Steve Kroll-Smith, *Volatile Places: A Sociology of Communities and Environmental Controversies* (Thousand Oaks: Sage, 2007), 140.

9. Maser, *Resolving Environmental Conflict*, 18.

10. Gunter and Kroll-Smith, *Volatile Places*, 4.

11. David Owen, *Green Metropolis: Why Living Smaller, Living Closer, and Driving Less are Keys to Sustainability* (New York: Riverhead, 2009).

12. Kelly Moore, "Powered by the People: Scientific Authority in Participatory Science" in *The New Political Sociology of Science: Institutions, Networks, and Power*, ed. Scott Frickel and Kelly Moore (Madison: University of Wisconsin Press, 2006), 306.

13. Gunter and Kroll-Smith, *Volatile Places*, 7.

14. Kia Gregory, "Cost among Hurdles Slowing New York City's Plan to Phase out Dirty Heating Oil," *New York Times*, April 6, 2014.

15. Michael Kimmelman, "River of Hope in the Bronx," *New York Times*, July 19, 2012.

16. Several of these counties include land in watersheds other than the Hudson River's. Because of the challenges distinguishing the watershed boundaries in Census tracts that overlap watersheds, our analysis includes some facilities located in other drainages, primarily the St. Lawrence River's. In addition, portions of a couple of other counties—Fulton and Sullivan, in particular, fall within the Hudson drainage but were not included because the relevant areas were small.

17. Our methods were guided by a seminal scholarly paper: Paul Mohai and Robin Saha, "Racial Inequality in the Distribution of Hazardous Waste: A National-Level Reassessment," *Social Problems* 54, no. 3 (2007): 343–70. Mohai and Saha detail a GIS-based methodology in which the demographic characteristics of those living within one mile of a given facility ("neighborhoods") may be computed and then compared to the characteristics of those living outside of the neighborhoods.

Following Mohai and Saha, we compiled Census data for the following demographic characteristics: percent black, percent Hispanic, percent nonwhite, percent living in poverty, percent unemployed, percent employed in a white-collar job, percent employed in a blue-collar job, percent without a high school diploma, percent with a Bachelor's degree or higher, percent of households receiving public assistance, mean household income, and mean housing value. Initially, we compared the neighborhood demographic characteristics of all locations of a given facility type (for instance, major air polluters) with the characteristics of each county, minus the facility neighborhood data. However, because our focus is on the region as a whole, we recomputed the data for the region, and that is what we report below.

18. Robin Saha and Paul Mohai, "Historical Context and Hazardous Waste Facility Siting: Understanding Temporal Patterns in Michigan," *Social Problems* 52, no. 4 (2005): 623. Also see: Robert D. Bullard and Beverly H. Wright, "Blacks and the Environment," *Humboldt Journal of Social Relations* 14 (Summer 1987): 165–84.

19. Max Weber, *Ancient Judaism* (New York: Simon and Schuster, 1967), 343.

20. Maser and Kirk, *Resolving Environmental Conflict*, 177.

21. Ibid., 183.

Chapter 6. How It All Adds Up

1. Edward Hopper, *Nighthawks*, Art Institute of Chicago, 1942. The Art Institute's description of the painting quotes Hopper as commenting that a Greenwich Avenue restaurant was the setting for the painting: http://www.artic.edu/aic/collections/artwork/111628.

2. Gertrude Stein, *Everybody's Autobiography* (New York: Random House, 1971), 289.

3. A notable, and controversial, take on the culture of poverty is William Julius Wilson's *The Declining Significance of Race* (Chicago: University of Chicago Press, 1980).

4. Owen, *Green Metropolis*, 40.

5. Langdon Winner, *The Whale and the Reactor* (Chicago: University of Chicago Press, 1986), 23.

6. Owen, *Green Metropolis*, 31.

7. Mitchell L. Moss, Carson Y. Qing, and Sarah Kaufman, "Commuting to Manhattan: A Study of Residence Location Trends for Manhattan Workers from 2002–2009" (New York: NYU Wagner, 2012): 20; available online at: http://wagner.nyu.edu/files/rudincenter/ManhattanCommuting.pdf.

8. Warren Karlenzing, "What Makes Today's Green City," in *Growing Greener Cities: Urban Sustainability in the TwentyFirst Century*, ed. Eugenie L. Birch and Susan M. Wachter (Philadelphia: University of Pennsylvania Press, 2008), 346–63.

9. Dennis D. Hirsch, "Ecosystem Services and the Green City," in *Growing Greener Cities: Urban Sustainability in the Twenty-First Century*, ed. Eugenie L. Birch and Susan M. Wachter (Philadelphia: University of Pennsylvania Press, 2008), 283.

10. National Trust for Historic Preservation, *The Greenest Building: Quantifying the Environmental Value of Building Reuse* (Washington, DC: National Trust for Historic Preservation, 2011), http://www.preservationnation.org/information-center/sustainable-communities/green-lab/lca/The_Greenest_Building_lowres.pdf.

11. Owen, *Green Metropolis*, 32–36.

12. Timothy Carter and Colleen Butler, "Ecological Impacts of Replacing Traditional Roofs with Green Roofs in Two Urban Areas," *Cities and the Environment* 1, no. 2 (2008): 3, 12.

13. For more information, see the U.S. Green Building Council's Web site at: http://www.usgbc.org/home. Critics of USGBC abound, and this article, appearing in *The Atlantic* magazine's online *The Atlantic Cities* site, is one of the most insightful: Kaid Benfield, "As Important as It Is, LEED Can Be So Embarrassing" *The Atlantic Cities*, January 18, 2013, http://www.theatlanticcities.com/housing/2013/01/good-and-important-it-leed-can-be-so-embarrassing/4435/.

14. Dickson Despommier, *The Vertical Farm: Feeding the World in the 21ˢᵗ Century* (New York: Thomas Dunne, 2010).

15. Ibid., 128.

16. Anonymous, "FarmedHere, Nation's Largest indoor Vertical Farm, Opens in Chicago Area," *Huffington Post,* March 3, 2013, http://www.huffingtonpost.com/2013/03/22/farmedhere-nations-largest-vertical-farm_n_2933739.html.

17. David Goodman, "For Bike Advocates, Delayed Gratification," *New York Times*, August 12, 2012.

18. The Transportation Alternatives Web site is at: http://transalt.org.

19. Matt Flegenheimer, "A Success, but Wobbly from the Start," *The New York Times,* March 27, 2014.

20. Jan Gehl, *Life between Buildings,* 6th ed. (Washington, DC: Island Press, 2011).

21. Owen, *Green Metropolis,* 118–19.

22. Ibid., 119.

23. Richard Louv, *Last Child in the Woods: Saving Our Children from Nature-Deficit Disorder* (Chapel Hill, NC: Algonquin, 2008).

24. City of New York, *PlaNYC* Update April 2011, http://nytelecom. vo.llnwd.net/o15/agencies/planyc2030/pdf/planyc_2011_planyc_full_report.pdf.

25. Owen, *Green Metropolis,* 2.

26. Ibid., 3.

Chapter 7. A Complete Disruption

1. Ecovative may be found online at: http://www.ecovativedesign.com.

2. Paul Hawken, Amory Lovins, and L. Hunter Lovins, *Natural Capitalism: Creating the Next Industrial Revolution* (Boston: Back Bay Books, 1999), 15.

3. BALLE's Web site is: https://bealocalist.org.

4. Shelby Siems, "Ecotrek Makes Backpacks That Are Entirely Recyclable," *Christian Science Monitor,* July 18, 1995, 9.

5. Bill McKibben, "Tilting at Windmills," *New York Times,* February 16, 2005.

6. D. B. Belzer, "Energy Efficiency Potential in Existing Commercial Buildings: Review of Selected Recent Studies" (Springfield, VA: U.S. Department of Commerce, 2009).

7. National Trust for Historic Preservation, *Realizing the Energy Efficiency Potential of Small Buildings* (Washington, DC: National Trust for Historic Preservation, 2013), http://www.preservationnation.org/information-center/sustainable-communities/green-lab/small-buildings/130604_NTHP_report_sm.pdf.

8. Schendler, *Getting Green Done,* 6.

9. Paul Tonko, "Green Technology Can Help the Economy," *Albany Times-Union,* July 22, 2011.

10. Mark Muro, Jonathan Rothwell, and Devashree Saha, "Sizing the Clean Economy: A National and Regional Green Jobs Assessment (Washington, DC: Brookings Institution, 2011), 27, http://www.brookings.edu/~/media/research/files/reports/2011/7/13%20clean%20economy/0713_clean_economy.pdf.

11. Ibid., 13–14.

12. James Gustave Speth, *The Bridge at the End of the World* (New Haven: Yale University Press, 2008), 111–12.

13. Robert Costanza et al., "Time to Leave GDP Behind," *Nature* 505 (January 16, 2014), 284.

14. Hawken, Lovins, and Lovins, *Natural Capitalism*, 5.

Chapter 8. A Landscape to Fight For

1. The Battenkill Conservancy may be found online at: http://www.battenkillconservancy.org.

2. In 1999 River Watch joined with River Network; their Web address is: http://www.rivernetwork.org.

3. The data and other information are available at: http://www.ldeo.columbia.edu/edu/k12/snapshotday/.

4. Sharon Behar and Martha Cheo, "Hudson Basin Riverwatch Guidance Document," (East Greenwich, NY: Hudson Basin River Watch, 2000), http://www.hudsonbasin.org/HBRWGD04.pdf.

5. Harry M. Collins and Trevor Pinch, *The Golem: What You Should Know about Science* (New York: Cambridge University Press, 2012).

6. Anonymous, "Copy of Old Hudson Sloop is Launched," *New York Times*, May 19, 1969.

7. Douglas Robinson, "Sloop Will Sail up the Hudson in Campaign for Clean Water," *New York Times*, August 2, 1969.

8. Ibid.

9. Social movement theory does a disappointingly poor job of distinguishing between "real" social movements and large interest groups. For a discussion of some of the distinctions that can be drawn between them, including the importance of culture in movements, see: Rik Scarce, "Earth First!: Deviance Inside and Out," in *Extreme Deviance*, ed. Erich Goode and Angus Vail (Thousand Oaks, CA: Pine Forge, 2007).

10. Pete Seeger, "Sailing up My Dirty Stream," Fall River Music, 1961.

11. Richard Severo, "Pollution? Tuck Calls It 'Purity,' " *New York Times*, December 1, 1974.

12. John Cronin and Robert F. Kennedy Jr., *The Riverkeepers* (New York: Touchstone, 1999).

13. Riverkeeper's Web address is: http://www.riverkeeper.org.

14. Boyle, *The Hudson*, 99.

15. Ibid., 45.

16. Joseph Berger, "Imperiled Fish are Monitored in Bridge's Construction Zone," *New York Times*, May 30, 2014.

17. Boyle, *The Hudson*, 156.

18. Ibid., 157.

19. Frances F. Dunwell, *The Hudson: America's River* (New York: Columbia University Press, 2008), 304.

20. Tom Lewis, *The Hudson*, 268.

21. Christopher D. Stone, "Should Trees Have Standing? Toward Legal Rights for Natural Objects," *Southern California Law Review* 45 (1972): 20. Also see: Christopher D. Stone, *Should Trees Have Standing? Law, Morality, and the Environment* (New York: Oxford University Press, 2010).

Conclusion

1. The ironies are tinged with social and environmental bitterness too, a result of the destruction of thousands of acres of Catskill Mountains habitat to create New York's massive reservoirs in the first place.

2. Though highly technical in places, this document gives a sense of what Malta's decade-long land use struggle was about and how it was resolved: http://www.cdrpc.org/Workshops/2013-06-20__Town_of_Malta_Form_Based_Code.pdf.

3. U.S. Energy Information Administration, "Recent Trends in Energy-Related CO2 Emisions Vary across Regions and States," June 3, 2014, http://www.eia.gov/todayinenergy/detail.cfm?id=16531.

4. All data from: http://www.rggi.org.

5. Ann Morrow, "Signs of the Times," *Metroland* 37, no. 18 (May 1, 2014): 6.

6. More information is available at: http://greenbank.ny.gov.

7. Andrew Zolli and Ann Marie Healy, *Resilience: Why Things Bounce Back* (New York: Free Press, 2012).

8. Andrew Zolli, "Learning to Bounce Back," *New York Times*, November 2, 2012.

9. The Resilient Design Institute's work is particularly insightful in this regard. See: http://www.resilientdesign.org.

10. Susan Solomon, Gian-Kasper Plattner, Reto Knutti, and Pierre Friedlingstein, "Irreversible Climate Change Due to Carbon Dioxide Emissions," *PNAS* 106, no. 6 (February 10, 2009): 1704–1709.

Methodological Note

Kathy Charmaz, *Constructing Grounded Theory: A Practical Guide through Qualitative Analysis* (Thousand Oaks, CA: Sage, 2006).

Index

Battenkill, 188–191
Battenkill Conservancy, 188–189, 190
Battery (southern tip of Manhattan),
    26, 187
Bayer, Eben, 161–166
Beacon, NY, 108, 192, 194
Beacon Institute, 30
Beardsworth, Alan, 80
beaver, 16–18, 26, 36, 162, 219
Beeman, Randal S., 74
Benjamin, Vernon, 19
Bennington, VT, 83, 216
Bennington, Battle of, 20
Berkshire Mountains, 66, 172, 174,
    218
Berry, Wendell, 1, 66, 110
Bicknell's thrush, 52
bicycling, 139, 151–155, 215
bioregion, 1
biotic integrity. *See* ecosystem health
Bloomberg, Michel, 121, 138, 141,
    151, 157, 222
Blooming Grove, NY, 91
bluejay, 43
Bollack, Françoise, 141–144, 213
Boyle, Robert, 17, 23, 24, 25, 103,
    197, 198, 205
BPA (bisphenol-A), 54
British, 2, 58
    colonization of region, 18–20
    promotion of slavery, 20
Bronx, NY, 3, 156
    See also South Bronx
Bronx River, 123
Bronxville, NY, 146
Brookings Institution, 185
Brooklyn, 70, 150, 154, 156
Brundtland, Gro Harlem, 9
Brundtland Report, 9–10
Bullard, Linda McKeever, 117
Bullard, Robert, 117, 126
Bump, Marirose Blum, 85–90, 96,
    100, 102, 213, 222

Burns, Doug, 49, 50–53, 95, 222
business. *See* capitalism, green
    business
Butler, Colleen, 147

Cal Tech (California Institute of
    Technology), 78
Calamity Brook, 25
Canada, 18
Canham, Hugh O., 22
Capital District Community Gardens
    (CDCG), 70
capitalism, 15–31, 96
    and community, 220
    and corporate social responsibility,
        173
    and exploitation, 16–31
    future of, 162
    See also green business,
        sustainability
Carey Institute for Ecosystem Studies,
    39, 45
Carter, Majora, 122
Carter, Timothy, 147
Caspian Sea, 44
Catskill Center for Conservation and
    Development, 7
Catskill Mountainkeeper, 204
Catskill Mountains, 7, 13, 21, 22, 38,
    96, 104, 140, 156, 158, 168, 213
    global climate change's effects on,
        50, 52
    See also logging
Catskill State Park
    creation of, 23
    Landscape, 7–8
Caucasus Mountains, 46
Central Park, 43, 114, 144, 156, 211
Chamber of Commerce, 173
Chesapeake Bay, 140
chestnut tree, 43
Chicago, 143, 150
Chile, 170

net metering, 180
regional shortcomings, 215, 216–218
solar, 3, 61, 70, 151, 178, 180, 181, 183, 207, 216, 217–218
tide-driven, 207
wind, 3, 20, 151, 174–181, 207, 216
England, English. *See* British
Entergy, 40
environmental movement, 187
See also environmental justice
environmental justice, injustice, 113, 115, 116–126, 130, 136, 148, 184, 187, 206, 215, 216, 220
and climate justice, 194
and community, 12
in Hudson region, 123–126
and institutional racism, 211
movement, 117–123, 133
See also Sustainable South Bronx, WEACT
environmentalism, 2, 13, 133
Hudson region's role in, 204–207
EOS Ventures, 181
EPA (U.S. Environmental Protection Agency), 36, 117, 197, 199
Toxic Release Inventory, 125
equity, 11, 185, 195, 221
and access
to opportunity, 136, 139
to power, 126
to quality environment, 93, 200, 214
to quality food, 61, 69, 82, 83
to transportation, 116, 139
through businesses, 165–166, 174
and cities, 139
and community, 113, 116–126
and land use, 92–93
sustainability's understanding of, 116–117
See also farming; global climate change; triple bottom line accounting

Erenzo, Ralph, 167–171, 182, 183, 213
Erie Canal, 20–21, 23, 39
Erling, Todd, 61, 62, 73–78, 82, 148
Everett, Melissa, 2–3, 89, 184–185
Exxon, 199

Fairbank, Brian, 177, 179, 180
farmers markets, 83
See also farming; GrowNYC
farming, 11, 38, 57–84, 183, 212, 215
acres in region, 59–60, 77–78
and cities, 215
Collaborative Regional Alliance for Farmer Training, 79
and community, 62, 68, 220
and conservation, 82
as development, 76
and ecology, 71–73, 74
economic value nationally, 62
economic value regionally, 76
and equity, 78, 81, 82–84
and health, 82–84
historical role of, 21
knowledge, 78–80
natural, 61
number of farms in region, 79
organic, 61–67
and place, 151
Right to Farm laws, 75
systems, 57
traditional, as outmoded, 149–151
U.S. Dept. of Agriculture, 75, 150
vertical, 138, 147–151, 215
economics of, 149–151
energy sources, 151
See also Columbia Land Conservancy; CSA; development; Farmscape Ecology Program; GrowNYC; New York City; Tuthilltown Spirits
Farmscape Ecology Program, 71–73
Federal Dam, 50
Federal Power Commission, 205

industrialization. *See* industrialism
inequality. *See* social inequality
insight, 4–5, 212
inspiration, 4, 211
intentionality. *See* Landscape
International Paper Company, 23
invasive species, 11, 34, 43–47, 211,
   214

Jackson, Jesse, 118
Jacobs, Jane, 153
Jenkins-Lueken Orchards, 168–169
Jiminy Peak Mountain Resort, 162,
   174–181, 182, 183, 185, 223
   energy conservation, 174–181, 216
   energy use, 175, 178
   water conservation, 175, 176, 181
Johnson, Lucille, 18–19
Just Food, 82

Kansas City, 135
Keil, Teresa, 80
Kellogg, Scott, 3, 126–130
Kennedy, Robert F., Jr., 198
Kinderhook Creek, 174
King, Martin Luther, Jr., 4, 192
Kingston, NY, 107, 182, 194
Kirk, Christine, 110, 113, 123, 132,
   133–134
Kiviat, Eric, 47, 51, 52, 54, 102, 107
Kleppel, Gary, 33, 34–35, 37, 39, 53,
   92, 95, 111–112, 113–114, 115,
   194
Kline, Keith L., 86
Knable, Richard, 197
Knab-Vispo, Claudia, 71–73, 82
Knox, NY, 111–112
Koch brothers (Charles G. and David
   H.), 217
Kooris, David, 88, 91, 104, 106, 184
Kroll-Smith, Steve, 117, 119, 120
kudzu, 44
Kurlansky, Mark, 23

Lake, Tom, 18, 110–111
Lake Champlain, 48
Lake Erie, 20
Lake Forest College, 118
land trusts, 13, 188, 200–201
   purchase of conservation
      easements, 201
   purchase of development rights,
      200, 201
   and wildlife preservation, 200
land use, 11–12, 85–108
   clustered development, 103
   and comprehensive plans, 86–90,
      100
   planning, 11, 85–93, 139, 202, 213,
      216, 218
   and zoning, 86
Landmark West!, 144
Landscape(s)
   business's, 161–186
   community's, 109–134
   consciously created, 5–6, 9, 58, 61,
      72, 131, 212
   defined, 4, 5
   dominant, 8, 10, 11, 18, 39, 46, 66,
      121, 169
   ecology's, 33–55
   environmentalism's, 187–209
   farming's, 57–84
   as fragmented, 115
   Hudson, historical, 18–26
   as incoherent, 115
   integration into, 115, 133
   intentional re-meaning, 9, 209, 214,
      215
   land use and, 85–108
   as layered, 158
   localization, 115, 133
   micro, 12
   stable, 16
   sustainable, 215
   transformation, 16–31
   urban influence on, 135–159

wolves, 36, 42
Woodbury, NY, 91
Woodstock, NY, 139
World Wide Opportunities in Organic
    Farms, 79

Yellowstone National Park, 41

Yosemite National Park, 41

zebra mussels, 44, 46, 47
"Zephyr" (wind turbine), 177–181,
    183, 185, 216
Zolli, Andrew, 219, 221
zoning. *See* land use